THE
WRITTEN
AND
ORAL TORAH

THE
WRITTEN
AND
ORAL TORAH

A Comprehensive Introduction

NATHAN T. LOPES CARDOZO

JASON ARONSON INC.
Northvale, New Jersey
Jerusalem

The publication of this work was made possible through the kind generosity of my dear friends, Aron and Bep Spijer, The Hague, Netherlands.

This book was set in 12 pt. Stempel Garamond by Alabama Book Composition of Deatsville, Alabama.

Library of Congress Cataloging-in-Publication Data

Lopes Cardozo, Nathan T.
    The written and oral Torah : a comprehensive introduction / by
Nathan T. Lopes Cardozo.
        p.   cm.
    Rev. ed. of: The infinite chain.   1989.
    Includes bibliographical references and indexes.
    ISBN 0-7657-5989-6 (alk. paper)
    1. Commandments (Judaism)   2. Bible.   O.T.   Pentateuch—
Hermeneutics.   3. Jewish law—Interpretation and construction.
4. Rabbinical literature—History and criticism.   I. Lopes Cardozo,
Nathan T.   Infinite chain.   II. Title.
BM520.7.L65   1997
296.1—DC21   97–1252
                                                           CIP
                                                           r97

Manufactured in the United States of America. Jason Aronson Inc. offers books and cassettes. For information and catalog write to Jason Aronson Inc., 230 Livingston Street, Northvale, New Jersey 07647.

To my mother,
Rivkah (Bertha) Lopes Cardozo

In memory of my father,
Jacob Lopes Cardozo, z"l
(November 14, 1910–February 7, 1977)

The publication of this work
was made possible through
the kind generosity of my dear friends
Aron and Bep Spijer,
The Hague, Netherlands.

CONTENTS

PREFACE

During 1977 and 1978, I delivered a series of lectures at various colleges on the nature, structure, and history of the Written and Oral Torah.

At my students' and colleagues' behest, I agreed to publish these lectures for the benefit of a wider public. As I went from the spoken to the written word, I found that considerable restructuring was necessary to produce a well-organized, readable book.

I have tried to explain the classical sources as expounded by the most renowned authorities on traditional Judaism. This does not preclude other approaches, some of which, in fact, are suggested by the sources themselves. However, the purpose of this book is to provide the reader with basic insights into the way in which most of the primary authorities dealt with the issues at hand. Therefore, I have not touched on lesser-known schools of thought.

Some of the concepts discussed herein may intially seem contradictory, but a careful reading will prove otherwise. The Jewish tradition is a multi-faceted phenomenon, and different levels of study reveal different levels of insight into its nature. Just as light diffused through a prism separates into individual beams, Judaism divides into a many-hued but harmonious spectrum of interpretation, all emanating from a single source. I hope that after studying this book, the reader will understand how each approach complements the other, forming an overall picture of the fundamentals of Jewish tradition.

The book commences with an overview of the purpose, nature, and weltanschauung of the Torah. This is followed by discussions of such important issues as revelation, the eternal nature of the Torah and its rules of exegesis, the power of the Hebrew language, and the essence of its mystical interpretation.

The second section deals with the categorization of the *mitzvot*. The Noachide laws and the Decalogue are discussed, as well as the 613 commandments—according to various scholarly classifications.

The third section explores the orally transmitted Torah, the reasons for its existence, and the authority of the Sages who formulated it. The section closes with a study of the authenticity of the oral law and the basis of the prohibition against comitting it to writing.

The fourth section concerns the categories of the orally transmitted Torah, including the statutes handed down to Moshe (*Halachah leMoshe MiSinai*), the laws debated in the Talmud, rabbinical decrees, and the philosophical meaning of talmudic conflicts of opinion.

The fifth section discusses the fundamental rules governing the halachic interpretation of the Torah.

The sixth section takes up *Aggadah*, and its relationship to *halachah*.

The work as a whole is only an overview; each chapter could have been expanded into a book of its own.

Thanks to the generous moral and financial support of

my late father, of blessed memory, I have been fortunate to study the Jewish tradition for many years under the guidance of the great teachers of Yeshivath Beth Joseph in Gateshead, England, and other institutions of Jewish learning.

Although this work is a long overdue tribute to my father's memory, it is also dedicated to my mother, who has gone far beyond her duties in providing for me. May God grant her long life and good health. I also wish to thank my mother-in-law, Rosa Gnesin, in whose Jerusalem home much of this book was written.

My secretaries, Channy Shapiro, Mimi Brilleman, Riva Unterman, and Shula Ben David, have shown great patience in typing and retyping the manuscript. Special thanks are due to Rabbi Dr. David Refson, dean of Neve Yerushalaim College, and Rabbi Dr. Yehudah Copperman, dean of Michlalah, Jerusalem College for Women, for their encouragement. I am grateful to Rabbis Aharon Feldman, David Open, and Avraham Kimche for reading parts of this work. Rabbi Moshe Herskovics and my dear friend Els Bendheim read the entire book and made many very important suggestions. This book was also carefully studied by a young scholar, Rabbi Avraham Lopiansky.

My dear friends Rabbi Hanoch Teller, Dr. Moshe Dann, and the Mishkovsky family of Jerusalem deserve special mention. I would also like to thank Rabbi David Landesmann for his editing of the original manuscript and, above all, Rabbi Leonard Oschry for his editorial consultation. This book is a simplified version of my forthcoming academic work on the Written and Oral Torah.

As always, my dear friends Aron and Bep Spijer from The Hague, Netherlands, encouraged me to write this book. Their generosity made this possible.

I owe more than I could possibly express to my dear wife, Frijda Rachel. Her love and encouragement enabled me to continue writing despite many difficulties. May God grant her and our children—Devorah Sara, Shimon Moshe Chizkiyahu, Michal Avigail, Nechama Shulamit, and Elisheva Yehudit—their rightful portions of His bountiful blessings, and may all of Israel and mankind be blessed with peace and tranquility.

It is a great privilege to have an expanded edition of this work, originally released as *The Infinite Chain* (Targum/Feldheim, 1989), produced by the distinguished publisher, Jason Aronson Inc., who also brought my latest book, *Between Silence and Speech: Essays in Jewish Thought*, to light.

I took this opportunity to add a few new chapters to make the work more complete:

1. A complete overview of all the hermeneutic rules of Rabbi Yishmael and Rabbi Akiva, with examples.
2. A new introduction to the *Aggadah* and its relationship toward the *halachah*.
3. A complete overview of the thirty-two rules of aggadic interpretation (with examples).
4. An addendum with:

    • An introduction to the halachic *Midrash*, the *Mishnah*, the *Beraita*, and the *Tosefta*.

- A discussion on the authenticity of the Torah text and the reasons why traditional Judaism does not agree with "modern" approaches toward the text as stated by Bible criticism.
- A short index to the Written Torah.
- A short index to the chapters of the *Mishnah*.
- A short index to the Maimonides's codex: *Mishneh Torah*.

My wife and I have been blessed with eight grandchildren. May all of them, together with their parents, merit to walk in the path of our holy Torah and be inspired by its wisdom.

Since its first edition, this book has been translated in Russian and is soon to be translated in Swedish and Spanish.

I would also like to mention my thanks to Rabbi David Aaron and Rabbi Les Fried, of the Isralight Institute in the Old City of Jerusalem, for giving me the opportunity to teach the Written and Oral Torah to a most fascinating audience of bright young people. My dear friend Rob Kurtz from Los Angeles was responsible for making me aware of this program. My very dear friend Rabbi Moises Benzaquen from the Sefardi Community of Los Angeles is another outstanding friend, who allowed me to teach his many followers.

I am thankful to the Hanhalla of Yeshivath Darchei Noam (Chapel) in Jerusalem, who gave me the pleasure of teaching at their school.

The writing of these new chapters took much more time than I had expected. I thank my dear friend Arthur Kurzweil of Jason Aronson for having so much patience with me.

My dear friends Aron and Bep Spijer, together with my

wife and children, again created the possibility for me to write these new chapters.

May the Holy One, Blessed Be He, bless them with all good.

                                                            Nathan T. Lopes Cardozo

THE
WRITTEN TORAH

THE TORAH

Torah Shebichtav (the written Torah—the Pentateuch), the most important portion of *Tanach* (the Bible), is nothing less than the voice of God communicating His Will to mankind through the written word. Through its narratives and precepts the Torah challenges mankind to pose questions. What is one to do with his life? How can one sanctify his life? And above all, how can one develop the understanding that life *must* be sanctified? The Torah provides the answers to those who ask. To those who have no questions, the Torah remains an enigma, for as the well-known dictum states, nothing is more irrelevant than an answer to a question nobody asks. The person who genuinely seeks meaning in his life will find the Torah replete with intellectual incisiveness, penetrating psychological insights, and an overwhelming reverence for life.

The Torah is the source of the universal and eternal truth: God is One, man is not alone, and life has both meaning and purpose. It proclaims that man *can* fulfill his

1

role in the cosmos, since God has granted him free will.[1] Man's periodic failures are no reason for despair, for God has enabled him to repent and begin again. The Torah presents man with his greatest challenge—"You shall be holy"[2]—and teaches him that to "love one's neighbor"[3] is the way of God.

The Torah acts as a blueprint for human perfection by recounting the deeds and thoughts of mankind since Creation. It retells the trials and tribulations encountered by man on the road to perfection, and both guides and goads him toward these heights. The Torah is not a history of man in the usual sense. Rather, it is a history of moral and ethical refinement, an analysis of what man can be.

In Judaism, the Torah is the book of life, for it discusses every aspect of the human condition. Its message, therefore, is relevant to every man, irrespective of his capabilities, qualities, or circumstances. Everyone finds himself depicted in its narratives.

According to Jewish philosophers, the very existence of the Torah is an indication of its divine origin, for it surpasses the creative skills of humanity. Its distinctive ideas regarding God's existence, man's creation in His image, and the human soul are major spiritual innovations. No truth has changed the history and behavior of man as drastically as the truth of the oneness of God. No word is more revealing, knowing, or indispensable than the word of the Torah. Biblical revelations about man's free will, capacity for holiness, and ability to repent display a profound wisdom not found within mortal men. Concepts

---

1. See *Devarim* 30:19.
2. *Vayikra* 19:2.
3. *Ibid.*, 19:18.

like the Messiah, redemption, Shabbat, the different dimensions of justice, prophecy, the afterlife, and contrition are much too deep to be the products of the human mind. No book loves man more, respects him more, or identifies with him more in moments of sorrow and distress.[4] For thousands of years man has pored over its pages and found guidance in every area. No work has ever replaced the Torah.

With this in mind, one starts to understand why the Torah must be of divine origin. Since none of man's many intellectual creations even approaches this extraordinary work, it becomes impossible for man to believe the Torah to be a human invention. Thus the question is not, "Could the Torah have been written by God?" but rather, "Could the Torah have been written by man?"

Yet modern man has conditioned himself to reject the Torah's concepts. Intellectually, he cannot relate to its frame of reference; psychologically, he may feel threatened by its content. Once man begins to comprehend its challenge, he must either change his lifestyle or risk the inability to face himself.

The Torah urges man to *be* rather than to *have*. Instead of equating freedom with lack of restraint, it defines freedom as the ability to live in accordance with the divinely ordained axioms that are the basis for happiness. How foreign this message is to societies whose every code is based on selfishness and the acquisition of property, profit, fame, and social status. The Torah teaches man that he must strive to become all that he can be. How different from contemporary social systems, which teach that man is

---

4. See *Tehillim* 91:15.

what he possesses[5] and one who has nothing is a failure. The Torah sees virtue only in one who strives to be better. It rejects social humanism, those who define happiness in terms of sexual license, and those who admire man for his ability to acquire and control. It is the antithesis of those who worship themselves rather than God.

The Torah is rooted in a world unknown to the average man: The world of the soul, not the body. Though transcribed in human terminology, its essence is divine. It is the revelation of how Heaven affects Earth, how every action and event is part of the relationship between the spiritual and the material. Its every sentence, word, and letter is in harmony with truth. Not surprisingly, its narratives and imperatives defy man's expectations. The Torah's definitions of good and evil, right and wrong, justice and inequity often differ radically from the conceptions of modern man. What might be considered superior, the Torah can view as inferior—for most people employ earthbound criteria, whereas the Torah uses the standards of the divine. The Torah's measuring rod is real rather than perceived truth, a yardstick that allows man to savor Heaven on Earth.

According to kabbalistic (Jewish mystical) doctrine, the Torah is the means of restoring God's Presence in the material world. Every *mitzvah* (precept) fulfilled by man has cosmic influence and hastens the eventual *tikkun* (the ultimate repair) of the break in the link between the spiritual and material worlds. Though the Torah is a work borrowed from the library of a higher and more sanctified world, it is written in a language intelligible to human

---

5. See *Kohelet* 10:19.

beings. It is man's key to unlocking the mystery of human purpose. Within the Torah man finds all that was, is, and will be. Unbound by time and space, it offers man the opportunity to enter a dimension based on truth and wisdom. Its narratives and imperatives, therefore, have far more meaning than we might think. Prohibitions of vices like adultery or theft exist on a spiritual as well as a material plane. The stories concerning Avraham, Yitzchak, and Yaakov reflect higher worlds as well as historical events. Consequently, man needs guidance in understanding the Torah, for even if he grasps the obvious, he must still deal with the allegorical, the homiletic, and the mystical.[6] Only after he has comprehended the totality of the Torah can he taste the heavenly flavor of this remarkable work. To afford him the opportunity to perceive this totality, God granted man the *Torah Shebe'al Peh* (the orally transmitted Torah), a *modus operandi* consisting of explanations, textual regulations, formulas, and logical deductions through which he can unlock the Torah's levels and secrets.

TORAH MIN HASHAMAYIM—REVELATION

And God said to Moshe, "Thus shall you say to the children of Israel: 'You have seen that I have spoken with you from Heaven.'"

(*Shemot* 20:19)

The basis of our knowledge of God . . . does not rest on belief, which . . . allows an element of doubt. It rests

---

6. Also known as *pardes: pshat, remez, drash,* and *sod.* See *Chagigah* 14b and Rashi ad loc., s.v. "*pardes.*"

solidly on the evidence of your senses, on what *you* have seen with your own eyes, on what you yourselves have experienced. . . . The two fundamental truths upon which the whole of Judaism rests—the exodus from Egypt and the giving of the Torah at Sinai—stand firmly on the actual evidence of your senses and as they were seen, heard, felt and experienced simultaneously by hundreds of thousands of people;[7] every possibility of deception is ruled out. Both these fundamental truths accordingly share the highest degree of certainty. They are completely out of the realm of mere believing or thinking, and within the bounds of what we know with certainty.

(*The Pentateuch, Translated and Explained by Samson Raphael Hirsch*, trans. I. Levy, Vol. II, p. 249)

Because God desired that doubt should never be raised as to the circumstances under which the Torah was given, He chose to elevate the entire nation to the status of prophets so that they might witness that Moshe was God's agent in presenting them with the Torah.

(Malbim on *Shemot* 19:9)

As is known, Christian and Mohammedan traditions also base their claims to veracity on divine revelation. But these revelations were purportedly to individuals, so their authenticity stands or falls on the reliability of these figures. In contradistinction, the Torah records that the *entire* nation of Israel stood at the foot of Mount Sinai and witnessed the manifestations of the Divine Presence.[8]

---

7. See R. Yosef Albo (1380–1440), *Sefer HaIkkarim*, first article, Chapter 20.

8. While the revelation at Sinai was unmatched, the elevated status allowing man to perceive the glory of God was not limited to Sinai

Indeed, the revelation at Mount Sinai is the fundamental axiom upon which all of Judaism rests, for it was the nation's willingness to accept the word of God without reservation that qualified them for their historical role as the *am segulah*[9] (the distinct people). The Torah relates that the revelation was so overwhelming that the people feared for their lives and pleaded: "You [Moshe] speak to us and we shall accept [the Torah], but let God not speak [directly] to us lest we die" (*Shemot* 20:16).

For a people that had but recently been released from servitude in Egypt, for a nation that was in the first stage of formation, hearing God speak without an intermediary was too awesome and frightening. Yet, as both Hirsch and Malbim point out, this direct contact with God was necessary since the nation had to accept the Torah as the word of God. Only then could Moshe's role as the faithful recorder of the Torah begin.

Unlike the rest of the nation, Moshe received the entire Torah at Sinai. Every detail, explanation, and tradition was revealed to him during the forty days he spent[10] on the mountain while God dictated the text of the written Torah.

---

alone. Thus, R. Eliezer (*Mechilta, Shemot* 15:2) says that even the maidservants who witnessed the miracles at the Red Sea saw God's glory in clearer form than Yechezkel the prophet.

9. *Shemot* 19:5; *Devarim* 7:6, 14:2, 26:18.

10. See *Megillah* 19b. In the introduction to his commentary on the Mishnah, *Tosfot Yom Tov* (R. Yom Tov Lipmann Heller, 1579–1654) writes that Moshe was made aware of the entire orally transmitted Torah, but not in a manner enabling him to transmit it to Yehoshua. Moshe's unique prophecy is described by the sages as being completely clear rather than an obfuscated vision (see Bamidbar 12:8, *Vayikra Rabbah* 1:14, *Sukkah* 45b, and *Yevamot* 49b). The commentators explain that while other prophets saw and heard God in dreams or

Much of its oral dimension, however, was withheld until the time for its transmission to the Jewish people had come.

> R. Levi bar Chama said in the name of R. Shimon b. Lakish, "What is the meaning of the verse ' . . . and I shall give you the tablets of stone and the Torah and the precepts that I have written to teach them' [*Shemot* 24:12]? 'Tablets of stone' refers to the Decalogue; 'the Torah' refers to the Pentateuch; 'the precepts' refers to the Mishnah; 'that I have written' refers to the books of the Prophets and Writings; 'to teach them' refers to the Talmud. Hence Moshe received all these at Sinai."
>
> (*Berachot* 5a)

> When God revealed Himself at Sinai to give the Torah to Israel, He taught Moshe the verses with the [explanations and derivations of the] Mishnah, the Talmud, and the Aggadah, for the verse states, "And God spoke all these things . . ." [*Shemot* 20:1]. Even the questions a student asks his teacher were disclosed by God to Moshe at that time.
>
> (*Shemot Rabbah* 47:1)

The description of revelation given by the Talmud and Midrash needs clarification. Were the visions of the prophets and the praises of the psalmists really no more than a reiteration of what had already been said? Are the thousands of pages of Talmudic discussions only a re-recording of what God taught Moshe? In *Tiferet Yisrael*,[11] Maharal (R. Judah Loew b. Bezalel, 1525–1609) explains that

---

visions, Moshe was in complete control of his faculties when he spoke to God.

11. Chapter 68.

though the entire Torah—from the Chumash to the debates in the Talmud—was taught to Moshe, God concealed many parts of it from the nation as a whole. Each generation was allowed to reproduce the exegesis so as to strengthen its bond with the Torah. Had Moshe recorded all the messages of the prophets and the sayings of the sages, the unique link between the Jewish people and its lore might have never been forged. Malbim[12] (R. Loeb b. Yechiel Michael, 1809–1879) and Sfat Emet[13] (R. Judah Aryeh Leib Alter, 1847–1905), in their commentaries on the Torah, add that although the information conveyed to subsequent generations already existed at Sinai, the medium used for its expression was established later. When God appeared to the prophets, He repeated ideas that he had taught Moshe at Sinai. Moshe had not transmitted these lessons in their entirety. Consequently, when the prophets, psalmists, and sages recorded their works or derived their exegesis, they were formulating ideas unknown to the people.

The Talmud (*Gittin* 60a) records a difference of opinion as to when Moshe transcribed the Torah. R. Yochanan maintains that he wrote separate scrolls at various times, whereas Resh Lakish contends that the entire Torah was recorded at one time.

Moshe himself wrote thirteen Torah scrolls: one for each tribe and one that was placed in the Ark in the Sanctuary.[14] The Torah was also written on stones when the Jews entered the land of Israel.[15] The Mishnah (*Sotah* 7:5) states

---

12. In his introduction to *Vayikra*.
13. On *Ki Tisa*.
14. See *Devarim Rabbah* 9:9.
15. *Devarim* 27:8.

that it was written in all seventy spoken languages so that all nations would be aware of its message. There is a difference of opinion as to what was recorded on the stones:[16] the entire Torah, the *mitzvot*, the Decalogue, or the seven Noachide commandments.

Another dispute is adduced by the Talmud (*Bava Batra* 14b) concerning the authorship of the last eight verses in *Devarim*, which deal with Moshe's death: It is the opinion of one school that Yehoshua served as the recorder, for "could Moshe have written the words 'Moshe died there'?" Another school maintains that "until now, God dictated and Moshe repeated and wrote. Henceforth, God dictated and Moshe wrote with tears." All agree that the words recorded were dictated by God:[17]

> Our sages taught, "For he has despised the word of God" [*Bamidbar* 15:31]—this refers to one who states that the Torah does not derive from Heaven. Even if he asserts that the entire Torah derives from Heaven with the exception of one verse, which [he claims] was said by Moshe, [he is considered] one who "has despised the word of God." And even if he admits that the entire Torah derives from Heaven with the exception of a certain deduction . . . he, too, belongs [in the category of] one who "has despised the word of God."
>
> (*Sanhedrin* 99a)[18]

---

16. See R. Baruch Halevi Epstein (1860–1942), *Torah Temimah*, *Devarim* 27:8, note 6.

17. As we shall see (pp. 16–18 and pp. 27–34), conflicts among the sages do not necessarily mean that only one viewpoint is correct. Originally, the Torah was written as a jumble of letters; later, these letters were assembled into words. It is possible that Moshe wrote the letters and Yehoshua formed them into the words reporting his master's death.

18. *Kesef Mishneh* (on Rambam, *Mishneh Torah, Hilchot Teshuvah*

The whole Torah transmitted by Moshe is entirely of divine origin (i.e., he received it wholly from God in a manner metaphorically referred to as speaking. . . .) He [Moshe] was like an amanuensis. There is no difference between "And the children of Ham were Kush and Mitzrayim . . ." [*Bereshit* 10:6] and "I am the Lord your God" [*Shemot* 20:2] or "Hear, Israel, the Lord our God, the Lord is One" [*Devarim* 6:4]. They are all of divine origin. . . .

> (*Rambam, Commentary on the Mishnah*, introduction to last chapter of *Sanhedrin*, eighth principle)

The *Zohar* poses the question: If the Torah was dictated by God and reflects the thoughts, ideas and messages of a higher order, why are instances of human failure such an integral part of its contents?

If it is undignified for a human king to engage in common conversation, let alone to record it, is it conceivable that the Highest King, the Holy One, blessed be He, lacked holy subjects with which to fill the Torah and had to collect topics such as the worldly stories regarding Yishmael and Hagar [*Bereshit* 16], the talks between Lavan and Yaakov [*Bereshit* 31], the dialogue between Bilaam and his ass [*Bamidbar* 22], or the tales of Balak [*Bamidbar* 22] and Zimri [*Bamidbar* 25]? Why do we call this the "Torah of truth"? Why do we declare, "The Torah of God is perfect . . . , the testimony of God is sure. . . . The edicts of God are just. . . . They are more precious than gold, yea, than fine gold . . ." [*Tehillim* 19:8–11]?

> (Vol. III, p. 52a)

3:8) notes that no differentiation is made between the written Torah and the oral Torah. One who denies the divine origin of either is categorized as "despising the word of God."

The historical narratives recorded in *Tanach* portray a way of life that enables man to face the challenges of society without abandoning his unique role as the creature to whom God revealed Himself. The sages say: "The actions of the fathers are a guide to the children,"[19] (i.e., the manner in which our forefathers resolved the inevitable crisis caused by material beings attempting to live spiritual lives is the means through which man can attain the goals for which he was created.) The stories in *Tanach* are not told to us to inculcate within us a sense of pride in the accomplishments of our ancestors. They are telling us that what transpired in the lives of the biblical personalities might well occur in our lives, albeit in a somewhat different form. These personalities were able to overcome their trials because they lived according to a code of behavior ordained by God. The instances of failure are recorded to make it clear that they were caused by abandoning this code. Man can succeed in his spiritual endeavors if he studies his forefathers' actions and emulates their responses.

The narratives in *Tanach* are real-life examples of the ongoing struggle between body and soul, between man's physical desires and his spiritual core.[20] This struggle is the

---

19. See *Bereshit Rabbah* 70:6; Ramban on *Bereshit* 12:6.

20. The Talmud (*Shabbat* 88b) relates that when Moshe ascended on high, the angels asked God, "Do You choose to present man with this treasure that You hid for 974 generations before Creation? 'What is man that You should remember him . . . ?' [*Tehillim* 8:5]." God told Moshe, "Answer their question" (i.e., prove that man is worthy of receiving the Torah). Moshe replied, "Master of the universe, in the Torah it states, 'I am the Lord, your God, who has taken you out of Egypt . . .' [*Shemot* 20:2]—were you [the angels] in Egypt? Were you enslaved to Pharaoh? Why should you have the Torah? Furthermore,

inherent dichotomy of Creation, for how can the soul, existing in the world of truth, survive when held captive in a vessel that has no relationship to that world? The Torah, a code emanating from that world of truth, but written in a form that man can understand, is the means God has provided for resolving the dichotomy. Man can be an Esav or a Yaakov, an Amalkite or a deeply moral person. He holds in his hands the power to allow his soul to flourish despite the encumbrances placed upon it, or to follow the dictates of his material desires. The lives of the patriarchs prove to man that he can bridge the gap between Heaven and Earth. Through his God-given gift of free will, man can choose not to fail, not to become an Esau or an Amalekite, who foundered because they abandoned God's way in their search for gratification, and not because they were faced with an impossible task.

If the Torah was dictated by God and reflects the ideas and messages of a higher order, and if the narratives of Torah exemplify how to resolve the ongoing struggle between body and soul, the next question must be, could man exist without it? Could he not, through his superior faculties and abilities, attain the same heights of righteousness and purity for which he was created, even without Torah? Alternatively, we can also ask, Is man worthy of revelation?[21] Can a being who has consistently proven his

---

the Torah states, 'You shall have no other gods before Me' [*ibid.*, 20:3]. Are you [the angels] forced to live among people who worship false gods?"

21. Malbim, in his commentary on Tehillim 8, writes that King David confronted this question and concluded that if man is unworthy, he defeats the purpose of Creation (i.e., taking the Torah from Heaven and revealing it on Earth).

inability to live in harmony even with nature ever reach a higher level? Does revelation serve any purpose and is it of any benefit for a people who uses its abundant gifts to find more efficient means of destroying itself?

Although reason and logic are the sanctified altars before which generations of philosophers and scientists have prostrated themselves, they leave man's thirst for knowledge unquenched, for they fail to answer so many of his questions. The very fact that man poses problems for which he can find no solutions indicates that there must be a truth beyond his innate comprehension. At the same time, man's ability to understand that he must ask such questions makes him inherently worthy of having that truth revealed to him through the Torah. Elaborating on this point, Maharal explains that man's conceptions of reality, an thus his ability to reason, are often fallacious, based as they are on individual perception, with its consequent bias and distortion. Real truth, as exemplified by the Torah, exists in a dimension uninfluenced by individual limitations. God revealed the Torah to allow man to gain insight into the world as it really is.[22]

Revelation, then, is both the ultimate kindness to man and his ultimate test. On the one hand, it is the sign that God desires that man fulfill his role. On the other hand, once man has knowledge of the Torah, he can no longer offer any excuses for his failures. The Torah is the vehicle God has provided to take man as far as he can go. It is left to man to decide whether to use it.

---

22. Introduction to *Netivot Olam*.

The Eternal Nature of the Torah

> "He [a king] shall not multiply wives for himself, and his heart shall not turn away [from God] . . ." [*Devarim* 17:17]. Reasoned Shlomo Hamelech: "Why did God command, 'He shall not multiply [*lo yarbeh*] . . .'? So that 'his heart shall not turn away.' But I will multiply [*arbeh*] and my heart still will not turn away." That moment, the *yud*[23] of the word *yarbeh* went up on high, prostrated itself before God, and said: "Didn't you say that not even one letter of the Torah shall ever be discarded? Yet Shlomo now wishes to discard me. Today he shall do away with me, tomorrow with another letter, and eventually the entire Torah will be abrogated." God answered, "Shlomo and a thousand like him will pass away, but even the lower protrusion of a *yud* will not be discarded."
>
> (*Shemot Rabbah* 6:1)

Because the Torah is the revealed word of God, even a man with the wisdom of Shlomo has no right to change its rules or reinterpret them to conform to his needs. As the very word of God, its contents cannot be tampered with so as to make them seem more relevant.

R. Saadiah Gaon[24] (882–942) points out that the Jewish people are a people only by virtue of the Torah (both written and oral). Since the Jewish nation is destined to exist as long as Heaven and Earth, its laws must endure eternally. Whereas other nations are bound by culture and geography, the Jews have their common heritage of being the recipients of God's unchanging message. One who

---

23. See *Yefeh Toar* and *Maharazav* ad loc.
24. *Emunot Vedeot* 3:7.

denies the eternal nature of the Torah severs the cord that unites them as a people.

> In addition, the fact that the Torah cannot be abrogated determines that it was presented in its entirety. The verse states, "It is not in heaven" (*Devarim* 30:12): No part of the Torah has been left behind in heaven.
>
> Nothing in the divine revelation which was necessary for its being understood and accomplished remained in heaven so that you could say, Where can we find a mind so super-humanly enlightened that it penetrates into the secrets of heaven for us, or brings us a new revelation from heaven that we still lack that will complement our present knowledge?
>
> (Hirsch, *The Pentateuch*, Vol. II, p. 602)

The Torah states unequivocally that neither the prophets nor the sages have the right to change the Torah by declaring certain precepts inapplicable.[25] However, if the Torah is eternal and unchanging, how can the kabbalists tell us that many Torah laws will cease to apply in the messianic age, when the evil inclination will no longer prevail? They answer that its text will undergo a metamorphosis in which its letters will combine into different words suitable for the messianic era:

---

25. See Rashi on *Devarim* 13:4; Rambam, *Mishneh Torah, Hilchot Yesodei HaTorah* 9:3. The Sanhedrin, however, can temporarily override any Torah precept—except the prohibition against worshipping false gods—if there is dire need to preserve the Torah. Thus, Eliyahu was permitted to offer a sacrifice on Mount Carmel—despite the ban on offering sacrifices outside the Temple Mount—since by so doing he proved the prophets of Baal false and glorified the name of God (*I Melachim* 18). See *Yevamot* 90b. Needless to say, the rules for this temporary measure are themselves God-given and part of Torah legislation. See R. Z. H. Chajes (1805–1855), *Torat Nevi'im* 3:6.

Concerning the new interpretation of the Torah that will be revealed in the days of the Messiah, it may be argued that the Torah remains eternally the same, but originally [after Adam's sin] it assumed the form of material combinations of letters adapted to the material world. One day, man will cast off his material body and . . . recover the mystical body inhabited by Adam before the fall. Then he will understand the mystery of the Torah, and its hidden aspects will become manifest. And later, at the end of the sixth millennium [i.e., during the era of the Messiah], man will become an even higher spiritual being, able to delve even more deeply into the mysteries of the Torah. . . . For the fundamental idea of the present disguise is that the Torah, like man himself, has donned a material garment. When man rises up and frees himself from his material garment [i.e., when he overcomes the influences of his evil inclination] in favor of a higher and more spiritual one, so also will the material manifestation of the Torah be transformed and its spiritual greatness will be abundantly apparent. The hidden faces of the Torah will become radiant . . . and yet, in all these stages, the Torah will be the same as before; its essence will never change.

(R. Avraham Azulai,
Chesed L'Avraham 2:11)[26]

---

26. The author offers the following example of the changing of the meaning of a precept: The Torah (*Devarim* 22:11) states, "You shall not wear clothing made of *shaatnez, tzemer u'phishtim* [wool and linen] together." According to the kabbalists, this precept will become irrelevant in the messianic era, for man will return to his spiritual state before Adam's sin and will have no need for clothing. R. Avraham Azulai therefore suggests that *shaatnez tzemer u'phishtim* will be emended to *satan az metzar v'tofsim* (insolent Satan afflicts, and they [transgressions] ensnare). See *Chesed L'Avraham* 2:27; R. Moshe Cordovero, *Shiur Komah*. This new reading is a warning to man not to exchange his spiritual garment for the skin of the serpent, which reflects Satan's power to gain possession of him and bring him to sin.

This does not mean that in the messianic age the Torah will be new or different. Rather, according to the kabbalists, the Torah is infinite and all-encompassing. The precepts and narratives we read are the result of a combination of letters best suited to our spiritual perception. In an era of greater spirituality, the letters will recombine to offer a different meaning, while their previous meaning will remain concealed within the "lower" combinations.

In other words, the *mitzvot* and their spiritual value will continue to be applicable, but they will be represented by a world of higher dimensions. Because the Torah stems from a higher world, it can contain messages that material beings are incapable of deciphering until they are released from their dependence on the material world. This does not mean that when "times have changed," the text can be arbitrarily reinterpreted; it means that a complete reordering of the frames of reference will take place.

The *Masorah*

The term *masorah* is used in a variety of ways in Jewish literature. At times it refers to the transmission of the oral tradition. In its narrowest sense, however, it refers to the traditions connected with the writing of Torah scrolls (i.e., the shape of the letters, the spaces, the paragraphs, and other distinguishing marks).

The *masorah* is of ancient origin: The main portion was transmitted to Moshe; some parts date back to Ezra the

---

See my booklets, *The Torah as God's Mind, A Kabbalistic Look into the Pentateuch* (New York: Bep-Ron Publications, 1988); and *Between Silence and Speech* (Northvale: Jason Aronson Inc.), 1997. Chapter 7.

Scribe and the *Anshei Knesset Hagedolah* (Men of the Great Assembly), the most important rabbinical body from 500 to 300 B.C.E. Rambam[27] points out that as long as a Torah scroll written by Moshe was extant, all other scrolls were compared to that scroll to ensure accuracy.

The *Masorah* comprises not only the spelling of the Torah's words but:

a. The script. The Talmud (*Sanhedrin* 21b) records a dispute as to which type of script was used by Moshe. Mar Ukva asserts that the Torah was originally written in ancient Hebrew and Ezra decreed that Torah scrolls henceforth be written in *Ashurit* (see page 30). R. Yehudah Hanasi maintains that the Torah was recorded in Ashurit, but that script was lost and Ezra reestablished it. R. Elazar Hamodai maintains that the script never changed. Ever since Ezra, all agree that Torah scrolls must be written in *Ashurit*.

b. The *parshiot*—sectional divisions. The division of the Torah into chapters (*Capitolae* in Latin) is inconsistent and of gentile[28] origin. It was probably introduced by the translators who rendered the Hebrew *Tanach* into Latin. R. Yitzchak Natan, who compiled *Meir Metiv* (a fifteenth-century concordance of bib-

---

27. *Commentary on the Mishnah*, introduction. Also see Jerusalem Talmud, *Taanit* 4:2; *Avot DeRabbi Natan*, version 2 (Schechter edition), Chapter 26, end.

28. This division was apparently carried out by either Hugo of St. Cher (1200–1263), a French cardinal who compiled the first biblical concordance, or Stephen Langton (thirteenth century), archbishop of Canterbury. It was made using the Vulgata translation of *Tanach* into Latin by St. Jerome (340–420).

lical Hebrew), found himself "compelled to adopt this division into chapters since there was no Jewish arrangement known to him." There is, however, a Jewish tradition of sectional divisions based on the contents of the verses. This division is made in Torah scrolls by leaving an empty space between the end of one verse and the beginning of the next. If the two verses have no connection in their subject matter, this space extends until the end of the line and the next verse starts on the following line. This type of division is referred to as *petuchah*—open—and is indicated in printed editions by the letter *peh*. If the verses have some connection, a space the width of nine letters is left between them. This type of division is referred to as *stumah*—closed—and is indicated in printed editions by the letter *samech*. There are six hundred sixty-nine sectional divisions in the Torah—two hundred ninety are open and three hundred seventy-nine are closed.[29] The weekly Torah readings are made up of varying numbers of sections.

c. The *nekudot*—dots above certain letters. There are ten instances in the Torah where dots are written over individual letters, words, or groups of words[30] to teach various lessons.[31]

d. The *ketarim*[32]—crowns above certain letters.

---

29. See Rambam, *Mishneh Torah, Hilchot Sefer Torah* 8, middle.

30. *Soferim* 6:3; *Avot DeRabbi Natan*, version 1, p. 100, or version 2, 37:49.

31. *Bamidbar Rabbah* 3:13.

32. The Talmud (*Menachot* 29b) states that the letters *shin, ayin, tet, nun, zayin, gimmel,* and *tzadi* must be written with three lines on top like a crown. Rashi notes that one line points to the right, one to the

e. The *otiot memuyanot*—isolated letters. This refers to the practice of setting *Bamidbar* 10:35–36 apart from the preceding and subsequent verses by adding an inverted *nun* before and after. *Sifri* explains that these isolated *nunim* were added because these verses should appear elsewhere.[33]

f. The *otiot gedolot* and *ketanot*[34]—enlarged and reduced letters.

g. Words written *malei* and *chaser—plene* or *defective* (i.e., with vowels fully delineated, as in סוכה, or only partially, as in סכה).[35]

---

left, and one straight up, and these crowning lines are added to the final *nun* and *tzadi* as well.

33. See Rashi on Bamidbar 10:35. Also see R. Shlomo Ganzfried, *Keset Hasofer*, where these letters are called *menuzarot*.

34. The Talmud (*Soferim* 9:1–7) states that the *bet* in the word *bereshit* (*Bereshit* 1:1), the *vav* in *gachon* (*Vayikra* 11:42), the *lamed* in *vayashlicheim* (*Devarim* 29:27) and the *yud* in *yigdal* (*Bamidbar* 14:17) should be written larger than usual while the *yud* in *teshi* (*Devarim* 32:18) should be smaller than usual. See M. Z. Segal, *Mevo Hamikra*, vol. 3, eighth edition (*Kiryat Sefer*), pp. 842–910.

35. Although Torah scrolls are written without vowels, the Talmud (*Nedarim* 37b) states that the vowels were given to Moshe at Sinai and passed down through the generations. These vowels are important in determining the laws based on the meaning of words. *Tzafnat Pa'neach* (*Devarim* 31:9) records a tradition that the Torah scroll written by Moshe and placed in the Ark had vowels and accents.

Rambam (*Mishneh Torah, Hilchot Sefer Torah* 7:11) invalidates any Torah scroll in which a word that is traditionally written *malei* is written *chaser*, or vice versa.

The musical notes used in reading the Torah were taught to Moshe—see *Nedarim* 37b. Interestingly, while there are different traditions among various communities as to the melody for each note, there is no disagreement about the placement of the notes themselves. The importance of these notes lies not in the melody associated with

   h. *Keri* and *ketiv*[36]—words pronounced at variance with the way they are written.

   i. The order of the books in the Torah. Because this order originates with Moshe, some authorities[37] maintain that laws can be derived from the juxtaposition of paragraphs or verses. Even those who disagree accept this opinion in regard to *Devarim* since this book was recorded at one time (*Yevamot* 4a).

   j. The order of Torah readings in the synagogue. The original custom in the land of Israel was to read the entire Torah over a period of one hundred fifty-four weeks. Our practice of reading the entire Torah in one year follows the custom of Babylon.[38]

It is truly amazing that despite the complexity and mass of material, the entire *masorah* was transmitted orally from generation to generation without major discrepancies. Only when the sages began to doubt the efficacy of their memories were the rules of the *masorah* formally recorded. Short notes were sometimes written alongside the text of the Torah; these are referred to as the *masorah ketanah*—

---

them, but in the meaning they assign the verse. Thus, a pause introduced by these notes defines the meaning of the sentence.

See R. David b. Shlomo Ibn Abizimra (1479–1573), *Teshuvot HaRadbaz*, vol. 3, no. 1068, where it is stated that the musical notes are, in fact, a commentary on the Torah, and were omitted from Torah scrolls lest they preclude other interpretations.

36. Certain words in the Torah are read differently than they are written. In some cases, a *yud* is substituted for a *vav* (e.g., *Shemot* 37:8), and in others an entire word changes (e.g., *Devarim* 28:27, 30; *Shemot* 21:8). These variant readings date back to Moshe.

37. See *Yevamot* 4a.

38. Rambam, *Mishneh Torah, Hilchot Tefillah* 13:1.

the abridged *masorah*. Lengthier notes—the *masorah gedolah*—were recorded at the end of some editions or published as separate works. The first reference to a written *masorah* is found in *Halachot Gedolot*.[39] In subsequent years, complete works were written about the rules of the *masorah*.

The Talmud uses the term *masorah* in reference to the traditional transcription of the *Torah Shebichtav*. The term *mikra*—reading—is used to refer to words pronounced other than how they are written. When *masorah* and *mikra* contradict each other, R. Akiva maintains that legal rulings should only be derived from the traditional pronunciations. R. Yishmael, on the other hand, contends that legal derivations can only be based on the way words are spelled.[40]

Because the manner in which Torah scrolls are written is of the utmost importance, their transcription was only assigned to *soferim*—scribes—who could skillfully and flawlessly duplicate the text. The Talmud (*Kiddushin* 30a) notes that they were referred to as *soferim*—literally, "people who count"—because they counted the letters of the Torah. These righteous scholars were also known as *katvanaim*[41] (transcribers) or *lavlarim*[42] (scribes). Portions

---

39. The authorship and date of *Halachot Gedolot* have been the focus of many studies and conflicting views. It is variously ascribed to R. Sherira Gaon (906–1006), R. Hai Gaon (939–1038), R. Simeon Kayyara, or R. Yehudai Gaon. See *Teshuvot Hageonim* 376; *Zikaron Larishonim Vegam La'acharonim* ¼ (1887); and *Teshuvot Geonim Kadmonim* (1848).
40. *Sanhedrin* 4b.
41. Jerusalem Talmud, *Megillah* 1:11.
42. *Eruvin* 13a.

of the *masorah* were forgotten in the course of time and reinstated by Ezra and later sages.[43]

Though the Talmudic sages used the same text as earlier generations did, it is not uncommon to find biblical misquotations in the Talmud. Often, these are no more than typographical errors. In other instances, they reflect the Talmud's practice of only quoting the part of a verse germane to a specific discussion. If one bears in mind that the exegesis that makes up the Talmud was initially transmitted orally, it is not surprising that the sages preferred to quote a verse in part rather than in toto. Moreover, it is prohibited to quote from the written Torah without the benefit of a text.[44] Thus, the Talmud often prefers to paraphrase.

Today, the term *masorah* has become synonymous with the oral tradition on its entirety.

TIKKUN SOFERIM

It is a cardinal principle of Judaism that there are no extra or redundant letters or words in the written Torah. Each and every letter of the Torah has a lesson to teach.[45] Yet several words and letters seem to appear needlessly in the text. These instances, known as *tikkun soferim*— scribal embellishments—were made by God to transmit certain educational or moral lessons that would have been impossible to deduce had the style been different. The sages spent their lives scrutinizing the text to uncover the

---

43. *Sukkah* 20a.
44. *Gittin* 60b.
45. See *Teshuvot HaRadbaz*, vol. 3, no. 1068.

messages contained in these seemingly superfluous additions. Thus, in *Bereshit* 7:8 we find: *u'min habehemah asher einenah tehorah*—"and of the animals that are not ritually pure." The text could well have stated simply *u'min habehemah hatemae'ah*—and of the impure animals—but the Talmud notes that the longer form is used:

> R. Yehoshua b. Levi says, "One should never use coarse language, for the Torah itself added eight [extra] letters [i.e., the difference between *asher einenah tehorah* and *hatemae'ah*] so as to avoid using a gross expression."
>
> (*Pesachim* 3a)

Rashi comments that though the term *tamae*—impure—is employed elsewhere, the Torah's circumlocution in this instance indicates a lesson that is not necessarily related to the text.[46]

Similarly, the Torah uses certain phrases when referring to God even though a simpler or more concise form could have sufficed. Thus, in *Bereshit* 18:22 we find: "And the men turned from there and went to Sodom and Avraham remained standing before God." The context clearly implies that God was waiting for Avraham. Nevertheless, the Torah changed the phrasing because it is undignified to suggest that Avraham had made God wait.[47] Again, by using a more complex construction, the Torah teaches a lesson that is not part of the subject under discussion.

---

46. For a discussion, see R. Baruch Epstein, *Torah Temimah*; R. Zalman Sorotzkin, *Oznaim LaTorah*. For a list of all cases of *tikkun soferim*, see *Minchat Shai* on *Mikraot Gedolot*, Zechariah 2:2.

47. See R. Shlomo Algazi (1610–1683), *Yavin Shemuah* (a commentary on *Halichot Olam* by R. Jeshua b. Joseph) (Tel Aviv: Shilo, 5730) 2:1, pp. 9b–10a.

Mizrachi (R. Elijah Mizrachi)[48] ad loc. emphasizes that the term *tikkun soferim* does not mean the sages made changes to convey lessons that were not originally part of the Torah. Rather, because the sages closely examined every word of the text so as to elucidate the full meaning of each verse, they discovered that the Torah itself deviated from a more concise form. Maharal adds: "Just as the Torah uses the language people speak, it employs the style of *soferim*. . . . This is the meaning of *tikkun soferim* (i.e., as *soferim* would have written)" (*Gur Aryeh, Bereshit* 18:22).

ITTUR SOFERIM

Another stylistic deviation is referred to as *ittur soferim*—literally, "scribal crowning." It takes three forms:

a. *Ittur* as *Halachah LeMoshe MiSinai*—embellishments made by the Torah itself to render the text more poetic or linguistically effective. Thus, in Bereshit 18:5 we find: "And I [Avraham] shall fetch a morsel of bread and you shall refresh your hearts; afterwards you shall go on [*achar ta'avoru*]." The text could have stated *veta'avoru*—"and you shall go on"—using the conjunction "and" instead of the extra word "afterwards."[49] The longer form, however, is more appropriate linguistically. This phrasing, which would seem to add an unnecessary word, was given to Moshe at Sinai (*Nedarim* 37b).

---

48. A fifteenth-century Turkish scholar who authored a super commentary on Rashi.

49. See Ran on *Nedarim* 37b and Rashi on Bereshit 18:5.

b. *Ittur* as a means of understanding a verse correctly. At one time, people made notes in their private scrolls (the only written study materials available) to ensure that they had interpreted the verse under discussion correctly. Thus, alongside the previously cited verse, people would mark *veta'avoru* since the longer form used by the Torah could be misinterpreted to mean that the food Avraham had prepared was meant for his guests to take along with them on their journey, (i.e., "I shall fetch a morsel of bread and you shall refresh your hearts after you go on.") There are over twenty[50] such instances known to us. The sages, concerned that these changes might be substituted for the original text, marked them as *itturim*.

c. *Ittur* as a means of abrogating these earlier emendations, once the traditional interpretation had become common knowledge. Such deletions were also referred to as *itturim*, for they crowned the beauty of the Torah by restoring the original text.

THE TEXT AND ITS KABBALISTIC MEANING

As we have noted, great efforts were made to ensure that no changes were made in the text. Because each letter and word was inserted in the Torah for a specific purpose, care was taken that the transmission of the text from generation to generation be completely faithful. This dedication to precision assumes an even more profound meaning when

---

50. See Segal, *Mevo Hamikra*, pp. 824, 861.

one considers the statement in the *Zohar* (*Yitro* 87a) that
"the entire Torah is the name of God."[51]

Ramban writes:

> We have yet another mystical tradition . . . [that] the
> whole Torah is composed of the names of God. The letters
> of the words separate themselves into divine names when
> the words are redivided. . . . For example, the words
> *bereshit bara Elokim* ["In the beginning, God created"]
> can be reformed into the words *barosh yitbareh Elokim*
> [three names of God]. This principle applies to the entire
> Torah. . . . Therefore, a Torah scroll in which even one
> letter has been added or deleted is unfit for use, even if
> the mistake does not change the meaning of the word
> [and even if the word is spelled this way elsewhere in the
> Torah]. Apparently, the Torah that was written with black
> fire upon white fire . . . , i.e., without the letters being
> separated into words, enabling it to be read either as
> God's names or as we read it . . . was given to Moshe
> using the word division that expresses the *mitzvot*, but it
> was also transmitted to him orally in the form of the divine
> names.

> (*Commentary on the Torah,*
> translated and annotated by
> R. C. B. Chavel,
> introduction)

According to Kabbalah, the entire Torah takes on a
different meaning when we read the letters as forms of
God's names. Thus, Torah scrolls contain no vowels,
punctuation, or accents, for they would preclude a higher-

---

51. The "name of God" in kabbalistic thought represents not so
much the essence of God as the qualities of God known to man.

level reading of the letters.[52] As R. Meir, one of the great teachers of the Mishnah, says:

> When I went to R. Yishmael he asked me, "My son, what is your occupation?" I answered, "I am a scribe." He said to me, "My son, be careful in your work, for it is the work of Heaven. If you were to omit or add a single letter, you would destroy the entire world."
>
> *(Eruvin* 13a)

R. Azriel of Gerona, a thirteenth-century kabbalist, stresses this point:

> Just as some of the human body's limbs, joints, and organs seem to be more vital than others, so it seems with the Torah. To one who does not understand their hidden meaning, certain sections of the Torah seem fit to be thrown into the fire. But to one who has gained insight into their true significance, they appear essential. Consequently, to omit so much as a letter, or even a point, is like removing part of a perfect unity. It also follows that as concerns the divine character of the Torah, no distinction can be made between the verses in Bereshit that detail the children of Esav [seemingly a superfluous portion] and the Decalogue, for all are parts of the whole.
>
> *(Perush Aggadot*, p. 37)

One of the most famous of kabbalists, R. Avraham b. Shmuel Abulafia (1240–1291), expands on this idea:

> The methods of *tzeruf*—combining letters—can be compared to music. The ears hear the different sounds by way

---

52. See R. Eliyahu Kohen Ittamari of Smyrna, *Devash Lefi; Teshuvot HaRadbaz*, vol. 3, no. 1068.

of various combinations, according to the temperaments of the melody and instruments. Two instruments can effect a combination and then the ear of the listener registers a pleasant sensation . . . and the enjoyment of these melodies produces ever new delight. It is impossible to produce [this delight] except by way of a combination of sounds . . . and the secrets that express themselves in these combinations delight the heart that knows its God and fill it with ever fresh joy.

(Sefer Hapeliah 52b–53a)

While the language of the Torah is *lashon hakodesh* (the holy tongue)—Hebrew—the script used for its recording is known as *Ashurit*. There is a difference of opinion as to what is meant by this term: Some understand it to refer to an Assyrian script, while others interpret the word to mean an upright and beautiful type of letter. According to the Talmud (*Berachot* 55a), God created Heaven and Earth with the help of this alphabet. The kabbalists understand this to mean that the twenty-two Hebrew letters are divine in origin and their very shapes are reflections of heavenly "letters," which are themselves the foundations of the physical world.

As an example of the kabbalistic significance of the letters, we can follow the discussion of the letter *alef* in *Sefer Temunah* (Catalonia, 1250), attributed to R. Nechunya b. Hakanah and R. Yishmael Kohen Gadol (second century).

(Before we begin, however, we stress that this example is no more than a minute particle of the mountain of Kabbalah. By understanding the author's interpretation, we do not automatically become masters of Judaism's mystical tradition. Too often, laymen have written works on Kabbalah as well as treatises on the numerical values of letters—*gematriot*—without grasping the underlying meaning of these concepts. Such superficial wordplay and numerology robs the Kabbalah of its essence. Even works of tremendous scholarship often lack insight into the philosophy of Jewish mysticism and few English works convey a proper understanding of the Kabbalah.)

Every letter of the Hebrew alphabet has a numerical value; thus, *alef* stands for one, *bet* stands for two, *gimmel* for three, etc. The name of God is written as *yud* (10), *heh* (5), *vav* (6), *heh* (5)—from the root *haya*, "to be"—and has a numerical value of twenty-six. The letter *alef* (1), which represents God's oneness, is itself made up of letters with a numerical value of twenty-six, for it is formed by combining two *yudim* (10+10) with a *vav* (6).

This is of great significance since God revealed Himself in twenty-six generations (i.e., from Creation until the revelation at Sinai). Moreover, just as the number twenty-six in the name of God is made up of four components— *yud, heh, vav, heh* (10, 5, 6, 5)—the twenty-six generations in which God revealed Himself are divisible into four periods: There were ten generations between Adam and Noach, five between Shem and Peleg, six between R'eu and Yitzchak, and five between Yaakov and Moshe. Each of these four sets of generations is introduced in the Torah with the phrase *eleh toledot*—"these are the generations" (*Bereshit* 2:4, 6:9, 11:10, and 37:2)—for in each case, a different attribute of God was revealed. Thus, God allowed

His essence to appear in this world through His name (*yud, heh, vav, heh*), and He put His stamp on these twenty-six generations. Furthermore, when the zenith of revelation was reached at Sinai after twenty-six generations, God's oneness—as represented by the letter *alef*, which is made up of letters with the numerical value of twenty-six—became fully apparent. When seen in this manner, the chronology of Torah history takes on a deeper meaning.

God's name can also be written without a *vav* for, as we have noted, it finds its root in the Hebrew word *haya*—*heh* (5), *yud* (10), *heh* (5). The combined numerical value of these root letters equals that of the two *yudim* that form the *alef*. These *yudim*, as we have seen, are separated by a *vav* (6), which mirrors them and links the *yud* of the upper world with the *yud* of the lower world, just as the six days of Creation connect both worlds. Because *yud* (10) represents unity and perfection—since it marks the point where single digits are replaced by doubles, signifying the completion of a series—it has limited relevance in this material world. Consequently, in the spelling of God's name, one *yud* was left complete to symbolize the perfection and completeness of the upper world, and the other was split into two *hehim* to represent the imperfection of the lower, material world. God's essence could not be revealed in the lower world in perfect form, only in a fragmented manner. This duality also reflects the difference between the two worlds—the upper one is completely spiritual whereas the lower one combines the spiritual and material.

The *alef*, composed of two *yudim* mirrored by the conjunctive *vav*, represents the yearning of the lower world to reunite with the upper world. This is the very purpose of Creation: to create a system that, though seemingly complete and self-sufficient, nevertheless longs to rejoin its source. The construction of the *alef* represents the ideal relationship of the two worlds. The *yud* of the upper world desires to descend, while the *yud* of the lower world strives to ascend. This is the relationship depicted in *Shir Hashirim*—the longing of the lovers to be reunited. When man reunites the two *yudim*, when his life is ruled by both the higher and lower orders, then life and death become meaningless. The dichotomies and paradoxes of human existence were only brought about to make man yearn for a combination that can free him from their constraints. All this is reflected in the letter *alef.*

Similarly, the Torah tells us that man was created in "God's image" (*Bereshit* 1:27). Consequently, just as God's name had to be split to have meaning in this world, man's original form had to be divided so that he might fulfill his role. This is the meaning of the Midrashic statement that man was created as both male and female. God saw that it was not good for man to be alone[53] (i.e., he could not fulfill the purpose for which he was created, to unite the spiritual and material). Only when man was split into male and female, into forms that long to be reunited, could he evolve into a being that can resolve the paradoxes of life by reuniting the upper and lower worlds. Just as man yearns for woman to make himself complete, the lower world yearns for the upper one.

Thus, the shapes of the letters of the Hebrew alphabet are not accidental but deliberate, representing spiritual forms. The Talmud (*Pesachim* 87b) relates that when

---

53. *Bereshit* 2:18.

Moshe broke the tablets, their letters flew upwards and reunited with their heavenly counterparts. By prostrating themselves before a material form, the people of that generation revealed that they were incapable of reunifying the two worlds. Therefore, Moshe shattered the tablets and released the letters, thereby enabling them to affect this reunification themselves.[54] For only a generation that recognizes the lower world's spirituality and God's incorporeality is worthy of being presented with tablets written in heavenly script.

When man realizes how to reunify the two worlds, he can rise above the limitations of nature and "create new beings," as the sage Rava once did. By studying the forms of the letters, man can unlock the secrets of the universe and reach a level of understanding so exalted that even the future is not a mystery.

> The desideratum of study for its own sake is for man to attach himself to the letters in holiness and purity. They will make him wise and radiate much light and true eternal life.
>
> (R. M. Margoliot, *Sod Yachin U'Voaz*)

THE HEBREW LANGUAGE

> And the whole earth was of one language.
>
> (Bereshit 11:1)

> One says [this teaches us that] they all spoke that language of the Unique One.
>
> (Jerusalem Talmud, *Megillah* 1:9)

---

54. See R. Moshe Cordovero, *Pardes Rimonim* 27:2.

This means that they spoke Hebrew, the language with which the world was created.

(*Penei Moshe*)

To understand the message of the *Tanach*, we must read the text in the Hebrew original. Unlike other languages, which merely reflect man's attempts to describe his surroundings, Hebrew is the vehicle through which God conveyed His will to mankind. Samson Raphael Hirsch explains that until man built the Tower of Babel, all men were united, not only in language but in their outlook on life and the world. This harmony of thought was only possible as long as their words were based on objective truth rather than individual, subjective views[55] (i.e., on terminology God Himself had used to describe the world):

If this one language was the language in which God taught the first man to look at things, and the words were the names with which God called things for man, so that they contained the right way that God wants man to look at things . . . then it is quite possible that 'call in the name of God' [*Bereshit* 4:26] means nothing else but to teach the world what things are and should be according to God's will for man. For it is only when we call things by their right names that Truth remains clear and not clouded for us.

(Hirsch, *The Pentateuch*, Vol. I, p. 215)

Moreover, the holy tongue is also the ideal linguistic instrument by which the text of the Torah, its great and secret treasures, and especially the true significance of its

---

55. See Rambam, *Guide of the Perplexed* 1:2.

messages are to be understood.[56] Only Hebrew allows for
the interchange of letters and multilevel readings. Its pro-
nunciation has great philosophical importance in clearly
understanding truth and falsehood.[57] As R. Yehudah
Halevi writes:

> The proverb states, "from the mouth of scholars and not
> from the mouth of books" [*Gittin* 71a]. Verbal communi-
> cation finds various aids: in pausing or continuing to speak,
> according to the requirements of the sentence; raising or
> lowering the voice to express astonishment, question, narra-
> tive, desire, fear, or submission . . . [or] gesturing. Without
> these, speech by itself would be inadequate. Occasionally
> the speaker even has recourse to movements of eyes,
> eyebrows or the whole head and hands in order to express
> anger, pleasure, humility, or haughtiness to the degree
> desired.
>
> Implanted in the remnant of our language, which was
> created and instituted by God, are subtle elements calcu-
> lated to promote understanding and replace the aforemen-
> tioned aids to speech. These are the accents with which the
> holy text is read. They denote pause and continuation, they
> separate question from answer, beginning from continua-
> tion, haste from hesitation, command from request. . . .
>
> (*Kuzari* II:72)

As the blueprint of the world, the Hebrew language has
a great metaphysical value. It reaches God because it comes

---

56. R. Samson Raphael Hirsch, *Horeb,* trans. Dr. I. Grunfeld,
London, 1962, vol. I, introduction, p. cvi.

57. See Dr. P. Biberfeld, *Universal Jewish History,* New York, 1948,
pp. 50–53, 100–105; M. Glazerson, *Sparks of the Holy Tongue,*
Jerusalem, 1980.

from God, and it offers the means whereby man can express his profoundest feelings and loftiest knowledge. This is the solution to the problem of how God could ever have revealed His will to man by "word of mouth."

THE *MITZVOT*

MITZVOT

The primary message of the Torah is *mitzvot*—precepts. As we have already stressed, the Torah is a moral code designed to train man for his mission on Earth. As such, it commands us to obey certain precepts, for they are the God-given directions for fulfilling our role. These precepts deal with societal organizations, the service of God, and man's responsibilities to himself and others. Some *mitzvot* are logical and understandable; others are beyond our comprehension. Regardless, man is obligated to observe them all, for the performance of the *mitzvot* fulfills the will of God and is the key to creating Heaven on Earth.

The precepts can be classified in several ways. The notes accompanying this chapter deal with how some rabbinical scholars have categorized them. First, however, we would be well-advised to examine the more familiar ways in which the *mitzvot* have been classified.

THE NOACHIDE LAWS

Not only does the Torah provide legislation enabling the nation of Israel to attain a high moral standard; it also ordains an educational and legal system for the non-Jewish world.

The Torah considers Adam and Chavah the progenitors of the entire human race. Until the building of the Tower of Babel[1] we find no distinction between nations or between Jews and non-Jews. Only after Avraham's birth do we read about the *Ivrim* (Hebrews), who developed into the nation of Israel.

The Torah is universal in its outlook, and contains a universal message as well as universal legislation. These legal norms are called the *sheva mitzvot b'nei Noach* (the seven laws of the children of Noach), or the Noachide laws—although they were actually given to Adam, the first man—and *b'nei Noach* refers to all gentiles.[2] They incorporate the minimal moral duties enjoined by the Torah for the whole of mankind.[3] The Talmud[4] lists them as follows:

1. to establish a legal and judicial system[5]
2. to refrain from blaspheming

---

1. *Bereshit* 11:1–9.

2. The human race is descended from the three sons of Noach, who survived the flood (*Bereshit* 8–10).

3. *Sanhedrin* 56–60; Rambam, *Mishneh Torah, Hilchot Melachim* 8:10, 10:12.

4. *Tosefta, Avodah Zarah* 8:4; *Sanhedrin* 56a.

5. This included the establishment of courts in all cities. The Noachide laws are often discussed within the framework of a Jewish state in the land of Israel, partly inhabited by non-Jews. In such a case the Jewish courts would enforce Noachide law among the non-Jewish inhabitants, or appoint a non-Jewish court to judge non-Jews by these seven commandments (*Hilchot Melachim* 10:11). Whether the establishment of such a system allows for an independent non-Jewish judiciary based on the seven laws is a matter of discussion (see *Responsa Chatam* Sofer 6:14).

3. to refrain from idolatry[6]
4. to refrain from murder
5. to refrain from theft[7]
6. to refrain from sexual immorality[8]
7. to refrain from eating flesh torn from a living animal[9]

Other laws are understood as subheadings of the seven (e.g., the bans on drinking the blood of a living animal, emasculating animals, practicing sorcery as outlined in

---

6. Non-Jews are not required to have a profound knowledge of God; rather, they must abjure false gods (*Megillah* 13a; *Kiddushin* 40a; and *Hilchot Melachim* 10:2). The prohibition refers only to actually committing idolatry, not to studying it. Furthermore, a non-Jew is not required to martyr himself as is a Jew, although he must give his own life rather than take another's (see *Sanhedrin* 74a; Jerusalem Talmud, *Shevuot* 4:2; and Rashi on *Pesachim* 25b). It has long been a matter of debate whether Christianity is a monotheistic religion and thus permissible according to the Noachide laws. Later Jewish scholars feel that the doctrine of the Trinity is a form of *shittuf*—associationism— and is not forbidden to the non-Jew. See *Shulchan Aruch, Orach Chaim* 156:1; *Tur, Yoreh Deah* 148 and *Beit Yosef* ad loc.; Meiri on *Bava Kamma* 37b; and *Noda BeYehudah*, first edition, introduction.

7. Including dishonesty in business or military conquest (*Sanhedrin* 57a).

8. i.e., relations with one's mother; with one's father's wife; with a married woman, whether she is married to a Jew or a gentile; or with a sister born of one's mother. Pederasty and bestiality are also forbidden (*Sanhedrin* 55).

9. It is generally assumed that this prohibition only became applicable after the flood, since before that time all men were forbidden to consume meat (Rashi, *Bereshit* 9:3) even before the flood, since it includes all types of cruelty to animals. It is questionable whether a gentile may eat the meat of an animal that dies naturally (see *Torah Shelemah, Bereshit* 9:13).

Devarim 18:10,[10] offering blemished sacrifices, crossbreeding, and grafting trees;[11] and the obligations to give charity, procreate, and honor the Torah.[12])

Similarly, the proscription of theft encompasses the biblical prohibitions of taking stealthily (*Vayikra* 19:11) or forcibly (*Vayikra* 19:13), shifting landmarks (*Devarim* 19:14), cheating (*Vayikra* 19:11), and coveting (*Shemot* 20:17; *Devarim* 5:18).[13]

All together, sixty-six biblical precepts are included in the Noachide laws:

Civil law 19
Blasphemy 8
Idolatry 10
Murder 1
Theft 16
Sexual immorality 10
Eating flesh torn from a living animal 2

Clearly, it is incorrect to claim that Jews are obligated to observe 613 precepts while gentiles need only observe seven.

The original Noachide legislation was probably exhaustive but much of it seems to have been lost through the

---

10. *Tosefta, Avodah Zarah* 8:6.

11. *Sanhedrin* 56b. Gentiles are permitted to wear clothing made of linen and wool and to sow diverse seeds together. See *Vayikra* 19:19; *Devarim* 22:11.

12. *Chullin* 92a.

13. For the halachic differences between all these prohibitions, see the commentaries and Aaron Lichtenstein, *The Seven Laws of Noah*, New York, 1981, chapter 11.

ages. *Sefer Hachinuch*[14] maintains that it could be reconstructed by means of the same hermeneutical principles used to redevelop the orally transmitted Torah.

Rashi notes that Noach's sons Shem and Ever founded an academy to teach the Noachide laws.[15] Rambam adds that Moshe was obligated to teach them to mankind.[16] Yet the sages never codified these precepts because the gentile world rejected them. Nevertheless, the scholars of the Babylonian Talmud remarked that at least their gentile neighbors "do not write marriage contracts for males, or peddle human flesh, and they respect the Torah" (*Chullin 92b*).

The prevalent opinion in the Talmud is that only the seven precepts are obligatory upon all mankind; other laws mentioned in *Bereshit* (e.g., circumcision[17] and the prohibition of eating the sciatic nerve) are only applicable to the Jews, even though they were ordained before the rest of the Torah. The following rule is laid down:

> "Any pre-Sinaitic law which was not repeated at Sinai applies solely to the Israelites and not to the Noachides."
>
> (*Sanhedrin* 59a)

Although they personally were given certain precepts that were not obligatory upon all mankind, Avraham, Yitzchak, and Yaakov are considered Noachides inasmuch

---

14. Ascribed to R. Aharon Halevi of thirteenth-century Barcelona. See precept 424.
15. *Bereshit* 28:11.
16. *Hilchot Melachim* 8:10.
17. See *Hilchot Melachim* 10:7.

as the Torah had not yet been revealed in their times.[18]
Rambam[19] notes that, with two exceptions (Shabbat and
Torah study), gentiles may choose to observe other laws.
Indeed, the Midrash[20] states that Moshe was commanded
to transcribe the Torah in all seventy languages on twelve
stones. Some commentaries maintain that this was done to
enable interested gentiles to acquaint themselves with the
Torah.

Since the Noachide laws were known from the beginning of human existence, it is understandable that all legal
systems—including the Code of Hammurabi[21]—have been
influenced by them. They are the foundation of international and natural law. The Dutch jurist Hugo de Goot
(Grotius), considered to be the father of international law,
quotes these laws frequently as the source of "the law of all
nations."[22]

John Seldon (1584–1654), an English jurist, based his
conception of international law on Jewish and Noachide
law. His treatise,[23] *De Jure Naturali et Gentium Juxta
Disciplinam Ebraeorum*[24] (1640), abounds in international

---

18. *Sanhedrin* 59a.

19. *Hilchot Melachim* 10:8–10.

20. *Yalkut Shimoni,* Yehoshua 4.

21. Often, scholars have voiced the opinion that the Code of
Hammurabi was a forerunner of Jewish law. The existence of the
Noachide laws from the beginning of Creation refutes this argument.

22. See his main study: *De Jure Belli ac Pacis* (1625).

23. Selden refers to the Noachide laws as "natural law." The
Talmud (*Yoma* 67b) expresses the opinion that five of the seven laws
would have been mandatory even if God had not revealed them.

24. See *Netherlands International Law Review* 5, 1958, pp. 128–
130; and Nathan Isaacs, *The Legacy of Israel* (Oxford, 1927), p. 385.

applications of Jewish law.[25] Since Selden's day, Noachide law has become a common element in all judicial systems.[26]

The Noachide laws are obligatory upon Jews as well, for "nothing is permitted to an Israelite yet forbidden to a non-Jew" (*Sanhedrin* 59a). However, the extent of liability sometimes differs and gentile transgressors are punished more severely (*Sanhedrin* 57b).

Rambam maintains that non-Jews are obligated to observe the Noachide laws only because they are divinely ordained and were revealed to Moshe: "If one observed them because of logical conviction, he is considered neither a resident alien nor a righteous person nor a wise man" (*Mishneh Torah, Hilchot Melachim* 8:11).

The Jerusalem Talmud (*Avodah Zarah* 2:1) records a difference of opinion as to whether the Noachide laws are an eternal code for the non-Jewish world or a provisional one, before humanity embraces the Torah.

Because a gentile who observes the Noachide laws is

---

25. Selden writes in his introduction, "Now the word 'naturalis' in the title refers only to that which in the opinion, beliefs, and customs of the Jews—and according to the scholars in the accepted colleges— is taken as universal/common to all, and as the law of the world, in all countries and ages, even from the very foundation . . . so that at one and the same time it was made for mankind by the Maker of all creation, disclosed, imparted and ordained. This the Jews call the 'precepts' or the 'law of the sons of Noah.'"

26. The late Dr. I. Herzog, former chief rabbi of Israel, wrote: "As illustrative of the lengths to which Selden can go, I may instance the view he expresses in the opening chapters that very probably Pythagoras heard Yechezkel delivering his prophetic addresses and hence, as a logical consequence, Greek jurisprudence was indebted to Jewish law." ("John Selden and Jewish Law," *Judaism: Law and Ethics*, London: Soncino. Edited by Chaim Herzog, 1974, p. 71.)

assured a place in the world to come (*Sanhedrin* 105a),
Jews have never seen any reason to proselytize so as to
offer eternal life. Contrast this with Christianity, which has
always viewed itself as man's only means of salvation.

THE DECALOGUE

The most well-known part of the Torah is the portion
in *Shemot* 20:1–14 and *Devarim* 5:6–18 known as the
Decalogue (Greek for "ten words"), or more commonly
referred to as the Ten Commandments. Presented to
Moshe during his forty-day sojourn atop Mount Sinai and
written by God upon stones of sapphire, the Decalogue
was proclaimed directly to the nation so that the entire
people could rise to the level of prophets and accept the
yoke of Heaven with complete conviction.

According to *Shemot* 24, God engraved the Decalogue
on stone tablets and presented them to Moshe. When
Moshe descended Mount Sinai and saw the people revel-
ling in their worship of the golden calf, he broke the
tablets. God subsequently commanded him to hew another
set of tablets, on which the Decalogue was to be rewritten.
Both the first and second tablets were placed in the Ark of
the Testimony.

The order of the precepts of the Decalogue has frequently been discussed. Many scholars note that the text
deals first with metaphysical truths (i.e., fundamentals of
belief in God, followed by nature's subservience to God,
and man's relationship to society.[27])

---

27. See Rambam, *Guide of the Perplexed* 3:17; R. Yosef Albo, *Sefer
Hakkarim* 3:26.

There is a difference of opinion as to the format of the tablets. The prevailing opinion is that the first five commandments were inscribed on one tablet and the second five on the other tablet, reflecting the division of man's responsibility to God and to his fellow man.[28] Another school maintains that the entire Decalogue was written on each tablet (Jerusalem Talmud, *Shekalim* 6:1). According to a third interpretation, since the text states that the tablets were inscribed on both sides,[29] the Decalogue was written on both sides of the tablets.[30] The Talmud (*Shabbat* 104a) understands from this verse that the letters of the words were incised through the stone and the unattached letters *mem* and *samech* miraculously remained in place rather than falling out.

Both tablets were of equal dimensions (Jerusalem Talmud, op. cit.) and, though fashioned from stone, they could be rolled like a scroll.[31] Though their volume was equivalent to forty *seah* (approximately 648 liters), as long as the letters were upon them they carried themselves. After the sin of the golden calf, however, the letters flew back to Heaven and the tablets dropped out of Moshe's hands (Jerusalem Talmud, *Taanit* 4:5).

In truth, one errs in referring to the Decalogue as the Ten Commandments for all authorities agree that the text includes more than ten precepts. This phrase never appears in *Tanach* or rabbinic literature and is based on a misunder-

---

28. Commenting on *Shemot* 20:12, R. Samson Raphael Hirsch explains how the precept of honoring one's parents can be understood as an obligation to God.

29. *Shemot* 32:15.

30. *Midrash Shir Hashirim* 5:14.

31. *Ibid.*

standing of the Hebrew term "ten sayings."[32] In Hebrew, "tablets of the covenant"[33] and "tablets of testimony"[34] are also used to describe this portion of the Torah.

Rambam[35] maintains that the Decalogue consists of fifteen *mitzvot*:

1. to believe in and recognize the existence of God (*Shemot* 20:2)
2. to refrain from accepting false deities (20:3)
3. to refrain from making or providing idols (20:4)
4. to refrain from prostration or pagan rites (20:5)
5. to refrain from any form of idol worship (20:5)
6. to refrain from pronouncing or swearing by God's name for no purpose (20:7)
7. to declare the sanctity of Shabbat at the beginning and conclusion of the day (20:8)
8. to refrain from creative activity on Shabbat (20:10)
9. to honor one's father and mother (20:12)
10. to refrain from murder (20:13)
11. to refrain from adultery (20:14)
12. to refrain from kidnapping (20:15)
13. to refrain from bearing false witness (20:16)
14. to refrain from coveting goods that cannot be acquired fairly by coercing a reluctant owner to transfer them (20:17)
15. to refrain from coveting any object whose owner shows no inclination to part with it (20:17)

---

32. See *Shemot* 34:28; *Devarim* 4:13, 10:4.
33. See *Devarim* 9:9, 11, 15.
34. See *Shemot* 31:18, 32:15, and 34:29.
35. *Sefer Hamitzvot*, positive precepts 1, 155, and 211, and negative precepts 1, 2, 4, 5, 6, 62, 243, 265, 266, 285, 289, and 320.

Abarbanel, renowned Spanish rabbi, philosopher, and
statesman (1437–1508), explains that they are nonetheless
called the "ten sayings" because there were ten statements,
each separated by a pause.[36]

According to the Jerusalem Talmud, the Decalogue
contains all 613 *mitzvot* of the Torah:

> Chanania, the nephew of R. Yehoshua, says: "Between
> each saying [of the Decalogue], the derivations and details
> of the Torah [were transmitted], for the verse states, 'His
> hands . . . are filled with gems . . .'" [Shir Hashirim
> 5:14]. R. Shimon b. Lakish used to say when he read this
> verse, "Chanania has taught us well; just as there are small
> waves between the large ones, we can find all of the
> derivations and details of the Torah between each saying [of
> the Decalogue]."
>
> *(Shekalim* 6:1)

In *Azharot*,[37] R. Saadiah Gaon derives all 613 *mitzvot*
from the Decalogue. Similar derivations were made by
Abarbanel, Ibn Ezra, and Ralbag (R. Levi b. Gershom).

The Decalogue was read as part of the Temple service
but it was never incorporated into the daily prayers, "to
prevent the *minim* [heretics][38] from finding grounds to

---

36. See his commentary on *Shemot* 20:2.

37. A book of liturgical poems on the 613 commandments. Although *azharot* means "warnings," the term is also used in connection
with positive *mitzvot*. Its numerical value is 613 when written without
a *vav*. For a full explanation, see Prof. J.M. Guttmann, *Bechinat
Hamitzvot*, Breslau, 1928, pp. 53–63.

38. The reference is probably to the early Christians, who were
known to emphasize the importance of the moralistic commandments
and generally observed only those precepts that fit into that category.
Interestingly, the early Reform movement took the same stand and

claim that these precepts alone were given to Moshe"
(*Berachot* 12a).

In his commentary on *Shemot* 20:14, R. Samson Raphael
Hirsch stresses that the Decalogue's separate presentation
does not indicate that its *mitzvot* are more important than
others. Rather:

> God clearly and expressly proclaimed them [the "ten
> sayings"] as being merely a preparatory introduction to the
> whole following, real giving of the Law. 'I come to you,'
> God has said in Chapter 19:9, 'so that the people may hear
> that I do speak unto thee and *so have belief in thee forever.*'
> The revelation on Sinai is expressly stated to have for its
> object solely the preparation of the people for the whole of
> the rest of the lawgiving which was to be transmitted to
> them by Moses and to prove to them beyond all possibility
> of doubt, by their own experience, that 'God does speak to
> man' so that they would receive all the following Torah
> with unshatterable belief and trust as the 'word of God.' . . .
> Nevertheless, they are fundamental laws, general headings
> of chapters to which the whole of the rest of the lawgiving
> is really ways and means of carrying them out.

Though the Decalogue was given specifically to the Jews
and was not meant to replace the universal Noachide moral
code, it was proclaimed in all seventy languages (*Shabbat*
88b) and in desert territory belonging to no specific people.[39]

Although the text implies that the people heard God
pronounce the entire Decalogue, the Talmud (*Makkot* 24a)
states that the first two sayings were spoken by God,
whereas the remaining eight were transmitted by Moshe.
Ramban explains:

---

declared the Decalogue its Torah (Isaac M. Wise, "The Law," *Hebrew
Review* I, Cincinnati, 1880).

39. *Mechilta,* Yitro 5, end.

Surely all Israel heard the entire Decalogue from the mouth
of God, as the literal meaning of the text indicates. However, in the first two commandments they heard the utter-
ance of speech and understood it. . . . Therefore, He
spoke to them directly [i.e., in first person] just as a master
speaks to his servant. From then on, they heard the sound
of speech but did not understand, and it became necessary
for Moshe to explain each commandment. As the rabbis
explained, "Moshe spoke and God answered him by a
voice" [*Shemot* 19:19]. Hence, the remaining commandments were addressed by God to Moshe so that he could
tell the people. The first two commandments were spoken
directly to the people so that they should all be prophets in
[respect of] their belief in God and the prohibition of
idolatry. These are the roots of the entire Torah. . . .

(*Commentary on the Torah, Shemot* 20:7)

There are two versions of the Decalogue in the Torah.
The first in *Shemot*, forms an integral part of the historical
narrative whereas the second, in *Devarim*, is part of
Moshe's farewell address. There is a difference of opinion
as to which text was actually inscribed on the tablets that
Moshe brought with him from on high. Some suggest that
the text in *Shemot* was written on tablets Moshe received
from God whereas the text in *Devarim* was written on the
tablets Moshe himself wrote after breaking the first ones.
Others maintain that the text on both sets of tablets was
identical. All opinions agree that no matter which text was
written, both versions were uttered simultaneously at Sinai,
transcending the human faculties of speech and hearing.[40]

There are textual and halachic differences between the
two versions. In *Shemot*, the commandment is to "re-

---

40. *Shevuot* 20b; *Rosh Hashanah* 27a.

member" the day of Shabbat (by sanctifying it), and in *Devarim*, to "observe" it (by refraining from creative activity). In addition, the Talmud (*Bava Kamma* 55a) notes that the phrase "that it may go well with you" does not appear in the *mitzvah* of honoring one's parents in *Shemot* because the first tablets were destined to be broken.

THE 613 *MITZVOT*

> R. Simlai expounded, "Six hundred thirteen *mitzvot* were transmitted to Moshe: 365 prohibitions, corresponding to the days of the solar year, and 248 imperatives, corresponding to the number of limbs of the body." R. Chanina said: "What is the scriptural source [for this tradition]? 'Torah was commanded to us by Moshe . . .' [*Devarim* 33:4]. The numerical value of the word 'Torah' is 611. [Add] the precepts of 'I am the Lord, your God' and 'You shall have no other gods,' which were heard from God [Himself, and the total is 613]."
>
> (*Makkot* 23b)

The tradition of there being 613 *mitzvot* in the Torah appears often in Tannaitic and rabbinic literature.[41] Interestingly, however, nowhere do we find a list of these precepts in the Talmud. Indeed, the tradition would seem to stand in direct contrast to the Torah, since a simple enumeration of the biblical commandments proves that the actual number far exceeds 613. This figure also contradicts the Talmud, where thousands of imperatives are derived

---

41. See *Shabbat* 87a, *Yevamot* 47b, *Nedarim* 25a, and *Shevuot* 29a. The Mishnah (*Oholot* 1:8) lists the 248 major limbs of the body.

from the verses of the Torah. Obviously the laws the rabbis derived through the use of the exegetical rules[42] must be considered divinely ordained and eternally binding. Why then limit the Torah to 613 precepts?[43]

In the eighteenth-century work entitled *Maalot Ha-Torah*, R. Avraham makes the following comments in the name of his brother, R. Eliyahu, the Gaon of Vilna:

> One can surely not argue that there are only 613 precepts, for from the beginning of *Bereshit* until *Shemot* 12:2 we find only three commandments [i.e., what then is the meaning of the rest of these books if not to obligate man to live a moral life?]. Many portions of the Torah do not contain any precepts and this is difficult to understand. The truth is that every word of the Torah, inasmuch as it comes from the Almighty, must be considered a commandment [i.e., including the narratives]. . . . Concerning this David said [*Tehillim* 119:96]: "I have seen an end to every endeavor but Your commandment is exceedingly vast." The 613 commandments, therefore, are no more than roots [general rules]. . . . The Torah is "a tree of life to those

---

42. See p. 169.

43. Some scholars (Solomon Schechter, Bacher and others) have suggested that R. Simlai was only teaching a moral lesson without troubling himself about the accuracy of his count. Such an assumption is baseless, for the wording of the Talmud clearly implies that R. Simlai was passing on a known tradition. Moreover, elsewhere in the Talmud the number is given as a statement of fact rather than a symbol. Finally, it is highly unlikely that the rabbis, "who counted every letter of the Torah" (*Kiddushin* 30a), would have used a number without having a basis for it. And if they had, they probably would have said that there are approximately 600 *mitzvot*; the fact that they used a specific number indicates that the moral lesson was derived to suit the number rather than the other way around.

who grasp it . . ." [*Mishlei* 3:18]. Just as a tree has but one trunk, which splits into many branches, they in turn split into many twigs, which hold much fruit and many seeds, and each has the potential to reproduce all the commandments. . . .

(New York: Peninim edition, 1946, p. 6)

In other words, the precepts in truth consist of 613 general rules, which are the basis for all the Torah's imperatives and narratives and for Jewish law in its entirety.

As noted, we find no listing of the 613 *mitzvot* in the Talmud. The earliest attempt to establish a compendium is found in the introduction to *Halachot Gedolot*. Shlomo Ibn Gabirol also compiled a list of the 613 *mitzvot*.[44] However, all these attempts failed to establish definitive criteria for including certain precepts and excluding others.

Rambam, in the introduction to his *Mishneh Torah*, was the first to attempt to set down a framework whereby rules could be established for labelling a specific imperative one of the 613 *mitzvot*.[45] His work, originally published in Arabic and now known as *Sefer Hamitzvot shel*

---

44. Also see *"Taryag Mitzvot," Kitvei Ramban*, Mossad Harav Kook.

45. The following principles are mentioned by Rambam (trans. R. Dr. C. B. Chavel):

1. We are not to include commandments having only rabbinic authority.
2. We are not to include derived *mitzvot*.
3. We are not to include *mitzvot* that are not binding for all times.
4. We are not to include commandments that encompass the whole body of *mitzvot*.
5. Reasons for a *mitzvah* are not to be considered separate *mitzvot*.
6. If a *mitzvah* contains both positive and negative injunctions the two parts are to be counted separately.
7. The details of a *mitzvah* are not to be counted separately.

HaRambam, is sharply critical of *Halachot Gedolot*. Later authors, especially Ramban and Ra'avad (R. Avraham Ibn Daud, 1110–1180), took exception to some of Rambam's conclusions.[46] Nevertheless, the work has become the

---

   8. A negative statement, excluding a particular case from a *mitzvah*, is not to be counted separately.
   9. The number of *mitzvot* is to be based not on how many times a *mitzvah* is repeated, but on the nature of the action.
  10. Preliminary acts leading up to a *mitzvah* are not to be counted separately.
  11. Different elements that together form one *mitzvah* are not to be counted separately.
  12. Successive stages in the performance of a *mitzvah* are not to be counted.
  13. If a *mitzvah* is performed on more than one day, it is not to be counted as a separate *mitzvah* on each day.
  14. A means of punishment prescribed for several violations is not to be counted more than once.

46. Rambam maintained that only those *mitzvot* explicitly stated in the Torah can be referred to as *deoraita*—biblical. All other *mitzvot*— even if passed on by Moshe himself—are to be considered *divrei soferim* (i.e., deduced by the scribes (see Principle 2 of *Sefer Hamitzvot*)). Ramban challenged this statement for it seems to oppose the Talmud, which states that all laws derived through use of the thirteen herme- neutical principles are biblical. In his glosses, he writes, "This book of the master [i.e., Rambam] is sweet and full of delight except for this rule, in which he tears apart great mountains of Talmud and breaks down fortified walls in the Gemara. For students of the Gemara it is evil and bitter. Let it be forgotten and not discussed." R. Shimon b. Zemach Duran in *Zohar Harakia* (Principle 2) and others contended that Rambam never intended to imply that derived laws were not biblical in origin or status. Rather, he was distinguishing between those *mitzvot* that could be considered part of the 613 and those that could not since they are not explicit. In their view, Rambam maintained that there are three divisions of law: 1) *deoraita*, the 613 *mitzvot* mentioned in the Torah; 2) *divrei soferim*, laws derived from the text, which are

standard compendium and shows "the incomparable Moshe ben Maimon in his workshop."[47]

Another definitive work on the 613 *mitzvot* is *Semak (Sefer Mitzvot Katan—The Small Book of Mitzvot)*, written by a French rabbi, R. Yitzchak b. Yosef of Corbeil, in the second half of the thirteenth century. The author accepts neither Rambam's nor Ramban's viewpoint. In later years, many additional works were published. Of special importance are *Semag (Sefer Mitzvot* Gadol—*The Comprehensive Book of Mitzvot)*[48] and *Sefer Hachinuch.*

If all the Torah's imperatives are binding, what difference does it make whether a specific precept is one of the 613 roots or an offshoot? Moreover, why did the questions of how to establish which *mitzvot* are to be included in the 613 and which are to be excluded play such an important role in the works of so many rabbis? While the criteria might be of theological interest, they would seem halachically irrelevant. In truth, however, the question is significant for there are legal differences between those laws that are part of the 613 *mitzvot* and those that are not. Though both types are obligatory, the authorities note that those precepts that are not part of the 613 carry no biblical penalties if violated, are no more than general prohibitions, cannot serve as the basis for the creation of rabbinical

---

also biblical; and 3) *derabbanan,* rabbinical ordinances. Many commentaries, however, rejected their explanations and insisted that Rambam had, in fact, meant that all derived laws had rabbinical rather than biblical status (see Ra'abad, *Hilchot Ishut* 3, end; Rivash, responsum 163; and *Sefer Hachinuch*, precept 282).

47. See *The Divine Commandments,* trans. R. Dr. C. B. Chavel (New York, 1940), Book I, p. XI.

48. By R. Moshe of Coucy, a twelfth-century scholar.

proscriptions, and cannot be interpreted by applying the hermeneutical principles of law.

Hence, the question of including or excluding specific *mitzvot* is first and foremost a legal problem and not simply a theological one. This again raises the question of why no such listing can be found in the Talmud. Some scholars have suggested that such lists did exist at one time and were lost. But if so, why doesn't the Talmud mention them, just as it often refers to other works that are unknown to us?

Rather, it would seem that the rabbis never felt compelled to publish a list, although they may have compiled several. The Talmud (*Gittin* 60b) states that the oral tradition—which introduces the concept of 613 *mitzvot*—was not to be committed to writing. Moreover, the rabbis preferred the method of Midrash *Halachah*—memorizing the rules of formulating laws—as a means of deriving the precepts; hence, more importance was attached to establishing the exegesis and its basis in Scripture than to committing a list of 613 *mitzvot* to memory. One should not underestimate the early rabbis' opposition to codifying Jewish law, for they felt that it must be allowed to develop and expand freely without being shackled by an unchanging code. Indeed, the works of Rambam and other codifiers met with much criticism precisely because they set out to canonize the law.

Of the 613 *mitzvot*, 369 are applicable today: 126 imperatives and 243 prohibitions. However, some of these precepts (e.g., those dealing with the laws of divorce or vows) may never apply to certain people. Two hundred seventy precepts—48 imperatives and 222 prohibitions—are binding upon all Jews under all circumstances, although some are limited to certain times of the year (e.g., eating matza on Pesach).

Six *mitzvot* are always obligatory:

1. to believe in God
2. to refrain from believing in other gods
3. to affirm His unity
4. to love Him
5. to fear Him
6. to refrain from being turned away [from God] by one's heart or eyes.

The rabbinical mnemonic for them is:[49] ". . . there shall be *six* cities of refuge for you" (*Bamidbar* 35:13).

OTHER CLASSIFICATIONS OF THE *MITZVOT*

The Torah establishes different categories of *mitzvot*—categories that have no halachic implications.[50] These are:

---

49. See *Sefer Hachinuch*, trans. Charles Wengrov, Vol. I, p. 54.

50. The term "*mitzvah*" is often used to describe all of the Torah's *mitzvot*. It is also frequently used in the sense of a good deed. The term has its root in the Hebrew word *tzav*, which means "order."
Responsibility for the performance of the *mitzvot* is formally assumed by boys at the age of thirteen and one day and by girls at the age of twelve and one day. Women are generally exempt from all affirmative *mitzvot* contingent upon a time or season, although there are some exceptions (for instance, the sanctification of Shabbat, the eating of matza on Pesach night). On the other hand all negative *mitzvot*, whether limited to a certain time or not, are binding upon both men and women, with the exception of three (*Kiddushin* 1:7). Maharal writes that women are not obligated to observe most of the affirmative

1. *chukkim*—statues (*Shemot* 27:21)
2. *mishpatim*—ordinances (*Devarim* 4:5)
3. *edot*—testimonies (*Devarim* 4:45)
4. *mishmarot*—observances (*Vayikra* 8:35)
5. *torot*—teachings (*Shemot* 16:28).

The *Sifra*[51] makes the following comments:

> "And you shall fulfill my ordinances"—this refers to *mitzvot* that logic would have dictated even if the Torah had omitted them (e.g., [the *mitzvot* concerning] stealing, forbidden sexual relations, worshipping false gods, cursing God, and murder). "And observe My statutes"—[this refers to *mitzvot*] that the evil inclination and the nations of the world reject (e.g., the prohibitions against eating pork and wearing garments containing linen and wool,[52] the law of *chalitzah*,[53] the purification process of one afflicted with *tzara'at*,[54] the red heifer,[55] the goat sent into the wilderness[56] . . . . The verse therefore concludes, "I am the Lord, your God," (i.e., you are not permitted to reject them).
>
> (*Vayikra* 18:4)

It is clear from the *Sifra* that though different terms can be used to describe the *mitzvot*, all of them—whether

---

mitzvot because their nature enables them to achieve the same moral level without these symbolic observances (*Derush al Hamitzvot*).

51. A slightly different version is quoted in *Yoma* 67b. See *Dikdukei Soferim* for an explanation of the differences.

52. *Vayikra* 19:19; *Devarim* 22:11.

53. The alternative to the *mitzvah* of *yibum*—levirate marriage (*Devarim* 25:5–11).

54. *Vayikra* 14.

55. The animal whose ashes were used in the ritual purification of one who had come into contact with a corpse (*Bamidbar* 19).

56. Part of the Temple service on Yom Kippur (*Vayikra* 16:10).

rationally derived or divinely decreed—are equally obligatory for they find their root in the Torah's declaration of "I am the Lord, your God."

In the Talmud, we find various classification systems employed, although they are not mutually exclusive. Some of them are:

1. *Mitzvot asey*—imperatives,
2. *Mitzvot lo taaseh*—prohibitions,
3. *Mitzvot bein adam laMakom*—*mitzvot* governing man's relationship with God,
4. *Mitzvot bein adam lechaveiro*—*mitzvot* governing interpersonal relationships,
5. *Mitzvot kallot*—*mitzvot* whose transgression carries a less severe punishment,
6. *Mitzvot chamurot*—*mitzvot* whose transgression carries a severe punishment,[57]
7. *Mitzvot hatluyot ba'aretz*—agricultural *mitzvot*, most of which are only obligatory in the land of Israel,
8. *Mitzvot she'einon tluyot ba'aretz*—non-agricultural *mitzvot*, which are obligatory everywhere.

Many sages and scholars through the years have divided the *mitzvot* into various categories. All agree that such classifications have no halachic significance.[58]

---

57. See *Chullin* 12:5; *Yevamot* 47b; *Avodah Zarah* 3a.
58. R. Saadiah Gaon divided the *mitzvot* into:

   a. *sichliyot*—rational laws, which can be explained by their effect; theft, for example, is proscribed because it undermines the economic basis of society.
   b. *shimiyot*—traditional law, primarily expressions of God's will (*Emunot Vedeot* 3:1–3).

It is important to once again note that *halachah*, in the juridical sense, does not recognize the difference between

---

Bachya b. Yosef Ibn Paquada (late eleventh century) expanded R. Saadiah's divisions by adding:

a. *chovot ha'evarim*—duties of the body, obligatory through reason or because they are divinely ordained (e.g., the prohibition of mixing meat and milk)
b. *chovot halevavot*—duties of the heart (*Chovot Halevavot*, introduction).

Yehudah Halevi (1080–1145) established entirely different criteria:

a. *sichliyot*—rational laws, also referred to as *nafshiot*—laws of the soul, e.g., those having to do with belief in God, His justice, and our obligations towards Him
b. *minhagiyot*—or *mediniyot*—governmental laws regarding the structure of society
c. *shimiyot* (or *elokiyot*)—revealed or divine laws, which we have received by tradition, and for which no rational explanation is given (*Kuzari* II:48, III:11, IV:13).

Avraham Ibn Ezra (1093–1169) departed completely from the earlier classifiers and divided the *mitzvot* into:

a. *ikkarim*—fundamentals man can comprehend without revelation
b. *zichronot*—commemorations of events in Jewish history
c. *emunot halev*—faith of the heart, *hapeh*—of speech, and *hamaaseh*—of action
d. *mitzvot ne'elamot*—arcane *mitzvot* (*Yesod Morah V'yesod HaTorah* 5:7).

Ra'avad mentions R. Saadiah's classification but used different terminology:

a. *mefursamot*—commonly known *mitzvot*
b. *mekubalot*—traditional *mitzvot*, which he subdivided into: laws of morality; laws of home life; laws regulating society; and general religious law (*Emunah Ramah*).

In his *Mishneh Torah*, Rambam made the following divisions for pragmatic reasons:

ritual and civil laws, for both are founded on the divine law
revealed at Sinai. Furthermore, the explanations we ad-

---

    a. *mada*—fundamental truths
    b. *ahavah*—daily religious laws
    c. *zemanim*—sanctified seasons
    d. *nashim*—laws of marriage
    e. *kedushah*—personal sanctification by refraining from immorality or proscribed foods
    f. *hafla'ah*—imposed vows and oaths
    g. *zera'im*—agricultural laws
    h. *avodah*—the divine service of sacrifices
    i. *korbanot*—individual sacrifices
    j. *taharah*—ritual purity
    k. *nezikin*—torts and damages
    l. *kinyan*—purchase and sale
    m. *mishpatim*—litigation
    n. *shofetim*—judicial administration.

R. Yosef Albo, influenced by his teacher, Hasdai Crescas, established new criteria:

    a. *devarim*—general religious truths
    b. *chukkim*—laws beyond our abilities to comprehend
    c. *mishpatim*—social morality.

On philosophical grounds he divided these laws into:

    a. *hadat hativit*—natural law
    b. *hadat hanimusit*—laws of virtue
    c. *hadat ha'elokit*—divine law (*Sefer Halkkarim* 1:7).

In the nineteenth century, R. Samson Raphael Hirsch charted a new system using the terminology of the Torah:

    a. *torot*—instructions or doctrines (i.e., the historically revealed ideas concerning God, the world, the mission of mankind, and the mission of Israel). These doctrines are not simply matters of faith but principles to be acknowledged and realized in life.
    b. *mishpatim*—judgments, i.e., statements of justice involving creatures similar and equal to oneself
    c. *chukkim*—statutes, i.e., statements of justice involving subordinate creatures, which are obligatory because of the obedience due to God.

vance for the *mitzvot* are not necessarily identical to the divine reasons for them.[59] Nevertheless, different terms are used in the Talmud for the various *mitzvot*, though the means of interpretation used to derive the *mitzvot* is consistent, whether the subject under discussion is logical (e.g., laws concerning society) or unknowable (e.g., laws concerning ritual purity). The principles of *halachah* (e.g., the ability to appoint an agent[60] to affect a transaction on one's behalf) apply equally to sacrifices and marriage. Similarly, ritual directives are often based on civil law and vice versa (*Gittin* 47b; *Ketubot* 49b). The Torah is a unified entity and in classifying its imperatives, we should never presume to grant extra importance to some *mitzvot*.

This unity notwithstanding, the halachic authorities have, for practical reasons, distinguished between financial matters and ritual prohibitions.

Within halachic literature other terms are sometimes employed.[61]

1. *dinim*—judgments; normally used for legal rights and duties having a monetary value. This category is

---

These include justice vis-à-vis the earth, plants, animals and one's own body and soul

d. *mitzvot*—commandments to love all beings without distinction, purely because we are so ordered by God

e. *edot*—symbolic observances that testify to the mission of man and Israel

f. *avodah*—service or worship, i.e., exaltation and sanctification of man's inner powers by word and deed, which clarifies our task and enables us to fulfill our mission.

59. See Ramban, *Devarim* 22:6.
60. *Kiddushin* 41b.
61. See Dr. I. Herzog, *The Main Institutions of Jewish Law*, Vol. I, Soncino, p. XXI.

virtually identical to "civil law" but family law is also partially included. It is subdivided into:

    a. *mamonot*—matters arising from commercial trans-actions or relations, as distinct from torts such as battery or theft.
    b. *kenassot*—laws relating to penalties and fines.

2. *malkot*—laws relating to corporal punishment. This classification is not synonymous with criminal law since it also includes punishment for ritual offenses (*Ketubot* 45b).
3. *nefashot* (also referred to as *onshin*—punishments)—acts punishable by death or exile (e.g., involuntary manslaughter); again, the category includes punishment for ritual offenses (*Kiddushin* 63b).
4. *ishut*—laws of marriage and divorce.
5. *hekdesh*—laws applying to objects or money transferred to the Temple.[62]
6. *sanhedrin*—the administration of the law.

Matters like procedure, public law, the law of persons and other terms of modern legal systems have no absolute equivalents in Talmudic terminology. Because ritual and secular laws are so intertwined in *halachah*, it is difficult to establish the kind of criteria that are commonly employed. Only Rambam, in his *Mishneh Torah*, seems to have attempted to establish an overall system of classification.

---

62. In this division of the law, the monetary and ritual aspects are inextricably bound together. This concerns consecrated property of all kinds and monetary obligations incurred towards the upkeep of the Temple.

THE ORALLY
TRANSMITTED
TORAH

THE NECESSITY FOR THE ORAL TRADITION

Despite the beauty of its messages and the profundity of its thoughts, with no traditional explanations and interpretations to unlock its secrets, the written Torah would remain a closed book. Indeed, it cannot really exist without the orally transmitted Torah, for its brevity and style presuppose that the reader has received instruction in decoding its message. For example, the Torah (*Devarim* 12:21) ordains that cattle and sheep must be slaughtered ritually before being eaten, and sums up the precept by stating: "as I have commanded you." Nowhere does the text explain what ritual slaughter is or how it is to be performed. Yet the phrase "as I have commanded you" indicates that the people must have been familiar with the method of slaughter. Therefore, there must have been an oral tradition, which permitted the written Torah to ordain *mitzvot* in a concise manner. It is this tradition that we refer to as the orally transmitted Torah.[1]

A clear knowledge of the orally transmitted Torah is essential for many reasons. In his introduction to *Sefer Mitzvot Gadol*, R. Moshe of Coucy writes: "The verses of the Torah often contradict each other.[2] The oral Torah frequently resolves these apparent contradictions." R. Yehudah Halevi notes: ". . . that which appears plain in the Torah is yet obscure, and much more so are the obscure passages, because the oral supplement was relied on" (*Kuzari* III:35).[3]

For instance, the Torah (*Bereshit* 1:28) states, ". . . and God said to them, 'Be fruitful and multiply . . .'" The written Torah does not explain whether this was a blessing or a commandment. Even if we assume that it is an injunction, several questions must be answered: Are both men and women obligated? How many children must one have to fulfill the precept? What if one has children only of one sex? What if one's children die? Or if they die after having children themselves? Are their children considered his children? Only an oral tradition can answer these questions and allow us a proper understanding of the *mitzvah*.

Many of the written Torah's *mitzvot* simply can't be fulfilled without an instructive tradition. For example, *Shemot* 20:10 and *Devarim* 5:14 state that one shall not perform *melachah* work on Shabbat, yet neither text defines *melachah*. *Shemot* 21:12 declares that a murderer shall be put to death, yet it does not describe the method of carrying out the sentence, while the Torah uses separate

---

1. See *Chullin* 27a.
2. For example: *Shemot* 34:18 and *Devarim* 16:8.
3. See *Menachot* 66a.

terms for different manners of execution without specify-
ing what each entails. Concerning Yom Kippur, the Torah
decrees (*Vayikra* 16:31), ". . . you shall afflict yourselves . . . ," but it does not explain what constitutes
affliction. Nor does it specify how much of the harvest one
should leave in his fields for the poor.[4]

At times the Torah mentions a specific case but does not
indicate whether the applicable law can be taken as a
general rule. For example, *Shemot* 21:26–27 states: "And if
a man strikes the eye of his indentured servant or his
maidservant and destroys it, he shall free him as compensation for his eye." Is this law particular to damaging an
eye or is it also relevant to injuries to other limbs?

Furthermore, many laws are mentioned only in passing,
even though society depends upon them. Nowhere does
the Torah explain how marriage is effected; the text only
notes that there are such an institution. Similarly, the only
reference to the method of property acquisition and transfer is a prohibition of overcharging![5] Since the purpose of
the Torah is to create a code of behavior for mankind, there
must be some vehicle for determining its intent. The orally
transmitted Torah is that vehicle.

R. Samson Raphael Hirsch comments:

> After all, it was not out of this book that the Law was to
> have been acquired. This book was to be given into the
> hands of those who were already well informed in the
> Law, simply as a means of retaining and reviving ever afresh
> this knowledge which had been entrusted to their mem-
> ories. . . . The written Torah is to the orally transmitted
> Torah like short notes on a full and extensive lecture on any
> scientific subject. For the student who has heard the whole

---

4. *Vayikra* 19:9–10.
5. *Vayikra* 25:14.

lecture, short notes are quite sufficient to bring back afresh to his mind at any time the whole subject of the lecture. For him, a word, a question mark, an exclamation point, a period, the underlining of a word, etc., is often quite sufficient to recall to his mind a whole series of thoughts, a remark, etc. For those who had not heard the lecture from the Master, such notes would be completely useless. If they were to try to reconstruct the scientific contents of the lecture literally from such notes they would of necessity make many errors. Words, marks, etc., which serve those scholars who had heard the lecture as [guides] to the wisdom that had been taught, and learnt, stare at the uninitiated like meaningless sphinxes.

(The Pentateuch, Shemot 21:2)

The Talmud expresses this view in a most remarkable story:

Our rabbis taught: A Gentile once came to Shammai and inquired, "How many types of Torah do you have?" He replied, "Two: a written Torah and an orally transmitted Torah." The Gentile said, "I accept the written Torah but not the orally transmitted Torah. Convert me and teach me the written Torah." Shammai became angry and banished him. The Gentile then approached Hillel, who converted him. On the first day Hillel taught him the [Hebrew] alphabet; the next day he taught him the alphabet in reverse order. The convert asked, "Yesterday you taught me differently." Hillel responded, "Just as you trusted me [to have taught you correctly yesterday], trust [the authenticity of] the orally transmitted Torah."

(Shabbat 31a)

Hillel was not attempting to trick the convert into accepting the orally transmitted Torah. Rather, he showed him that even our understanding of something as seemingly simple as the alphabet is dependent upon an oral transmission. The orally transmitted Torah is the vehicle that brings order to the written Torah; it serves as the means of comprehending what God wants of us. Deny its authenticity or endeavor to observe only the written Torah and you are faced with an insurmountable dilemma—for how do you know you are even reading the words correctly? Man's ability to live in accordance with his divinely assigned role is completely contingent on an oral tradition.

Our acceptance of this tradition is ultimately a leap of faith, as Hirsch writes:

> There is no evidence or guarantee for the truth and reality of a historic fact save our trust in tradition. All sorts of documents and evidences, all manner of internal and external circumstances, may lead you to the conclusion that it is probable, or almost certain, that such-and-such an event did really happen; but who tells you that what you consider probable has really happened? or that the very documents from which you draw your conclusions are not in reality forged? What other assurance have you that the conclusions you draw are a safe enough basis for both your present and future course of action, if not your trust in the genuineness of tradition?. . . . The fact is that the written Torah contains no direct documentary evidence of the truth of the orally transmitted Torah. Yet an entire nation has joyfully committed the preservation of its existence during more than 3,000 years to this authority. . . . How deeply convinced all these generations were of the truth of this tradition . . . so completely assured was the people of the faithful transmission of this tradition that it required no other legitimization.
>
> (*Gesammelte Schriften*, Vol. I, pp. 97ff., as quoted in *Horeb*, trans. Dr. I. Grunfeld, London, 1962, Vol. I, p. 30)

The very dependence of the written Torah on an orally transmitted explanation belies the attacks of generations of critics of the former. The textual inconsistencies and contradictions they use to pronounce the Torah no more than a collection of manuscripts from different sources are, in truth, the evidence that the written Torah must have been revealed together with an oral explanation. Inadvertently or not, these critics have overlooked the orally transmitted Torah as a source for resolving the problems they encountered. Using Hirsch's imagery, we can say that they found the notebook but missed the lecture (see also Bible Criticism and its Counter-arguments, pp. 201–232).

THE NATURE OF THE ORALLY TRANSMITTED TORAH

The written Torah, given at Sinai, is the "voice" of God in the world. Although it can be heard and read, it is not immediately meaningful. Rather, it represents that which is capable of assuming meaning. It needs interpretation to be understood. The orally transmitted Torah[6] is that part of revelation that makes the written word accessible to the human being.

The Torah was originally in Heaven,[7] meaning that its form transcended the physical realm of existence. It predated the creation of the world, encompassed all knowl-

---

6. It is important to remember that the orally transmitted Torah is called Torah and not "explanation" or "interpretation," because—as discussed above—these terms do not describe its purpose. Nor is *Torah Shebe'al Peh* called "the unwritten Torah," which would suggest "a Torah not given" (as in natural law). Rather, the distinctive meaning of *Torah Shebe'al Peh* is a "given Torah not written."

7. *Bereshit Rabbah* 8:2.

edge, and was, according to the kabbalistic interpretation, the "mind of God."[8]

This *Torah kedumah* (primordial Torah), explain the kabbalists, burned before God in "black fire on white fire" and was divided into two "forms": the form that encompassed all knowledge and reflected God's essence, symbolized by the white fire; and the form of the written Torah and the oral Torah given to man, symbolized by the black fire. Within the process of Creation, the *Torah kedumah* coalesced into a Torah men could delve into, the Torah we study today. The relationship of the orally transmitted Torah to the written Torah is also likened to this image of "black fire on white fire" (Jerusalem Talmud, *Shekalim* 6:1, end). Just as a white background contains no meaning for man, representing the metaphysical world beyond his grasp, the written Torah given at Sinai carries no meaning for man until it is "humanized" by the orally transmitted Torah. In effect, the Torah given to man is the primordial Torah what the oral Torah is to the written Torah.[9]

This kabbalistic doctrine reveals the very nature of the written and orally transmitted Torah. The white fire, in which the letters are not yet distinct, only finds meaning through the black fire, the orally transmitted Torah, which forms the consonants and vowels. Only the orally transmitted Torah can give meaning to the written Torah;

---

8. *Zohar* II, 60a; Recanati, *Ta'ame Hamitzvot.*
9. *Sefer Habahir* 99; *Tikkunei Zohar, tikkun* 21, p. 52b. Also see Isaac the Blind on *Midrash Konen*; Ramban, *Commentary on the Torah*, Introduction. For a full explanation, see my previous booklet, *The Torah as God's Mind, A Kabbalistic Look into the Pentateuch* (New York: Bep-Ron Publications, 1988). Also see *Between Silence and Speech*, Northvale, NJ: Jason Aronson Inc. Chapter 7.

without it, the written Torah could never be understood. The mystical white space between the letters on the Torah parchment is the written Torah, but the black letters—the orally transmitted Torah—make the knowledge of a higher world accessible to man through the human language of narratives and laws. Just as the primordial Torah is fixed and unalterable, so is the written Torah. Just as man needs the written Torah to act as a "filter" for the *Torah kedumah*, which would otherwise be inaccessible to us, we need the oral Torah to bring meaning to the written Torah.

For this reason, the orally transmitted Torah is a supernatural phenomenon, dynamic, flexible, ever-fresh, and rejuvenated, but only when interpreted in accordance with the Lawgiver's intention. Only then does it become the eternal spring, the inexhaustible and infinite outpouring of Judaism.

That the orally transmitted Torah is the essence of both all knowledge and the covenant God made with Israel is not surprising.

> Things were said orally and things were said in writing, and we would not know which are paramount. When the verse states, ". . . for by the 'mouth' of these words I have made a covenant with you and with Israel" [*Shemot* 34:27], we must conclude that those communicated orally are primary.
>
> (Jerusalem Talmud, *Peah* 2:4)

Therefore, when the sages interpret the written Torah through the orally transmitted Torah and its rules, they unfold the real, intended meaning of the text and bring wisdom to this world.

Just as musicians playing a symphony they did not compose still participate significantly in its performance, the sages, in their great wisdom, sound the heavenly notes of the Torah within the limits of the lower world.

In *Seder Eliyahu Zutta*, we are given an even deeper understanding of this concept:

> A heretic once told me: "The written Torah was given to us at Mount Sinai but the orally transmitted Torah was not." I said to him: "But were not both the written Torah and the orally transmitted Torah spoken by God? Then what difference is there between them?"
>
> To what can this be compared? To a king who gave each of his two beloved servants a measure of wheat and a bundle of flax. The wise servant took the flax, spun a thread, and wove a cloth. Then he ground the wheat, made flour, baked bread, and spread the cloth over it until the king came. But the foolish servant did nothing at all. When the king returned, he said to them: "My sons, bring me what I gave you." One servant showed him the bread with the cloth spread over it, and the other servant presented his raw wheat and flax. How great was his shame and disgrace! Similarly, when God gave Israel the Torah, He presented it only in the form of wheat and flax, leaving us to extract flour and make a garment.

This Midrash points out that the written Torah is not yet fully revealed, and still needs to be elaborated, just as the physical world requires human labor before it assumes its full purpose. Only man, by applying the rules of the orally transmitted Torah to the written text, brings this revelation to life and cultivates its contents. In that sense, man becomes a partner in the revelation of the Torah.

In other words, the divine word given at Sinai is an open-ended message to be elaborated upon by learned men throughout the generations. The *Zohar* (II:99) explains that the sages, through assiduous study, are capable of penetrating the barriers and unfolding some of the Torah's deeper hidden meaning.

Verily the Torah lets out a word and emerges a little from her sheath, only to hide herself again. But she does this only for those who know and obey her. Like a beautiful and stately maiden, she knows her lover haunts the gate of her house. So she opens the door to her hidden chamber ever so little, momentarily reveals her face to her lover, and then immediately hides it again. If anyone is with her lover, he perceives nothing. Her lover alone sees and is drawn to her with his heart and soul. He knows that because of her love for him she has disclosed herself. . . .

So it is with the word of the Torah, which reveals itself only to those who love it. The Torah knows that the *chacham libba*—the wise heart—haunts the gate of its fortress. From within the hidden palace it peeks out and then immediately hides again. The passersby perceive nothing. The lover alone sees and is drawn with his heart and soul.

The Authority of the Sages and Their Intellect

The sages' authority to interpret the text is based on *Devarim* 17:11—"According to the [interpretation of the] Torah they shall teach you, and the judgment they shall tell you, shall you do. You shall not deviate from the word they shall tell you, neither right nor left."

This verse empowered the Sanhedrin as well as the later sages of the Talmud[10] to interpret the Torah. In differences of opinion, majority rules.[11] While they used specific rules in interpreting the Torah, they were granted extraordinary authority, as the following episode indicates:

---

10. Rambam, *Mishneh Torah*, introduction; *Rosh Hashanah* 25a.
11. See *Shemot* 23:2 and Rashi ad loc.

R. Eliezer ruled that [a certain object] was ritually pure and the sages ruled it ritually impure. . . . On that day, R. Eliezer offered every imaginable argument [to support his ruling] but they did not accept them. He said, "If the *halachah* is in accordance with my view, let this carob tree serve as proof." Thereupon, the carob tree was uprooted and moved one hundred cubits. . . . The sages answered, "No proof can be derived from a carob tree." He then said, "Let this stream of water prove that the *halachah* is in accordance with my opinion," whereupon the stream began to flow backwards. The sages said, "No proof can be derived from a stream." He then said, "Let the walls of the study hall serve as proof," and the walls of the study hall buckled, about to fall. But R. Yehoshua rebuked them and said, "What right do you have to intervene when sages argue about *halachah*?" So the walls did not fall in deference to R. Yehoshua but they did not straighten up out of respect for R. Eliezer. . . . Whereupon R. Eliezer said, "Let the Heavens prove that the *halachah* is in accordance with my opinion." A voice from Heaven proclaimed, "Why do you argue with my son Eliezer when the *halachah* accords with his view?" R. Yehoshua stood up and declared, "It [the Law] is not in Heaven" [*Devarim* 30:12]. What did he mean? R. Yirmiyah says, "Once the Torah was given at Sinai we pay no heed to heavenly voices, for it says in the Torah, 'you shall follow the majority' [*Shemot* 23:2] [and the majority in this case differs with R. Eliezer]." R. Natan later met the prophet Eliyahu and asked him, "What did God do [when R. Yehoshua made this statement]?" He said, "God smiled and said, 'My sons have defeated me.'"

(*Bava Metzia* 59b)

Once the Torah was given at Sinai, God wanted man to interpret it without paying attention to supernatural intervention. To be sure, there are rules governing this interpretation, but as long as one explains the Torah in a manner consistent with these axioms, he can determine the law with complete confidence that his rulings are acceptable. In a sense, God has limited His right to intervene in the halachic process. He prefers orderly legal procedures to miracles and heavenly voices.[12] Were supernatural phenomena allowed to influence the decision of *halachah*, the entire structure of Torah study—the pillar upon which all of Judaism rests—would collapse. Remove the sages' ability to interpret the law and you render the debates and dialogues of the Talmud meaningless. The sages' right to determine the *halachah* must be independent of divine negation if Judaism is to be an ever-fresh and dynamic way of life. The episode recounted was a test. Had the sages agreed to accept R. Eliezer's opinion because of the voice from Heaven, they would have misunderstood the basis of revelation: the Torah is not in Heaven. Everything man needs to know concerning the Torah was given to him at Sinai. It is man's responsibility to use this knowledge and these tools to develop the system of living the Torah demands.

The sages, as interpreters of Torah law, can use their faculties of reason to declare that a given ruling reflects the intent of the Torah. In fact, their intellectual abilities are given more credence than the vision of a prophet:

> They [the sages] and the prophets are like two agents sent by a king to a province. With regard to the latter he wrote: "If they show you my signet, trust them, but otherwise do not." With regard to the former he wrote: "Even when they do not show you my signet, trust them." Thus, about the words of prophecy it is written: "If there arise among you

---

12. For other examples, see *Temurah* 16a; *Bava Metzia* 86a.

a prophet . . . and he gives you a sign . . ." [*Devarim* 13:2], but of the words of the sages it is written: "According to the Torah they shall teach you . . ." [*Devarim* 17:11].

(*Shir Hashirim Rabbah* 1:2)

Given that this extraordinary authority made the sages the arbiters of Torah law, how can we be sure they were objective in developing their exegesis? Is it not possible that they fixed the outcome to reflect their own ambitions or prejudices? Moreover, as we shall later see, *sevarah*— logic—is given great weight in determining a halachic ruling. Can we be certain that the logic of the sages was indeed incorruptible?

A host of factors can affect man's objectivity, and the different forces at work within his subconscious mind can blind and mislead him. Only through self-discipline and a lifelong effort to live morally can true objectivity be achieved. It is not so much a denial of the inner forces that is called for, as an awareness of their effects and a conscious attempt to balance them so that they play no role in workings of the mind. The means of attaining this balance is the focus of the works of Jewish ethics. In Jewish tradition the sages are credited with many ways of reaching this balance, and their authority is predicated on the assumption that personal advantage, pride, and other factors were not a force in their lives. Throughout the Talmud and later rabbinic literature, we find great emphasis placed upon how the scholars avoided unethical or immoral behavior and unhealthy spiritual environments, always striving to improve their temperaments and habits. This quest for complete personal integrity may well explain why so many of the sages grew elderly before their opinions were accepted.

This does not mean that these men were infallible. The children of Israel were told, "Do it [i.e., construct the Sanctuary as accurately as you can] and whatever you are able to do will be satisfactory" (*Bechorot* 17b). Similarly, once the sages have done everything within their power to reach objectivity, no more can be expected of them. The law they establish is considered to meet the highest requirement of the human intellect. This is the meaning of the phrase "it is not in Heaven": God Himself agrees with the sages from the outset. That is, once the sages have given their ruling, even if they declare right left and left right,[13] it is the law.[14] Because the Torah has empowered them to rule, their decisions carry the authority of the Torah itself.

THE AUTHENTICITY OF THE ORALLY TRANSMITTED TORAH

As we have stressed, the orally transmitted Torah is not a development of later generations—its principles existed at the time of the revelation at Sinai. The interpretation Moshe taught Yehoshua[15] is precisely the same interpretation taught today. Throughout Jewish history, however, dissenting groups have challenged this tradition. Most of these factions have not denied that there was an orally transmitted Torah, for the very text of the written Torah points to the need for one. Rather, they have maintained

---

13. *Sifri* on *Devarim* 17:11.

14. Unless, for example, these rulings lead to inadvertent violations of *mitzvot* that, if willfully transgressed, would carry the punishment of *karet* (extirpation). See *Horayot* 1.

15. *Avot* 1:1.

that the sages developed an interpretation that departed radically from the intent of the original.

The first of these sects were the Sadducees (c. 200 B.C.E.), who rejected the orally transmitted Torah as taught by the sages. They generally insisted on a more rigid and literal understanding of the written Torah than the Pharisees—as the sages were known.

The classic example of a disagreement between the two schools is the principle of *Lex Talionis* (the law of retribution), as described in *Shemot* 21:24 and *Vayikra* 24:19–20: "An eye for an eye, a tooth for tooth, a hand for a hand, a foot for a foot." The Pharisees, basing themselves on the traditional interpretation, which was later incorporated into the Talmud, explained that the verse referred to financial compensation, whereas the Sadducees sought to interpret it literally.[16]

Sadducee claims that the Pharisees created a new Judaism are partly refuted by evidence from *Nach* indicating that the interpretations of the Talmudic sages were consistent with the practices of earlier periods. Indeed, if anyone was guilty of creating a new Judaism, it was the Sadducees, whose interpretations were often based on personal interest and prestige. Their efforts to curry favor with their Greek protectors[17] recall the attempt by German reformers to make Judaism more palatable to the gentile world they so envied.

---

16. The eighth century C.E. saw the rise of a similar sect known as the Karaites. They were referred to as *Karaim* in Hebrew, for they based their practices on the *mikra*, the literal text. The Karaites believed that the oral interpretation depended on the insights of each generation, whereas the Sadducees rejected it altogether.

17. See R. Yitzchak Isaac Halevi, *Dorot Harishonim*; R. Saadiah Gaon, *The Book of Refutation* (in Arabic).

As stated, the books of the Prophets[18] and Writings demonstrate that the Talmudic orally transmitted interpretation was, from the very beginning, incorporated into Jewish life.[19] For example, *Shemot* 20:22 commands: "And if you make Me an altar of stone, do not build it of hewn stones, for if you lift up your [iron] tool upon it, you have profaned it."[20] *Mechilta* explains that the prohibition of building with cut stone applied not only to the altar, but partially to the rest of the Temple: the building could be constructed from hewn stones only if the cutting was done at the quarry rather than at the building site. The stones used for the altar, however, could not be cut at all. This interpretation is consistent with *I Melachim* 6:7:

> And the house [i.e., the Temple built by Shlomo], when it was being built, was constructed out of complete stones transported [to the site]; neither hammer nor axe nor any iron tool was heard in the house during construction [i.e., iron tools were not used at the building site but could have been used at the quarry].

Another illustrative prohibition is that of transferring articles from one domain to another on Shabbat. This

---

18. Although *Nevi'im* is seen as an explanation of the written Torah, it differs from the Mishnah and Talmud in that it was prophetically transmitted to each prophet according to his capacity for revelation. However, the explanations derived from or specified in *Nach* are part of the orally transmitted Torah. Thus, a law elucidated in *Nach* reflects a traditional interpretation rather than a new decree promulgated by a prophet.

19. D. S. Shapiro, *Torat Moshe Vehanevi'im* (Jerusalem: Mossad Harav Kook, 1961).

20. See *Devarim* 27:5–6; *Sotah* 48b, concerning the *shamir*, a creature about the size of a barley corn, which could cut stones.

proscription is the subject of extensive discussion in the Talmud. Yet it is not specified in the written Torah. However, in Yirmiyahu 17:21–22 we find:

> Thus has God said, "Protect your soul and bear no burden on the Shabbat day, nor bring any into the gates of Jerusalem. Neither shall you remove a burden from your homes on the Shabbat day . . . and you shall sanctify the Shabbat day, as I commanded your fathers."

Mezudat David notes that the prohibition referred to by Yirmiyahu indeed involves transferring from one domain to another—from outside the city into the gates of Jerusalem and from one's home to the outside. Here again we find evidence that the orally transmitted Torah's explanation of one type of prohibited work was already known and enforced at the time of the prophets. Thus, the traditions of the Pharisees were not their own innovations, as claimed by the Sadducees.

An additional classic controversy between the Pharisees and the Sadducees concerned the proper time for the *omer* offering. The basis for the controversy is the following passage:

> Speak to the children of Israel and say to them: "When you come to the land that I give you, and harvest its produce, you shall bring an *omer* [a measure of grain] of the first of your produce to the *Kohen*. And this *omer* shall be waved before God so that it shall be favorably received from you; *on the day after Shabbat the Kohen shall wave it.*"
>
> (*Vayikra* 23:10–11)

The Pharisees understood "the day after Shabbat" to refer to the day following the first day of Pesach, since the word "Shabbat" may also refer to a holiday. The Sadducees, on the other hand, interpreted the phrase literally and maintained that the *omer* offering was to be brought on a Sunday. Thus, if the first day of Pesach fell on a Tuesday, according to the Pharisees the *omer* would be offered on Wednesday, whereas according to the Sadducees it would only be brought on the following Sunday.[21] However, in Yehoshua 5:11 we find: "And they ate of the produce of the land on the day after Pesach. . . ."[22]

There are numerous other examples of interpretations found in the orally transmitted Torah and reflected in *Nach*. The utilization of *chalifin*—exchange—and money as a means of transferring title (*Bava Metzia* 47a) are already noted in *Megillat Ruth* (4:7) and *Yirmiyahu* (32:9). In addition, one of the Temple laws later stated in the Talmud (*Moed Katan* 5a) appears in *Yechezkel* (44:9). Hence, the orally transmitted Torah—as recorded in the Talmud—is not a later interpretation or a new body of laws, but a record of traditions dating back to the time of revelation.[23]

Further evidence of this fact can be drawn from the Mishnah. *Makkot* 2:4 discusses whether the three cities of

---

21. The dispute had other ramifications (e.g., the day on which Shavuot is celebrated). The Torah states that it is to be celebrated fifty days after the *omer* is offered. According to the Pharisees, Shavuot would always be on the same Hebrew date since the *omer* was offered on the day after Pesach. According to the Sadducees, however, the date would change yearly since it was dependent on a count beginning from the Sunday after Pesach.

22. Regarding whether this day could have been Shabbat, see Rambam, *Mishneh Torah, Hilchot Temidim Umusafim* 7:11; *Haketav Vehakabbalah* ad loc.

23. For more examples, see Prof. Ch. Albeck, *Mevo LaMishnah*, Chapter 2. Also see *Sanhedrin* 49a; *Yevamot* 47a; *Pesachim* 20a.

refuge established on the east bank of the Jordan[24] functioned while the west bank was being conquered by Yehoshua. The Mishnah rules that they only became operative when the land was conquered and three such cities had been established on the west bank as well. The entire question deals with a reality of early Jewish history. Thus, to argue that the orally transmitted Torah was formulated later ignores the fact that it explains issues only relevant to earlier periods.[25]

Traces of the orally transmitted traditions can even be found in non-Jewish literature, predating the Talmud by centuries. The Septuagint—the famous third-century B.C.E. Greek translation of the Bible[26]—is often remarkably consistent with rabbinical tradition. For example, in *Shemot* 12:15 we find: "For seven days you shall eat unleavened bread; but on the first day, *tashbitu*—you shall remove—the leaven from your homes. . . ." The Septu-

---

24. See *Devarim* 4:41–43.
25. See Dr. David Zvi Hoffmann, *The First Mishnah and the Controversies of the Tannaim*, trans. P. Forchheimer; A. Kurman, *Mevo LaTorah Shebichtav U've'al Peh*.
26. The Septuagint (literally, "seventy") is the oldest extant Greek translation of the Bible. It probably owes its name to *The Letter of Aristeas* (written by an anonymous Alexandrian Jew of the third century B.C.E.), according to which seventy-two scholars (a number rounded off to seventy in the work's title), summoned from Jerusalem by Ptolemy II Philadelphus, translated the Pentateuch into Greek. The story is quite similar to one related in *Soferim* 1:8–9, where the rabbis comment: "The day the law was translated into Greek was as unfortunate for the Jews as that on which the golden calf was made."
   In Hebrew, the translation is referred to as *Targum Hashivim*—the translation of the seventy. Interestingly, according to tradition, though each of the sages worked independently, their finished products were identical.

agint translates *tashbitu* as destruction rather than removal. So do the sages of the Talmud (*Pesachim* 21a, 27b), who considered simple removal inadequate. This parallelism indicates that the Septuagint's authors were aware of the rabbinic interpretation of the Torah's command.

Similarly, the Septuagint renders the aforementioned phrase "the day after Shabbat" (*Vayikra* 23:11) as "the day after Pesach," consistent with the Pharisees rather than the Sadducees.[27]

Other Hellenistic works also reveal a familiarity with the traditions of the orally transmitted Torah. Thus, the Aramaic Elephantine Papyri of Yeb (fifth century B.C.E.) cite the laws of the *ketubah*—the marriage contract—as well as many Pesach observances that are not obvious from the text of the written Torah. Demetrius, an author who lived in the second century B.C.E., mentions that the prohibition of eating the sciatic nerve only applies to cattle, and Pseudo Aristeas (second century B.C.E.) describes the *halachot* of *tefillin, tzitzit*, and mezuzah in detail. All of these laws are dependent upon the orally transmitted Torah for their clarification.

Archaeological remains of the Second Temple period further confirm the authenticity of the orally transmitted Torah. The *mikvaot* (ritual baths) found at Masada, Maon (Nirim) and Herodion were built in accordance with the specifications outlined in *Shulchan Aruch*—the sixteenth-century code of Jewish law written by R. Yosef Karo!

Similar support can be drawn from the discovery of tefillin at the Dead Sea. The tradition of laying tefillin is based on a rabbinic interpretation of the following verse:

---

27. For more examples, see Albeck, Chapter 2.

> And these words, which I command you this day, shall be
> upon your heart. . . . And you shall bind them for a sign
> upon your hand and they shall be ornament between your
> eyes.
>
> *(Devarim* 6:6, 8)

Nowhere does the written Torah describe this sign and ornament. The *tefillin* we use today are the result of the tradition of the orally transmitted Torah. Yet not only are the fragments of *tefillin* found in the Qumran excavations similar to our own;[28] the order of the biblical passages written on these fragments indicates that the difference of opinion between Rashi (eleventh century) and Rabbenu Tam (twelfth century) dates back to the earliest moments of Jewish history, for *tefillin* of both types were found! Centuries later as well, "in Nehardea and Jerusalem they found two sets of *tefillin*: one according to the order of Rashi and the other according to Rabbenu Tam" *(Piskei Tosafot, Menachot* 34b).

Though our acceptance of the orally transmitted Torah is ultimately a matter of faith, several arguments support the traditional interpretations of the sages. Throughout our history, many commentators have taken it upon themselves to show that no other form of exegesis is logical or even plausible. This is especially true of commentaries written during the period of emancipation in Europe, when certain "enlightened" circles attempted to divorce the written Torah from its traditional interpretation. While we shall not analyze the motives of those who sought to rid Judaism of what they considered archaic practices, it is

---

28. For more information, see Y. Yadin, *Tefillin from Qumran* (1969).

worth our while to at least examine how much of our tradition is implicit in the text of the Torah.

In *Ayelet Hashachar*, the foreword to his commentary on *Vayikra*, Malbim outlines six hundred thirteen rules used by the sages in interpreting *Vayikra*: two hundred forty-eight linguistic principles and three hundred sixty-five guidelines for deciphering verbs and synonyms. Though it is beyond the scope of this work to examine every rule, his basic premise was that even if the orally transmitted Torah had been forgotten, it could have been reconstructed from the written Torah by employing these methods.[29]

Because the question of authenticity is so important, we cite the following example of Malbim's approach. The Torah states:

> If his sacrifice be a burnt offering brought from cattle, he shall sacrifice a male without blemish; at the entrance to the *Ohel Moed* he shall offer it, as an expression of his will [*lirtsono*] before God.
>
> (*Vayikra* 1:3)

Torat Kohanim, a midrashic work, understands the phrase "he shall offer it" as an imperative, deriving that one

---

29. Other commentators have also shown the unity of the written and orally transmitted Torah; most notable among them are the Gaon of Vilna (1720–1797), in *Aderet Eliyahu*; R. Yaakov Tzvi Mecklenburg (1785–1865), in *Haketav Vehakabbalah*; R. Samson Raphael Hirsch (1808–1888), in *The Pentateuch*, trans. I. Levy; and R. Baruch Halevi Epstein (1860–1942), in *Torah Temimah*.

Another work of great importance is *Matteh Dan*, by R. David Nieto (1654–1728), who defended the orally transmitted Torah against the attack of ex-Marranos who found the rabbinic tradition unacceptable.

can be forced to offer a sacrifice. How, then, is this "an expression of his will"? The sages answer that we coerce him until he agrees.

Why did the sages interpret the phrase as indicating that he is to be forced to offer the sacrifice? Why not simply explain that the sacrifice is only offered if he is willing? Malbim proves that the structure of the verse itself leaves no room for an alternative explanation. Had the Torah meant to tell us that this sacrifice could only be brought by someone willing to do so, the verse would have stated, "as an expression of his will he shall offer it."[30] Because "he shall offer it" comes first, it must be an independent statement, and therefore the Torah must be teaching us that he can be compelled to offer the sacrifice.

Furthermore, Malbim notes that there are two Hebrew terms for "will": *chefetz* and *ratson*. The former describes an emotional desire, whereas the latter refers to an intellectual one. By convincing a person that offering a sacrifice is a divine imperative, one can win his intellectual agreement even though his emotions might view the act as undesirable.[31] Hence, although one can be compelled to offer a sacrifice, this can still be seen as an expression of *ratson* (intellectual will). Thus, the Torah's phraseology indicates the interpretation offered by the sages.

Another example of this phenomenon is the aforementioned case known as *Lex Talionis*, the law of retribution:

> And if a man injures his fellow man, as he has done so shall it be done to him. A fracture for [*tachat*] a fracture, an eye

---

30. Rule 194 of *Ayelet Hashachar* establishes that an imperative is always stated at the beginning of a verse, while a mere repetition of a word in the same verse is always at the end.

31. See Rambam, *Mishneh Torah, Hilchot Gerushin* 2:20.

for an eye, a tooth for a tooth; as he has injured a man, so shall it be done to him.

(*Vayikra* 24:19–20)

I might think that if a man blinded his fellow man, he, too, should be blinded, or if he cut off the hand of his fellow man, his hand should be cut off. . . . We are therefore taught [by the juxtaposition of the verses] that damaging another's animal is comparable to injuring one's fellow man; just as one who damages another's animal must pay financial compensation, so must one who injures another man.

(*Torat Kohanim*)[32]

Perhaps no text of the Torah is more misinterpreted than the above verses in *Vayikra* (which are also recorded in *Shemot* 21:24–25). Countless critics and scholars have cited this as an example of the sages changing the literal meaning of the text (i.e., whereas the written Torah seemed to have demanded retribution in kind, the sages reinterpreted it to mean financial compensation).

These accusations are baseless, for if the sages were indeed changing the law of the written Torah, why did they not change the text as well? Moreover, the text itself shows that no other interpretation is possible:

The Torah concludes the section pertaining to personal injuries with this verse: "You shall have one law, the stranger shall be as the citizen, for I am the Lord, your God" (*Vayikra* 24:22). W. F. Albright, a well-known biblical archaeologist, points out:[33]

---

32. See *Bava Kamma* 84a.
33. See W. F. Albright, *History, Archeology and Christian Human-*

This principle was in actuality an outstanding revolutionary change in law. In ancient oriental jurisprudence, men of greater social standing or wealth were able to escape punishment for the most heinous of crimes simply by paying a fine. In primitive law revenge was dominant and if a member of a clan was killed the penalty was the destruction of the offender's entire clan.[34]

With *Lex Talionis*, however, the principle of equal justice for all came to dominate all punishments for injury or homicide. So *Lex Talionis*, far from being something which is completely outworn today, is something which we have not begun to attain—the principle of equal justice for all![35]

Were we to interpret "an eye for an eye" as exact retribution, how could we understand the Torah's demand for "one law"? As the Talmud (*Bava Kamma* 84a) poses the question: "If a blind man blinded another man, or if a cripple crippled another man, how could we fulfill the imperative 'an eye for an eye'?"

---

ism (1964). The quote is a paraphrase of Albright by E. Feldman in *Tradition* (winter 1965).

34. The Code of Hammurabi rules: "If a man knocked out the tooth of his equal, one shall make his tooth fall out." This retaliation principle is carried to grotesque extremes. For example, if a jerrybuilder's faulty construction causes the death of a homeowner, the jerrybuilder is killed, but if he causes the death of the homeowner's son or daughter, then *his* son or daughter is killed (*Pentateuch and Haftorahs*, ed. Dr. J. H. Hertz [London: Soncino Press, 1975], pp. 405–406).

35. Prof. Johann David Michaelis (1717–1791), in *Gruendliche Erklaerung des Mosaischen Recht* (Frankfurt, six volumes), writes, "It is a law appropriate only for free people, in which the poorest inhabitant has the same right as his most aristocratic assailant. . . . It deems the tooth of the poorest peasant as valuable as that of the nobleman; strangely so, because the peasant must bite crust while the nobleman eats cake."

The conclusion reached by the Talmud is that the text can only be referring to financial compensation, for no one is identical to his fellow man. The courts are adjured to determine the financial implications of the loss of an organ and assess damages accordingly. In this sense, "an eye for an eye" is fulfilled and no attention is paid to the bodily condition of the perpetrator, for the Torah states, "You shall have one law. . . ."

Benno Jacob[36] (1862–1945), a rabbi and Bible scholar, notes that "an eye for an eye" is stated in the context of injuries caused by accident. In the preceding verses, the Torah refers to cases of deliberate assault but does not call for exact retribution. Were we to interpret "an eye for an eye" literally, we would have to conclude that the Torah viewed accidental injuries as more serious than deliberate ones!

The terminology used by the Torah also indicates that the verse cannot be interpreted literally. Throughout *Tanach,* the word *tachat* means "below," "beneath" or "instead of" rather than "for," which would imply exact retribution. Had the Torah intended the verse to be taken literally, the Hebrew would have read not *ayin tachat ayin* (an eye instead of an eye) but *ayin b'ayin*—the *bet* indicating "for." R. Samson Raphael Hirsch, in his commentary on *Shemot* 21:27, points out that the concept of replacement is only expressed by financial compensation— for by blinding his attacker, the injured person would in no way be replacing his loss.[37]

---

36. Quoted by N. Leibowitz in *Studies in Vayikra,* translated and adapted from the Hebrew by Aryeh Newman (Jerusalem, 1980), p. 251.

37. In *Devarim* 19:21, however, the prefix *b'* is used, but there the

Moreover, from the verse "You shall not take ransom for the life of a murderer, who is condemned to death . . ." (*Bamidbar* 35:31), the Talmud (*Bava Kamma* 83b) deduces that for the life of a murderer one may take no ransom but for the main organs of the human body, which do not grow back, one may take ransom (i.e., cash compensation).

Maharal notes that the Torah uses the phrase "an eye instead of an eye" rather than unequivocally stating "financial compensation for an eye" to teach us a moral lesson.

> Had the Torah [specified] "financial compensation" I would have assumed that just as one who kills his friend's animal and pays damages is free from further punishment, one who injures another and pays damages has no further need to compensate. In truth, however, even though he paid for the injury, he is still obligated to ask forgiveness. . . . The Torah thus states that were it possible, his hand should also be cut off [to show his remorse].
>
> (*Gur Aryeh*, *Vayikra* 24:20)

In summation, "an eye for an eye" is anything but a brutal call for retribution.[38] Rather, it is an indication of the divine nature of Torah law, a system that realizes that man cannot simply acquit himself through monetary compensation—he must also seek the forgiveness of the person he has wronged. And it teaches us the impossibility of interpreting the written Torah without the orally transmitted Torah, for though they may have been given in separate form, they are indivisible.

---

injury was only attempted, not inflicted, so there could be no question of indemnification. Hence the more general term *b'* is used. See Hirsch, *The Pentateuch*.

38. See R. Travers Herford, *Talmud and Apocrypha*, p. 119: "There is nothing to show that the literal was ever inflicted."

A third example is the prohibition of mixing milk and meat. In all three references to this prohibition,[39] the relevant verse states simply, ". . . you shall not cook a kid in its mother's milk." R. Samson Raphael Hirsch, in his commentary on *Shemot*, writes:

> The *Halachah* teaches that these words forbid the cooking of the flesh of any *behemah tehorah*, (i.e., beef, mutton or goat-flesh) with the milk of a *behemah tehorah* (i.e., with the milk of cows, sheep or goats). But *behemah temae'ah, chayah*, and *oaf* [ritually impure domesticated animals or non-domesticated animals or fowl] are not included in this prohibition.[40] We can accordingly understand why the text chooses *gedi* [a kid] and *chalev imo* [its mother's milk] to sharply define the objects affected by this prohibition. It would be difficult to express [the prohibition of mixing] *besar behemah tehorah* [the meat of a ritually pure domesticated animal] in *chalev behemah tehorah* [the milk of a ritually pure domesticated animal] with equal brevity and precision otherwise. *Basar* and *chalav* alone would be too comprehensive, and would include meat and milk of any kind, including venison and fowl, etc. Even adding *behemah* and saying again *besar behemah tehorah* would not suffice, as we find quite clearly that under the term *behemah* (e.g., in Deut. XIV, 4 & 5) *chayah* is included, and here *chayah* must be excluded. If, as is remarked in Chullin 113b, the word *gedi* used by itself includes the young of *parah* and *rachel* (cow and sheep)[41] there is hardly any other word that on the one hand includes the species *bakar vetzon* [cattle and sheep] and on

---

39. *Shemot* 23:19, 34:26, and *Devarim* 14:21.

40. i.e., the mixture is not proscribed by Torah law. It is, however, forbidden rabbinically.

41. Hoffmann, in *Das Buch Deuteronium*, p. 208, notes that *gedi* does not refer solely to young goats, for the Hebrew term for that is the more specific *gedi izim*. See Rashi on *Shemot* 23:19.

the other excludes all other species, and no shorter expression to limit the milk, too, to that of these species, than *chalev imo*.

(p. 407)

In addition, the sages point out that the Torah reflects common practice when citing examples. For instance, when the Torah prohibits the flesh of a live animal, the text states, ". . . neither shall you eat any meat torn in the field . . ." (*Shemot* 22:33). In fact, there is no difference whether the meat was torn from the animal in the field or at home; the prohibition is simply worded in this manner to reflect common practice. Similarly, August Dillman (1823–1894), a German Orientalist, Bible scholar and theologian, points out that it is common practice in the Arab world to cook lamb in sour milk.

R. Hirsch remarks that the formulation of the verse could also imply that "even this flesh and milk, which after all were so intimately connected (mother and kid), are to be kept apart in cooking; i.e., one may not even cook *gedi bechalev imo* [a kid in its mother's milk]."

THE PROHIBITION AGAINST RECORDING THE ORALLY TRANSMITTED TORAH

> The words that are written you are not at liberty to recite by heart, and the words transmitted orally you are not at liberty to read from writing.
>
> (*Gittin* 60b)

Though the written Torah and the orally transmitted Torah were presented simultaneously and the latter is the only means of understanding the former, the sages insisted that the orally transmitted Torah remain oral,[42] while allowing the heads of the courts and the prophets to write memoranda of the oral traditions for private use. But amid dire political and economic conditions and a diminishing number of students, these scholars feared that the Jews might forget the oral Torah, which had been meticulously preserved since it was handed down by Moshe.[43] Only then, in approximately 250 C.E., did they agree to record it for posterity.

In truth, the very nature of the orally transmitted Torah does not allow for its full recording. In the words of David: "I have seen an end to every endeavor but Your commandment is exceedingly vast" (*Tehillim* 119:96).

The totality of the Torah's message is immeasurable and beyond our ability to condense into a written form. The wisdom and truth it contains can never be expressed completely in writing. Recording the orally transmitted Torah would turn it into an archaic code of statutes. Instead of serving as a fountain of spiritual grandeur, the Torah would become a stagnant pool devoid of dynamism and flexibility. Moreover, certain forms of information can only be explained orally, and some dimensions of the orally transmitted Torah can only be passed on from teacher to pupil:

> In modern times, where reflection threatens to swallow up all life, where everything has been reduced to dead, abstract concepts, and it has been thought possible to educate men by theory alone, that old inherent reciprocal relationship

---

42. Also see *Temurah* 14b: "Those who record the *halachah* are like those who burn the Torah."

43. Rambam, *Mishneh Torah*, introduction.

between the written and spoken word, between theory and practice, has been totally displaced. When everything practical is incorporated into theory, when everything transmitted orally is put into writing and nothing left over for life, true theory along with genuine practice in life are lost. In the ancient worlds, however, where men still related to each other in much simpler, more natural ways, this natural relationship of the written to the spoken word, of theory to practice, was likewise much more properly observed.

(J. F. Molitor, *Philosophie der Geschichte oder Ueber die Tradition* [Frankfurt, 1857], Vol. I, p.4)

The goal of the Torah is to transform man into the carrier of its message. When man becomes permeated with the Torah, he can then serve as a transmitter to the following generation. When his thoughts, emotions and behavior indicate that he has embraced the Torah, only then can he share his knowledge with others. By recording the orally transmitted Torah man would be provided with a shortcut allowing him to pass on the tradition without assuming a personal obligation.

Furthermore, the written word quickly becomes dated. To remain meaningful, the oral Torah must therefore transcend text and time, creating harmony between the unchanging divine message and the challenges arising in history. Whereas a rigid written law would immobilize the Torah, an oral tradition enables it to constantly unfold, allowing new facets of the divine word to shine forth.

In addition, practically speaking, it would simply be impossible to record all the words of the sages.[44]

The prohibition against fully recording the orally trans-

---

44. R. Yosef Albo, *Sefer HaIkkarim* 3:23.

mitted Torah was also a powerful expression of the sages'
concern that the Torah would fall into the hands of the
very often anti-Semitic non-Jewish world, which would
then claim it as its own.

> Moshe asked God, "Shall I write it [the Torah] down for
> them?" God answered, "I chose not to give it entirely in
> writing for I foresee a day when they shall be subservient to
> other nations, who will then take the Torah [and claim it as
> their own]. . . . Therefore, I shall give the Torah in writ-
> ing but the Mishnah, Talmud, and Aggadah shall be trans-
> mitted orally, so that even when they become subservient to
> other nations, they shall remain distinct."
>
> (*Shemot Rabbah* 47:1)

The *Tanach* is shared by many faiths. However, the relationship between the Jews and the Torah is unique, for we
consider the Torah not merely a divinely inspired work,
but the constantly fresh word of God eternally applicable
to man. Maharal[45] points out that the bond between Israel
and the Torah is strengthened and renewed in every
generation because the Jews are living links in the tradition
that dates back to Sinai. Had the *Torah Shebe'al Peh* been
recorded, this link would never have been forged, for
Israel's relationship with the Torah would not have differed
from that of other nations and religions. Because the Torah
was orally transmitted, each generation had the opportunity to reestablish and reproduce the message conveyed to
Moshe. Recording it would have denied them the ability to
form a relationship with their Torah. A stagnant written
interpretation of the Torah would deny man his right to

---

45. *Tiferet Yisrael* 68.

find truth on his own. Thus, God permitted Moshe only to "take notes" in the form of the *Torah Shebichtav*, whose incomprehensibility indicated that there was another repository of revelation. By orally transmitting the explanation of these notes and the rules through which the correct interpretation could be derived, Moshe ensured that the Torah would remain an inexhaustible spring of knowledge, ever ready to flow into the minds of those who know how to draw from its waters.

Rambam offers an alternative explanation.[46] He notes that the written word is more subject to misinterpretation than ideas transmitted orally. No writer, no matter how skilled, can be sure the reader will not misconstrue his intent. An orally transmitted lecture, on the other hand, is less prone to misinterpretation, for the student can immediately clarify ambiguous or difficult points. Thus, the interpretations of the Torah were transmitted orally to ensure that the meanings of the *mitzvot* and codes were understood clearly and consistently in each generation.

When the sages reached the conclusion that the times demanded the recording of the orally transmitted Torah, they wrote it in a manner that preserved its oral essence. The Mishnah and Talmud are explicable rather than readable, for our ability to discern their meaning is dependent on the chain of tradition. R. Mendel of Kotzk, a nineteenth-century Chassidic leader, once explained that when the rabbis permitted the orally transmitted Torah to be recorded, they did not violate the prohibition, for the meaning of the Torah can never be contained in books.

---

46. *Commentary on the Mishnah*, Introduction.

THE CATEGORIES OF THE ORALLY TRANSMITTED TORAH

INTRODUCTION

In the introduction of his *Commentary on the Mishnah*, Rambam divides the orally transmitted Torah into five categories:

1. Explanations received and transmitted by Moshe, which are also indicated in the verses of the Torah and can thus be extracted by analysis. There can be no disagreement among the sages concerning these laws.
2. Laws termed *Halachah LeMoshe MiSinai*, which have no scriptural source. About these there can also be no disagreement.
3. Laws subject to debate, derived by reasoning (*sevarah*) and analysis (*drash*).
4. *Gezerot* (decrees), enacted by prophets and sages to preserve laws of the Torah.

5. *Takkanot* (ordinances), instituted by the sages for the welfare of society and the enhancement of individual moral standards.

The last two categories are normally designated as rabbinic law, and do not have the status of Torah law.

EXPLANATIONS RECEIVED AND TRANSMITTED BY MOSHE

The orally transmitted Torah came directly from God. After Moshe received it at Sinai, the prophets and sages passed it on to subsequent generations.

Why does the Talmud endeavor to deduce laws from the text of the Torah if they were conveyed to Moshe? Rambam points out that it is not because these laws were instituted by the sages (and therefore subject to conflicts of opinion). "Rather, these proofs were adduced later, when the rabbis sought textual support for an explanation already well-known." Among his many examples, Rambam cites the obligation to take "the fruit of a beautiful tree" (*Vayikra* 23:40) on the first day of the Sukkot festival. The written Torah does not designate the fruit by name, and the sages debated the intent of the text (*Sukkah* 35a). Through the method known as *drash*, they concluded that it had to be the *etrog* (a citrus fruit). If the sages derived this *halachah* from the text alone, no one could have fulfilled the *mitzvah* until they had completed this derivation.[1] Rambam continues: "The general rules and specific details

---

1. See *Bava Kamma* 84a; *Sifri* on *Devarim* 25:12; *Sanhedrin* 50b.

of the entire Torah were revealed at Sinai. However, even though they were stated by Moshe and there is therefore no disagreement as to their validity, these specifications can, in addition, be extracted from the verses of the written Torah through the scientific method of Torah exegesis transmitted to us." Yet why did the sages seek to reconcile the text with known oral laws? Perhaps to show how the oral Torah is contained in the written law[2] and to connect the two as a mnemonic device, because the oral Torah was not allowed to be written down.[3]

In addition, to corroborate well-established laws, the sages frequently cited texts that only implied such a law without explicitly indicating it.[4] Such corroboration is called an *asmachta* (literally, "support").

HALACHAH LEMOSHE MISINAI

Another indisputable class of the orally transmitted Torah is called *Halachah LeMoshe MiSinai* (laws given to Moshe at Sinai).[5] The difference between the explanations received and transmitted by Moshe and *Halachah LeMoshe MiSinai* is that the former are somewhat indicated in the text of the Torah, while the latter is not, nor can it be

---

2. Ritva on *Rosh Hashanah* 16a.

3. Rambam, *Commentary on the Mishnah*, introduction. Also see R. Yehudah Halevi, *Kuzari* III:73.

4. This was often done by means of the rules of interpretation discussed in Chapter 5.

5. The term occurs only three times in the Mishnah—in *Peah* 2:6, *Eduyot* 8:7, and *Yadayim* 4:3—but it appears frequently in the Talmud.

deduced by *sevarah* or the rules of interpretation.[6] Yet the
Talmud occasionally finds allusions to these *halachot* in the
Torah text. For instance, it detects a reference to the Sukkot
water libation in the passage describing the festival offerings,[7] while legal quantities pertaining to the *mitzvot* are
alluded to in: "A land of wheat and barley, and vines and
fig trees and pomegranates; a land of olive oil and [date]
honey" (*Devarim* 8:8).[8] These hints are also called *as-
machtaot*.

Halachah LeMoshe MiSinai needs no intellectual justi-
fication,[9] it is accepted because it was handed down at
Sinai, although sometimes reasons were offered.[10]

Other *Halachot LeMoshe MiSinai* concern the defects
that render an animal *terefah* (prohibited for consump-
tion);[11] the laws of tefillin,[12] such as the parchment and ink
to be used; some rules of ritual immersion;[13] levitical
defilement;[14] and many other matters.[15]

Sometimes *Halachot LeMoshe MiSinai* refer to events in
the messianic era. For instance:

> R. Yehoshua said: "I have received a tradition from R.
> Yochanan b. Zakkai, who heard it from his teacher, and his
> teacher from his teacher, as a *Halachah LeMoshe MiSinai*,

---

6. Rambam, *Commentary on the Mishnah*, Introduction.
7. *Sukkah* 34a.
8. *Berachot* 41a.
9. See Rashi on *Gittin* 14a, s.v. "*kehilchatah*."
10. *Bava Batra* 12b.
11. *Chullin* 42a.
12. *Menachot* 35a.
13. *Eruvin* 4a.
14. *Chullin* 9b.
15. See Rambam, *Commentary on the Mishnah*, Introduction.

that [when he comes to herald the arrival of the Messiah] Eliyahu will not pronounce objects clean or unclean. . . ."

(*Eduyot* 8:7)

Some post-Talmudic authorities observe that not all *Halachot LeMoshe MiSinai* actually came from Sinai, since some are rabbinical laws:

I have received a tradition from R. Yochanan b. Zakkai, who heard it from his teacher, and his teacher from his teacher, as a *Halachah LeMoshe MiSinai*, that Ammon and Moav must separate the tithe for the poor in the seventh year.

(*Yadayim* 4:3)

This is definitely a rabbinical law since the Torah only obliges us to tithe produce grown within the land of Israel. Yet it is like *Halachah LeMoshe MiSinai* since it is beyond doubt.[16]

Similarly, other terms designating a *Halachah LeMoshe MiSinai* indicate certainty e.g., "in truth they said" (*be'emet amru*),[17] *halachah*,[18] (or *halachot*),[19] "the *halachah* was told to Moshe at Sinai" (*ne'emru leMoshe miSinai*),[20] "we have learned,"[21] and "it is a *halachah* from a received tradition."[22]

---

16. Rosh, *Hilchot Mikvaot* 1.
17. See Jerusalem Talmud, *Shabbat* 1:4; Rashi on *Bava Metzia* 60a, s.v. *"be'emet."*
18. For example, *Nazir* 25a.
19. For example, *Kiddushin* 49a.
20. For example, *Chullin* 42a.
21. For example, *Niddah* 49a, and Rashi ad loc., s.v. *"shonin."*
22. See Rambam, *Mishneh Torah, Hilchot Nezirut* 2:13.

Although this type of *halachah* does not allow any dispute, we sometimes find differences of opinion concerning such laws because certain sages were not aware that they belonged in this category.[23] On occasion there may also be disagreement about the details of such laws, but not about the laws themselves.[24]

Some *Halachot LeMoshe MiSinai* were forgotten and later reinstated.[25]

LAWS SUBJECT TO DEBATE

Although the orally transmitted Torah was handed down by Moshe to the people, this great teacher remained the arbiter whenever doubt arose. Thus, in his last days we find:

> Moshe gathered the people and said, "The time for my death is near. If anyone has heard a *halachah* and forgotten it, let him come to me and I shall explain. And if anyone is uncertain about any part of the Torah, let him come forward and I shall clarify," as the verse states [*Devarim* 1:5], ". . . Moshe explained the Torah, saying. . . ."
>
> (*Sifri, Devarim* 1:5)

The sages (*Temurah* 15b) stress that Moshe possessed a unique comprehension of the entire Torah. In fact, his understanding was so great that he knew "all that a

---

23. See *Yevamot* 76b; *Responsa Chavot Yair* 192:25.
24. See *Chavot Yair*, loc. cit.
25. See *Yoma* 80a.

conscientious student would produce in the future"[26] and all the wisdom of the different worlds. This knowledge was imparted to him on Mount Sinai[27] in only forty days, for "God Himself taught Moshe, and is anything too difficult for Him?"[28]

One should not infer that Moshe was consciously aware of all the Torah insights that were to originate with future generations. Rather, he was a complete master of the fundamentals of the Torah, upon which all later deductions were based.[29] However, given Moshe's elevated status, the following aggadah becomes somewhat difficult to understand:

> When Moshe ascended on high [to study the Torah], he found God affixing crowns to the letters [of the Torah]. He asked Him, "Master of the universe, who is holding You back [from giving the Torah without crowns]?" God answered, "After several generations, a man named Akiva b. Yosef shall come forward and expound many *halachot* [based] on each point of the crowns." Moshe thereupon said, "Permit me to see him." God instructed, "Turn around." Moshe went and sat at the end of the eighth row, but he could not understand what was being said and became ill at ease. When R. Akiva came to a certain point, his students asked, "Rabbi, what is your source?" He replied, "It is a *halachah* given to Moshe at Sinai." Consoled, Moshe asked God, "Master of the universe, a man like this is destined to come forward and You choose me to

---

26. See Jerusalem Talmud, *Peah* 2:4; *Megillah* 19b.

27. See *Sefer Mitzvot Gadol*, Introduction.

28. *Leshem Shevo Ve'achlamah, Derushei Olam* 2:4. Also see *Sotah* 36b; *Yalkut Shimoni* on I Shmuel 129:19.

29. See Rambam, *Sefer Hamitzvot*, Principle 2; *Kreti Uphleti* on *Yoreh Deah* 29:5; R. Z. H. Chajes, *Mevo LaTalmud*, introduction.

transmit the Torah?" God replied, "Be silent, for this is My decree."

(*Menachot* 29b)[30]

On the surface, it would seem that R. Akiva's knowledge surpassed that of Moshe. Commenting on *Vayikra* 13:27, however, *Or Hachaim* explains that everything R. Akiva taught was indeed part of the orally transmitted Torah passed on by Moshe. However, Moshe was aware of these teachings by virtue of having received them from God. He had no need to resort to allusions, inferences or rules of interpretation.[31] By contrast, R. Akiva, who was not present at this revelation, had to find sources for his deductions in the written Torah.

As stated, this does not mean that Moshe knew all future halachic rulings. Rather, he mastered all the halachic guidelines, with all their nuances. Nevertheless, later sages were confronted with new situations that had no clear halachic precedents. A steady stream of important halachic questions begged for elucidation. The Torah therefore had to contain provisions for deriving *halachot* in any eventuality. These are the laws that Rambam writes were extracted by *sevarah* and *drash*.

Another reason for the aforementioned provisions involves the human factor in the chain of tradition.

When Moshe became aware that he would soon depart from the world, he called Yehoshua and said, "Ask me all

---

30. See also *Tanchuma, Chukkat* 24; *Bamidbar Rabbah* 19:6.

31. See R. Moshe Chaim Luzzatto, *Ma'amar HaIkkarim*; Maharal, *Tiferet Yisrael* 63. Also see my booklet, *The Torah as God's Mind, A Kabbalistic Look into the Pentateuch* (New York: Bep-Ron Publications, 1988). See also *Between Silence and Speech*. Northvale, NJ: Jason Aronson Inc. Chapter 7.

the questions you have [regarding the Torah]." Yehoshua replied, "Teacher, have I left your side for a moment? Have you not written: '. . . and his servant Yehoshua never left the tent' [*Shemot* 33:11]?" Moshe thereupon became weak and Yehoshua promptly forgot three hundred *halachot*, and seven hundred doubts confronted him. . . .

(*Temurah* 16a)

Maharsha explains that because Yehoshua so confidently maintained that he knew all of the Torah, he was punished and made to forget. This would seem to have been an isolated incident and indeed, the Talmud goes on to state that the next generation was able to reestablish all the teachings. Yet:

From the time of Moshe until the death of Yose b. Yoezer [in the second century B.C.E.] all of the towering Torah masters studied the Torah in the same manner as Moshe. Afterwards, however, the Torah was not studied this way.

(*Temurah* 15b)

From the time of Yose b. Yoezer it would seem that moral regression became more prevalent and more and more of the orally transmitted Torah was forgotten. This naturally led to conflicts of opinion, with different schools insisting that their interpretations or traditions were correct.

R. Yosi said: "At first there were few conflicts of opinion [those that did arise were settled by a majority vote of the Sanhedrin]. . . . But the disciples of Shammai and Hillel [first century C.E.] did not serve their teachers with proper dedication, and when they multiplied, so did the conflicts.

(*Sanhedrin* 88b)

Hillel himself said that had the leaders of his generation served their teachers—Shemayah and Avtalyon—properly, there would never have been a doubt about any *halachah*.[32]

The sages indicate that other factors led to conflicts of opinion. First, Moshe could not communicate the orally transmitted Torah perfectly, for while he had been taught by God, his students were taught by man.[33] Second, Moshe was not permitted to transmit all that he knew, lest certain points be misinterpreted. When this knowledge was necessary, it was derived through the rules of interpretation.[34] Third, although God revealed the different sides of each question to Moshe, He did not always tell him which opinion would prevail in the end. Each side in a Talmudic debate has merit[35] and it was left to the sages to determine which opinion would become the *halachah*.[36]

The last point would seem to suggest that God deliberately fostered conflicts of opinion. While we shall discuss the Talmud's positive attitude towards disagreements later, we should point out that the debates as to the proper interpretation of the Torah have guaranteed that the Torah remain a dynamic force to be studied.

If forgetfulness and new circumstances caused parts of the orally transmitted Torah to be debated, how can we be sure that a newly derived *halachah* is consistent with the text or with the law taught to Moshe? Our certainty stems

---

32. *Pesachim* 66a.

33. *Tosfot Yom Tov*, introduction to the Mishnah.

34. Jerusalem Talmud, *Avodah Zarah* 2:7; R. Pinchas b. Tzvi Hirsch Halevi Horowitz, *Panim Yafot*, Beshallach.

35. See "Conflicts of Opinion and Their Philosophical Value," later in this chapter.

36. *Midrash Hagadol, Shemot*, p. 557; Ritva on *Eruvin* 13b.

from the fact that whenever doubts arose, or new halachic rulings became necessary, the rules of *sevarah* and *drash* were employed.

Rambam, moreover, points out that the conflicts of opinion were always limited in scope:

> From the time of Moshe until the present day, we have never found a dispute among the sages wherein one opinion interpreted "an eye for an eye" [*Devarim* 19:21] literally and the other maintained that the verse was referring to monetary compensation.
>
> (*Commentary on the Mishnah,*
> introduction)

Ra'avad elaborates: "Conflicts of opinion never arose concerning principles—only concerning specifics" (*Sefer Hakabbalah*, p. 1).

The fundamentals of the orally transmitted Torah were never forgotten. Rather, their applications became unclear. The major points of the lecture transmitted by Moshe and subsequent teachers were consistent; the "notebook"—the written Torah—ensured that whatever had been forgotten could be reinstated.

One method of redeveloping the orally transmitted Torah involves the hermeneutical principles of R. Yishmael and others, which shall be dealt with in a subsequent chapter. It should be noted that although these rules are ascribed to R. Yishmael, they were known and used before his time.

Following the deaths of Moshe and Yehoshua, we find that, in conjunction with the sages of his day, Otniel ben Knaz—the first Judge—deduced from the written Torah the *halachot* that had been lost (*Temurah* 16a). Later, Ezra reconstructed the forgotten parts of the orally transmitted Torah together with an assembly of sages known as the *Anshei Knesset Hagedolah*. These courts—also known as the Sanhedrin—had a juridical function as well as a responsibility to reestablish the exegesis. Their authority was based on the court of Moshe and the Elders and the *nasi* (prince) took the place of Moshe as president of the court. He was assisted by a vice-president known as the *av beit din.* The court's seventy-one members were all renowned for their erudition in Torah, their secular knowledge,[37] and their honesty and integrity.

The Sanhedrin served as the supreme arbiter of ritual and civil law, and all halachic controversies were resolved by a vote of its judges. When the Temple was constructed in Jerusalem, the Sanhedrin met in the *Lishkat Hagazit* (the Chamber of Hewn Stone), which stood within the Temple precincts. In the Talmud we find the following description:

> Originally, there were not many disputes in Israel but one court of seventy-one judges convened in the *Lishkat Hagazit* and two courts of twenty-three judges also functioned: one at the entrance to the Temple mount and one at the door to the Temple court. Other courts of twenty-three members were established in each city. If a matter of inquiry arose, the local court was consulted. If its members had a tradition [as to the correct ruling of the orally transmitted Torah], they stated it; if not, they went to the nearest court. If that court's members had a tradition, they stated it; if not, they went to the court at the entrance to the Temple mount. If that court's members had a tradition, they stated it; if not, they went to the one situated at the entrance to the Temple court and a dissenting judge declared, "Thus have I expounded [the *halachah*] and thus have my col-

---

37. Mishnah, *Sanhedrin* 1:5.

leagues expounded, thus have I taught and thus have they taught." If that court's judges had a tradition, they stated it, and if not, they proceeded to the Chamber of Hewn Stone [where the Sanhedrin] was in session from the time of the morning sacrifices until the afternoon sacrifice. . . . The question was then put before [the judges of the Sanhedrin]. If they had a tradition, they stated it; if not, they voted. If the majority[38] voted "impure," they declared it so; if they voted "pure," they declared it so.[39]

(Sanhedrin 88b)

These early disputes are not recorded in the Talmud, for they were settled by the court and became part of the orally transmitted Torah once again. Once the Sanhedrin ceased to function, in the days of Hillel and Shammai (first century C.E.), or a little later, disputes could no longer be settled in this fashion and the different viewpoints were incorporated into the Mishnaic and Talmudic discussions. The later authorities, who delivered halachic rulings in accordance with certain priorities, determined which view was to be accepted as binding.[40]

While we would be hard-pressed to find a conflict of opinion in the Talmud concerning the major principles of Jewish law, there is hardly a detail of these principles that

---

38. See *Shemot* 23:2 and Rashi ad loc.

39. i.e., the Sanhedrin had the power to declare its rulings part of the oral law even if it could not agree on a scriptural basis for them. The majority vote—though usually used to establish rabbinical laws— could also be used to determine Torah laws whose derivation was impossible or controversial. See the introduction to Rambam's *Commentary on the Mishnah*.

40. i.e., rules were established as to whose opinion was to be considered binding. See, for example, R. Shmuel Hanaggid, *Mevo HaTalmud*.

was not the subject of discussion. Again we must stress that these debates reflect the sages' insistence on finding sources within the Torah as a basis for establishing *halachah*. Thus, for example, there was never a disagreement as to the Torah obligation to eat in a sukkah, only as to the maximum height of a sukkah, the minimum number of walls, which materials were fit for the roof, etc. (Mishnah, *Sukkah* 1).

The Talmud (*Bava Kamma* 43b) states that every sage had the right to express his opinion, even if it conflicted with the viewpoint of his greatest contemporaries.

Rambam[41] notes that it is not surprising to find many undecided controversies in the Talmud since it was left to human intelligence to apply the exegetical rules, and not all minds reach the same conclusions. R. Chisda resolved numerous Mishnaic disputes by ruling that some opinions reflect exceptional piety rather than a halachic requirement (*Bava Metzia* 52b, *Shabbat* 120a, *Chullin* 130b). Indeed, this distinction would seem to suggest that dissenting views were recorded to give people an option to adopt higher moral standards.

Before the period of Hillel and Shammai, only one controversy seems to have remained unresolved: whether it is permissible to perform the *mitzvah* of *semichah*—leaning on the sacrificial animal—on festivals (*Chagigah* 3:2).[42] Shammai and Hillel themselves only disagreed on three *halachot* (*Shabbat* 14a).

The major differences of opinion in the Talmud begin with the schools of Shammai and Hillel. Of these almost

---

41. Rambam, *Commentary on the Mishnah*, Introduction.
42. In *The First Mishnah and the Controversies of the Tannaim*, trans. P. Forchheimer, p. 82, R. David Tzvi Hoffmann discusses why this conflict could not be decided by a vote of the Sanhedrin.

three hundred fifty conflicts, the overwhelming majority deal with Jewish law in general (e.g., blessings, the tithes and gifts due the *kohanim*, marriage and divorce, ritual purity, sacrifices, the divine service, and civil and capital law).

Generally speaking, the school of Hillel ruled more leniently than the school of Shammai. The Mishnah (*Eduyot* 4) enumerates twenty-four to fifty instances where the school of Shammai ruled more leniently. While there are several instances where the school of Hillel accepted the viewpoint of the school of Shammai (*Yevamot* 15:3, *Eduyot* 1:12), there is only one record of the school of Shammai yielding to the school of Hillel (*Terumot* 5:4).

It would seem that the differences of opinion among the sages were kept to a minimum, which prevented "two Torahs" from taking hold among the people. Indeed, *Sifri* interprets the injunction of *lo titgode'du* (*Devarim* 14:1) as forbidding not only self-destructive mourning practices but *gedudim*, factions.[43] The schools of Shammai and Hillel observed this prohibition scrupulously:

> Though one school permitted what the other prohibited and forbade what the other declared permissible, the school of Shammai did not refrain from marrying women connected with the school of Hillel[44] . . . nor did either refrain from borrowing utensils for the preparation of food. . . .
>
> (*Yevamot* 1:4)

---

43. Though Abaye and Rava understood the verse differently (*Yevamot* 14a), both agreed that the gist of the *Sifri*'s ruling was to establish uniformity of practice.

44. See *Yevamot* 14b.

Similarly, Rabban Gamliel II (first century C.E.) once accepted the testimony of two witnesses claiming to have seen the new moon, whereas R. Yehoshua rejected it. By starting the new month on different days, these two scholars and their followers would inevitably observe Yom Kippur on different days as well. To prevent this rift in the Jewish community, Rabban Gamliel exercised his authority as president of the Sanhedrin and ordered R. Yehoshua to desecrate "his" Yom Kippur. After consulting with R. Akiva and R. Dosa b. Hyrkanus, R. Yehoshua complied, whereupon Rabban Gamliel kissed him and hailed him as both his teacher and his disciple (*Rosh Hashanah* 2:8–9).

The halachic process, while allowing for disagreements, is rigid in the sense that once the law is laid down, all parties are bound to accept it. Theoretical differences and debates are permitted only until the *halachah* is established; afterwards, there is only the decision of the Sanhedrin, which is as legally binding as a proclamation by Moshe himself.

GEZEROT—PROTECTIVE MEASURES TO PRESERVE THE TORAH

According to *Vayikra* (18:30), "And you shall guard My ordinance . . . ," the rabbis are empowered to enact precautionary legislation. This verse is taken to mean: "You shall build a fence to safeguard My *mitzvot*."[45]

The reasons for many *gezerot* are quite apparent: The rabbis often observed people transgressing the *mitzvot*,

---

45. Rambam, *Mishneh Torah*, Introduction.

and felt obligated to safeguard the law by protective decree. According to *Shabbat* 40a, for example, the rabbis forbade hot baths on Shabbat because people had begun to heat the water for these baths on Shabbat itself. In addition to Shabbat violations, many *gezerot* in the Talmud are directed against dishonest business practices and sexual immorality.

Rambam states[46] that the obligation to observe rabbinical law is found in *Devarim* (17:10): ". . . and you shall act in accordance with all that they teach you." According to Rambam, one who deliberately violates a rabbinical law also violates this imperative, as well as the commandment not to ". . . deviate from all that they instruct you . . ." (*Devarim* 17:11). Often, the Talmud will cite a scriptural text as support for a rabbinical law. As in the case of oral law, this is referred to as an *asmachta*. However, the text is not to be taken as proof of the validity of the rabbinical enactment; rather, it is an indication that the Torah considers this law fitting,[47] in keeping with the principle that "there is nothing that is not intimated in the Torah."[48]

An example is offered by R. Yechiel Michel Halevi Epstein regarding the rabbinical prohibition of sounding the shofar if Rosh Hashanah falls on Shabbat.[49] *Bamidbar* 29:1 refers to Rosh Hashanah as *yom teru'ah*, "a day of sounding." In *Vayikra* 23:24, however, we find reference to a *zichron teru'ah*, "a remembrance of sounding." R. Ep-

---

46. *Sefer Hamitzvot*, Principle 1. Also see *Shabbat* 23a; *Hasagot HaRamban* ad loc.; and *Meshech Chochmah, Devarim* 17:11.

47. *Chiddushei HaRitva* on *Rosh Hashanah* 16a.

48. R. Yechiel Michel Halevi Epstein, *Aruch Hashulchan, Orach Chaim* 588:9.

49. See *Shabbat* 29b.

stein points out that the verse in *Vayikra* refers to the first
Rosh Hashanah after the Exodus, which the Jews observed
on Shabbat. Thus, when Rosh Hashanah coincides with
Shabbat, the Torah refers to it as "a remembrance of
sounding," clearly alluding to the rabbinical decree[50] that
prohibited sounding the shofar.

Rabbinical law presents a problem regarding the prohibition stated in *Devarim* (4:2): "You shall not add to the
word I command you, nor shall you diminish it. . . ."
However, Rambam explains that the prohibition is not
violated if the rabbis unequivocally declare their ordinances rabbinical and *not* a part of Torah law.[51] But were
they to claim that the Torah itself demands, for instance,
that Sukkot should be observed for eight days instead of
seven, they would transgress this proscription.[52]

Finally, it should be mentioned that rabbinical law can
only be introduced when the majority of the population is
in a position to observe it.[53]

Takkanot and Minhagim

A *takkanah* is a directive enacted by the sages for the
religious or general welfare of society or the individual.

---

50. See Maharal, *Be'er Hagolah* (London edition by L. Hoenig), pp.
14–15; R. Baruch Halevi Epstein, *Torah Temimah*, *Shemot* 17:14.

51. *Rambam, Mishneh Torah, Hilchot Mamrim* 2:9. See, however,
Ra'avad ad loc. Also see *Sefer Hachinuch*, precept 454; Ramban on
Devarim 4:2.

52. *Rosh Hashanah* 38b. The rabbis introduced a second day of
each festival outside the land of Israel only to ensure that the correct
first day was kept, since it was not always clear when the first day was.

53. Rambam, *Mishneh Torah, Hilchot Mamrim* 1:3.

Takkanot are found throughout the Talmud—especially in the Mishnaic order of *Nezikin*, which concerns torts and damages—and in later rabbinical literature. Many involve financial agreements, the relationship of husband and wife,[54] proper standards of honesty,[55] laws concerning divorcées and widows,[56] and the protection of the interests of young girls[57] and women.[58] Numerous *takkanot* were instituted "for the sake of peace and equity."[59] Aside from these we find purely religious enactments of blessings and the festivals of Chanukah and Purim.

The primary purpose of *minhag* (custom) is similar to that of *takkanah* (i.e., to fill the void when the *halachah* offers no solution to a new problem). However, *takkanot* are enacted by the rabbis, while *minhagim* arise out of people's observance.[60]

The sages extended authority to *minhag* on the basis of verses such as "Remove not the ancient landmark, which your fathers have set up" (*Mishlei* 22:28)[61] and "Hear, my son, the instruction of your father, and forsake not the teaching of your mother" (*Mishlei* 1:8).[62] A classic example of this authority concerns the tithing of fruit grown in a tree's fourth year. The Jerusalem Talmud (*Peah* 7:6) states that whenever the court has no means of deciding an issue but there is an established custom, one is to follow the

---

54. For example, *Bava Kamma* 82a.
55. For example, *Sanhedrin* 25b.
56. For example, *Ketubot* 95b.
57. For example, *Shulchan Aruch, Even Ha'ezer* 112.
58. For example, *Yevamot* 62b.
59. For example, *Gittin* 59a, b.
60. *Berachot* 45a; *Pesachim* 54a.
61. See *Midrash Mishlei*.
62. See *Pesachim* 50b; *Chullin* 93b.

custom. In this case, the custom was not to tithe, probably in keeping with ancient, forgotten *halachah*.

On occasion, *minhag* may actually override the law in civil matters. For example, deeds that are not signed as required by law are nevertheless valid if prepared in accordance with local custom.[63] Similarly, payment of debts that by law may only be recovered from the debtor's immovable property may also be exacted from his movable property when such is the local custom.[64] This practice gives Jewish law great flexibility in adapting to changing economic realities.

Customs frequently assume the authority of *halachah*,[65] but only if they are clear,[66] frequently observed,[67] and practiced by the entire country, locality, or class.[68]

CONFLICTS OF OPINION AND THEIR PHILOSOPHICAL VALUE

Although the Talmud states that conflicts of opinion arose because of moral decline and negligence in study, the sages also saw them as beneficial:

> Every controversy that is for the sake of Heaven shall endure and every one that is not for the sake of Heaven shall not endure.

> (*Avot* 5:20)

---

63. *Kiddushin* 49a; *Bava Batra* 10:1, 165a.
64. See *Ketubot* 51a; Jerusalem Talmud, *Gittin* 5:3.
65. See *Menachot* 20b, *Tosafot* ad loc., s.v. *"nifsal."*
66. Rambam, *Mishneh Torah, Hilchot Ishut* 16:7–9, 23:12.
67. *Responsa Maharshdam, Choshen Mishpat* 436.
68. *Responsa Rivash* 475.

Both viewpoints are the words of the living God.

(*Eruvin* 13b, *Gittin* 6b)

The dynamism of Torah permits two or even more opposing viewpoints to be correct at the same time. Even though practice demands that we establish a law in accordance with one opinion, we can still maintain that these different viewpoints are true.

The *halachah* discusses life in all its aspects, and life is full of contradictions, as are human beings. Each person relates differently to life. Only by being put in a state of both interdependence and independence does one come to understand the complexity and totality of life. For this reason it becomes necessary for the *halachah* to allow, and even encourage, disparate opinions. Our desire to establish one way of doing things is a weakness of being human, for we find it hard to comprehend opposing theories as being simultaneously valid. Because the human condition dictates that something be either true or false, rules were made for establishing *halachah*. Yet, in the world of real truth, both theories might be valid or the first might apply to one situation and the second to another.

The debates of the sages show different sides of the same coin. Maharal writes:

> One can maintain that wood is related to the element of water and be correct and one can maintain that it is related to the element of air and be correct. The same is true of the Torah. Nothing is totally impure, without a pure aspect. If someone declares an item pure and presents his arguments to prove it, he has only demonstrated one aspect of reality. Similarly, when one declares an item impure, he has only considered another aspect. One who declares something pure and one who declares it impure have both learned the

Torah but each one saw the item differently. However, God created that item as a whole and He has the ability to create it in a manner that can be viewed in different ways.

(*Be'er Hagolah* [Tel Aviv, 1955], pp. 13–14)

Thus, no opinion in the Talmud is incorrect; rather, each reveals one side of the real truth: "For the differences and contradictions originate not from different realms but from the place in which no contradiction is possible . . ." (*Avodat Hakodesh*).[69]

Practical *halachah* is determined by which side of the coin reveals the most important representation of the issues involved. As Maharal continues:

. . . to establish the *halachah* one must assume that one aspect is more important than another . . . though the other aspects should not be neglected. Indeed, one who takes account of all aspects will perceive the thing as a whole. . . .

In nature, the work of God, one can also establish one element as being more important in the composition of something, even though the other elements are also present. . . .

The schools of Shammai and Hillel started from different directions in their journey towards the same goal: to carry out the word of God. The Talmud (*Eruvin* 13b) states that their arguments were settled when a divine voice proclaimed that both were the words of the living God, but that the ruling of the school of Hillel was to be followed in practice. However, this divine voice had no bearing on

69. By R. Meir b. Gabbai of sixteenth-century Turkey. Also see R. Yeshaya Horowitz, *Shenei Luchot Habrit* (Amsterdam, 1689), pp. 25b–26a.

establishing the *halachah*; it simply confirmed what man had already decided.[70]

The school of Shammai was generally strict whereas the school of Hillel preferred leniency. Both are God-given attributes and were employed when God created the world.[71] As such, it is easy to understand how they can both be the words of the living God though they seem to contradict each other, for they reflect different perspectives. Yet the establishment of a practical *halachah* dictates that one viewpoint be declared binding. Maharal writes that the school of Hillel's view became law because the world is more dependent on kindness than on strictness. R. Alexandre Safran expands on this:

> In the view of the school of Hillel, the Torah was made for man as he is in his present condition, weakened by his own sins. It must be expected, according to the kabbalists, that in the messianic age—when man finally turns back to God and regains his full strength and his original power of sight—the *halachah* will be applied in the strict form of the school of Shammai, the original conception of the Torah. Indeed, God originally intended to create the world using the strict criterion of judgment. It was only when He realized that the world could not thus survive that He added the criterion of generosity or mercy. The messianic age will see the glorious restoration of the first age and man will calmly endure the divine strictness because he will recognize in it the true mercy which human weakness will no longer be able to reduce to mere pity.[72]
>
> (*The Kabbalah*, p. 128)

---

70. See *Yevamot* 14a; *Tosafot* ad loc., s.v. "*Rabbi Yehoshua.*"

71. See Rashi on *Bereshit* 1:1.

72. This seems to contradict the kabbalistic view, stated earlier, that the laws of the Torah will undergo a complete transformation in which the letters of the Torah will allow for a new text. Probably the

The polarity of ideas found in the Talmud is the very proof of the vitality of the Torah, just as the polarity within nature is its grandest aspect. Modern physics has its complementary principles, as seen in the wave theory and the corpuscular theory of light. We can profitably view light as consisting of either waves or particles, even though the terms are contradictory. Similarly, the arguments in the Talmud are simultaneously true. "Through the constant tension they create, they guarantee the equilibrium of the Torah and the universe" (ibid.). As the Mishnah states: "There will be no end to conflicts of opinion until the Messiah comes" (*Eduyot* 8:7).

---

kabbalists see the messianic age as spanning many stages—initially the readings of the school of Shammai will be adopted, and then the transformation of the text will occur.

THE RULES OF INTERPRETATION

SEVARAH

Wherever the oral interpretation was forgotten or new halachic rulings were necessary, the sages of the Sanhedrin made use of two methods: *sevarah* (logical deduction) and *drash* (the hermeneutical principles, or deductive method).

Both methods were revealed to Moshe as authentic means of uncovering the message of the Torah. By utilizing them properly, the sages of the later generations could confidently reestablish the *halachah* and interpretations obscured over time, or rule on new matters.

When the logic of *sevarah* appears insufficient, the Talmud adduces scriptural proof. If this, too, yields no results, the hermeneutical principles are applied.[1] The order of method is highly significant: logical reasoning precedes actual scriptural proof. And if there are no objections to a *sevarah*, it is sufficient and no further proof is required. Hence the Talmudical statement: "Why should I require scriptural proof? *Sevarah hi*—it is logical!"[2]

---

1. See, for example, *Kiddushin* 13b.
2. See, for example, *Ketubot* 22a.

There is a very profound belief behind this: human reasoning, when practiced by the sages, is as authoritative as the Torah. This is even true in matters of life and death:

> How do we know that one should allow himself to be killed rather than commit murder? It is a *sevarah*: A man once came to Rava and said: "The ruler of the city ordered me to kill a certain person or I myself would be killed." Rava replied: "Let yourself be killed rather than killing him, for who is to say that your blood is redder than his?"
>
> (*Sanhedrin* 74a)

Moreover, when the Talmud ad loc. concludes that one should likewise forfeit his life rather than commit adultery, it bases itself on a scriptural analogy to the case of murder: ". . . for just as when a man rises up against his neighbor and kills him, even so is this matter" (*Devarim* 22:26). Thus, although the Torah does not explicitly state that one should sacrifice his life rather than murder, it considers this law so self-evident that Scripture alludes to it to clarify the ban on adultery![3]

Many other cases are decided by *sevarah*, such as those involving monetary and ritual laws; consequently, they have scriptural force. For instance, *Bava Metzia* 46b states that according to the Torah, monetary payment effects the transfer of title. There is no scriptural support for this assertion, but it stands to reason.[4]

Some forms of analogy, often utilized by the Talmud, are

----

3. R. Z. H. Chajes, *Mevo LaTalmud*, chapter 4.
4. Ibid.; *Nimukei Yosef* on *Bava Metzia* 46b. There is, however, some disagreement among the authorities concerning this matter. For an example of ritual law, see *Yoma* 14a, *Tosafot* and Ran ad loc.

also founded on *sevarah*. For example, in *Kiddushin* 13b, a widow's right to remarry is held analogous to the abrogation of the consecrated state of sacrificial animals.[5] Similarly, in *Shabbat* 59b, problems of Shabbat observance are compared to cases of ritual impurity.

In truth, the entire Talmud is dependent on *sevarah*. As Rashi comments (*Berachot* 47b): ". . . they used to expound the logic of the Mishnah, and gather together and engage in it. This is the format of the Gemara arranged by the *Amoraim*."

Thus, it is quite understandable that a sage is culpable not for being unaware of a tradition, but for being unable to properly use *sevarah*.[6] It is not surprising that the Torah was given on the authority of the sages since every rule founded on their logical reasoning originates from the Torah itself. In the introduction to *Ketzot Hachoshen*, his famous commentary on *Shulchan Aruch*, *Choshen Mishpat*, R. Aryeh Leib b. Yosef Hakohen Heller (1745–1813) states this explicitly:

> The Torah was given not to the angels, but to man, who possesses human intelligence. . . . The Torah was given to be determined by his intelligence even if he errs . . . and the truth is established by agreement of the sages. . . .

Chazakah

One form of *sevarah* deals not with the interpretation of the Torah but with the application of *halachah*, by verify-

---

5. See Ritva on *Yoma* 14a, who clearly shows the factor common to both.
6. See *Berachot* 47b and *Gittin* 6b.

ing human characteristics and normative behavior. It is
rooted deeply in common sense alone. There is no basis for
it either in Torah or in the oral tradition, but as explained
above, rulings derived from common sense are equal in
authority to those derived directly from the Torah.[7]

One of the most common forms of this type of *sevarah*
is the principle of *chazakah*—legal presumption.

The fact that *chazakah* may be used to establish a ruling
is derived from a verse,[8] but the criteria for *chazakah* are
determined by the logical observations of the sages (i.e., by
sevarah).

Chazakah is established in the following cases:

1. Status quo—i.e., we presume that a situation remains
   unchanged until there is evidence to the contrary.[9]
   For example:

   a. If a messenger delivering a bill of divorce from a
      different city testifies that the husband was alive
      when he left, we assume that he is still alive and the
      document is therefore valid, though the husband
      may have been ill when the agent departed (*Gittin*
      28a). This has tremendous legal ramifications, for if
      the husband died before the bill of divorce was
      presented, his wife is a widow and may be subject
      to levirate marriage.[10]

   b. Two parties might lay claim to an object, one

---

7. See *Mevo LaTalmud*, chapter 1.

8. *Chullin* 10b.

9. See R. M. L. Wagenaar, *Algemene Talmoedische Pricipien* (Dutch),
Amsterdam.

10. See *Devarim* 25:5–6.

maintaining that its former owner pledged it to him on his deathbed, and the other countering that this owner was healthy at the time—in which case his verbal declaration was insufficient to transfer ownership. Unable to prove either claim, we presume that the owner was in the same physical condition then as he is now (*Bava Batra* 153b).

2. Normative behavior as indicating certain conditions. For instance:

a. We presume that a woman is the mother of a child if we observe the child clinging to her (*Kiddushin* 80a). Thus, if the woman and child engaged in sexual relations, the fact that we had observed him clinging to her (for an extended period) would be sufficient to establish the relationship as incestuous and no further corroborating evidence would be necessary.

b. If a person lived or worked on a plot of land for three years and the former owner never protested his presence, we assume that he legally acquired the property. Thus, after three years, the person need not produce title to the land; the lack of protest is sufficient proof that it is his (*Bava Batra* 28a).[11]

c. No one is entitled to keep what he finds, unless the loser has abandoned hope of recovering it. Since people are constantly examining the contents of

---

11. Unable to produce scriptural support for this law, the Talmud ultimately bases it on common sense (Chajes, chapter 15). Others understand this to be a *takkanah*.

their pockets, we presume that whoever loses money is aware of his loss and has given up hope. Therefore, anyone finding money in the street may keep it (*Bava Metzia* 21b).

3. Recurring events involving the same causes and individuals. For instance, if a mother's first two sons die because of circumcision, her subsequent sons are not to be circumcised, for we presume that their lives are endangered by circumcision (*Yevamot* 64b). Although such presumptions are usually adopted after a three-time occurrence, we make the assumption in this case after death occurs twice, as an extra precaution.

Miggo

Another rule deeply rooted in common sense is *miggo* (literally, "because"). *Miggo* could be described as follows: A person is presumed to be telling the truth, for had he wished to lie, he could have advanced a better plea, enabling himself to win the case.[12]

Rov

Jewish law also employs the principle of *rov*, majority rule. Like *chazakah*, *rov* is essentially a means of making an assumption based on statistical probability. But unlike it, *rov* relies on neither the status quo nor psychological motives. The Talmud (*Niddah* 18b) rules that when *rov*

---

12. See Shach on *Shulchan Aruch, Choshen Mishpat* 82. The principle of *miggo* has many limitations.

and *chazakah* lead to contradictory rulings, we follow the principle of *rov*, which is rooted[13] in *Halachah LeMoshe MiSinai*.

There are two types of *rov*:

1. "A majority that is before us" (*ruba d'ita kaman*), i.e., a definite number (observable) in reality or hypothetically. For example:

   a. A vote of the Sanhedrin. Here the Torah rules that one must follow the majority.[14]
   b. Assuming that a specific item is similar to the majority of other such items. Thus, if there are ten butcher shops in an area, nine of which stock kosher meat and one non-kosher meat, we can assume that a piece of meat found in the street came from a kosher butcher shop. For any item is considered to have originally been part of the majority of similar items. This applies to the status of people as well (*Pesachim* 9b, *Kiddushin* 73a).

2. "A majority that is not before us" (*ruba d'leta kaman*), i.e., an indefinite number that precludes exact numerical proof but allows us to make an assumption based on observations. For example: We assume that most men engaging in ritual slaughtering (*shechitah*) are competent (*Chullin* 3b). Where the *shochet* is not available for examination, we rely on this assumption.

---

13. See *Chullin* 12a; Rashi ad loc., s.v. *"Pesach"*; Chajes, chapter 15.
14. See Rashi on *Shemot* 23:2.

Kavua

The principle of *rov* is invalidated by that of *kavua* (literally, "fixed"), which is rooted in Scripture[15] rather than in *sevarah*.[16] For instance, in the case of the butcher shop, *rov* allowed us to assume that the meat found in the street was kosher since the majority of the shops stocked kosher meat. However, if one purchased meat directly from a butcher shop without knowing whether it was one of the kosher establishments, we cannot rely on *rov* because the meat was not separated from its fixed place— the shop. Instead, we proceed as though there were an equal number of kosher and non-kosher shops, which leaves the status of the meat in doubt.

In such a case, when all the aforementioned principles are inoperable, we invoke the axiom of *safek deoraita lechumrah*—a doubt concerning a Torah law, such as the *kashrut* of meat, is resolved stringently. Therefore, the meat may not be eaten. Similarly, if two authorities of equal stature differ on a matter of Torah law, we are obligated to follow whoever rules more stringently (*Avodah Zarah* 7a). The early Talmudic commentators debated whether this obligation is itself biblical[17] or rabbinical.[18]

On the other hand, if the matter in doubt is a rabbinical precept, the guiding principle is *safek derabbanan lekulah*— in doubts concerning rabbinical law the more lenient view is followed.

---

15. *Ketubot* 15a; *Tosafot* ad loc., s.v. *"Perat."*

16. See, however, R. Shimon Shkop, *Shaarei Yosher* 2:1.

17. See Rashi on *Kiddushin* 72b; Rashba, *Torat Habayit Ha'aruch*, 4:1; *Hasagot HaRamban* on Rambam's *Sefer Hamitzvot*, Principle 1.

18. See Rambam, *Mishneh Torah, Hilchot Issurei Biah* 18:17.

Even though doubts concerning Torah laws are resolved stringently, where the doubt is compounded, we rule leniently. For example:

> A learned, meticulously observant man died and left a storeroom full of produce[19] and we are not sure if he tithed it.[20] However, even if he did not, it is doubtful whether this produce needed to be tithed in the first place.[21]
>
> (*Avodah Zarah* 41b)

This is referred to as a *sfek sfeka* (double doubt): The doubt as to whether this produce needed tithing is the first *safek*, while the possibility that it was indeed tithed constitutes the second *safek*.

The subject of *sfek sfeka* is quite complicated and beyond the scope of this work. Suffice it to say that it has been discussed in halachic literature for generations.

DRASH

The second method employed to reconstruct the forgotten portion of the orally transmitted Torah (or to create new halachic rulings) involves the hermeneutical principles. These rules are actually means of *drash,* or more formally, *Midrash halachah*, which can be translated as

---

19. See *Vayikra* 27:30.

20. The time of tithing varies for different kinds of produce.

21. The biblical obligation to tithe applies only to grain that is winnowed before being brought into the storeroom (*Bava Metzia* 88a). Rabbinically, however, grain must be tithed even if it is winnowed only later.

"deduced *halachah.*" *Drash* is an investigation into the inner, logical, intended and true meaning of a particular text and the inter-relationship of its words, based on specific rules of interpretation. Thus, we find:

> "These are the rules that you [Moshe] shall set before them" [*Shemot* 21:1]. R. Yishmael says: "These are the thirteen rules through which the written Torah shall be interpreted, which were handed down to Moshe at Sinai."
>
> (*Midrash Hagadol, Shemot*, p. 459)

Although these rules are popularly attributed to R. Yishmael, it is clear from the Midrash that they were already known to Moshe. R. Yishmael served as their compiler, organizing them into thirteen categories. The number of *drashot* by means of which the sages expounded the Torah so as to deduce *halachot* totals many thousands, yet they are all reducible to the framework of the thirteen hermeneutical principles.[22] Similarly, while certain types of *drash* are not strictly part of these rules,[23] the classical methods of interpreting the Torah and reconstructing exegesis generally fall into one of these categories.

Although we have differentiated between *drash* and logical reconstruction through the use of *sevarah,* the former method is also dependent upon logic. However, *drash* differs from *sevarah* in that it relies upon guiding principles and often is only applicable if there is a tradition that a specific derivation was made.

---

22. R. Moshe Avigdor Amiel, *Hamidot Lecheker Hahalachah* (Tel Aviv, 1938), introduction, chapter 6.

23. Ra'avad on *Sifra,* introduction, regarding the *baraita* of R. Yishmael.

The use of *drash* is analogous to the mathematical formula of the scientist. To the layman, the formula is meaningless. But to the scientist, it is both comprehensible and logical. Similarly, the rules of *drash* may seem to be illogical word games. Yet the sages, through their familiarity with the Torah and its intentions, were able to utilize *drash* to reestablish that which had been forgotten, or to find a source for new *halachot* within the words of the written Torah. The derivations produced through *drash* are not new. Rather, they give expression to fundamental truths that would have remained hidden had they not been formulated.

As we have observed, *drash* also provides scriptural basis for many well-known *halachot* and facilitates the memorization of the orally transmitted Torah.[24] It is the mechanism employed to ensure continuity in *halachah* (i.e., through its use we can be certain that the precepts we observe are the same as those given at Sinai).

The process of interpreting the Torah began immediately after it was given. According to *Temurah* 16a many laws were also forgotten when Moshe died. Thus, we find that ". . . Ezra dedicated himself to interpreting the Torah and to fulfilling [it], to teach within Israel statutes and justice" (Ezra 7:10).

The Talmud (*Pesachim* 70b) refers to Shemayah and Avtalyon—two of the earliest *Tannaim*—as "great sages and great *darshanim*—interpreters." Yet the first time rules of interpretation are mentioned is in connection with Hillel, who enumerated seven categories.[25] Again, he did

---

24. See p. 100, "Explanations Received and Transmitted by Moshe."
25. See *Sifra*, introduction, regarding the *baraita* of R. Yishmael; *Tosefta, Sanhedrin* 7:11.

not invent these rules—he formulated them in a manner that could be used by others.

Towards the end of the first century C.E., two students of R. Yochanan b. Zakkai—R. Nechunya b. Hakanah and R. Nachum of Gamzu—formulated two additional rules of interpretation. These rules reveal two approaches to Torah exegesis, which found expression in the schools of R. Yishmael and R. Akiva.

R. Yishmael—a disciple of R. Nechunya b. Hakanah—based his interpretations on the principle that "the Torah speaks in the language of man" (*Sanhedrin* 64b) (i.e., not every word of the text is there to teach new *halachot*, for the Torah might repeat something for stylistic reasons).[26] On the other hand, R. Akiva maintained that each verse and word was open to interpretation, as were the crowns on the letters. He even interpreted all the "and"s in the Torah (*Yevamot* 68b). R. Yishmael's exegesis was primarily concerned with clarifying the meaning of the text as a whole, whereas R. Akiva's focused more on interpreting each part.

Generally, the two schools disagreed not about the actual *halachah* but about how to derive it from the text. For example, both R. Yishmael and R. Akiva agree that placing a bill of divorce in a woman's domain is tantamount to handing it to her. They differ, however, on the scriptural basis for this law. R. Yishmael asserts that when the Torah states that a bill of divorce should be placed "in her hand" (*Devarim* 24:1), the term "hand" should be taken not literally, but as a reference to domain, as in Bamidbar *21:26* ". . . and he took all his land out of his

---

26. See *Menachot* 29b.

hand, even up to Arnon." R. Akiva maintains that the Torah repeats the phrase two verses later to broaden the concept of "hand" to include domain as well.[27]

Although R. Yishmael's approach was generally accepted by the majority of sages, important works of halachic exegesis by both schools are extant. It was R. Yishmael who expanded the seven rules of Hillel into the thirteen hermeneutical principles. Indeed, both R. Yishmael's and R. Akiva's methods should be viewed as "the words of the living God."[28]

OTHER RULES OF INTERPRETATION

Aside from the specific rules of R. Yishmael and R. Akiva, the Talmud is replete with other examples of halachic exegesis based on textual analysis. Thus, the Mishnah (*Berachot* 1:3) records a dispute between the schools of Shammai and Hillel regarding the obligation to recite the *Shema. Devarim* 6:7 states: "You shall speak of them [these words] when you are sitting in your home and when you travel on your way, when you lie down and when you rise up." The school of Shammai maintains that the verse must be understood literally. Therefore, one must recite the Shema at night when lying down and in the morning while standing up. The school of Hillel, on the other hand, contends that the verse obligates us to recite the Shema at the times when people generally lie down and arise.

---

27. See Jerusalem Talmud, *Gittin* 8:11.
28. See R. Naftali Tzvi Yehudah Berlin, *Ha'amek Davar*, introduction.

Similarly, R. Yoshiah and R. Yonatan offered conflicting elucidations based on the Torah's use of conjunctives. *Sanhedrin* 66a relates:

> What does the term *ish ish*—every man—teach us in the verse "For every man who curses his father and mother shall surely be put to death: his father and mother he has cursed; his blood is upon him" [*Devarim* 20:9]? It comes to include a daughter, a person of indeterminate sex, and a hermaphrodite [i.e., they, too, are subject to the death penalty]. The phrase ". . . who curses his father and mother" only teaches us that the law applies to one who curses both his father and mother. How do we know that it also applies to one who curses either his father or his mother? Because the verse states, ". . . who curses his father and mother . . . [and then adds] his father and mother he has cursed. . . ." The term "curse" is juxtaposed to both "father" and "mother," implying that the law applies to one who curses either parent. This is the view of R. Yoshiah. R. Yonatan says: "The first half of the verse implicates one who curses either parent . . . since it does not state "his father and mother together." The second half teaches a different lesson."

Unlike the schools of Hillel and Shammai, both R. Yoshiah and R. Yonatan agreed on the *halachah*. Their only disagreement concerned the manner in which it could be deduced from the text.

Another form of halachic deduction prevalent in the Talmud is called *Midrash hahigayon*—logical exegesis. This differs from *sevarah* for it is a method of interpreting the text, not of indicating unstated *halachot*. For example, *Devarim* 24:6 charges: "No man shall take the lower or upper millstone as a security, for it is [the debtor's] livelihood that he takes." In *Bava Metzia* 9:13, the sages expanded this principle to include not just millstones but any item used for food preparation, for the Torah declares, ". . . it is [the debtor's] livelihood that he takes."

The rabbis made this type of logical deduction whenever the text suggested it. For instance, *Shemot* 12:6 states: ". . . and the entire congregation of Israel shall slaughter [the Pesach offering]. . . ." The Talmud poses the obvious question:

> Does the entire congregation slaughter this offering? Surely only one person slaughters it [on behalf of the others]! Thus, we see that one's agent's actions are equivalent to one's own.
>
> (*Kiddushin* 41b)

Finally, halachic exegesis can serve to restrict the application of a law rather than expand it. Thus, the Torah states: "A [male] Ammonite or Moabite shall not enter the assembly of God [i.e., may not marry a Jew] . . . for they did not meet you with bread and water when you left Egypt . . ." (*Devarim* 23:4–5). The sages inferred that female Ammonites and Moabites *could* marry into the Jewish people, however, since the male noun form is used in the verse and since men were expected to meet and greet visitors but women weren't (*Yevamot* 77a).

Rabbi Yishmael's Hermeneutic Rules

The thirteen rules of Rabbi Yishmael may be divided into two parts:

> *Midrash Hamekish*—Analogical interpretation, that is, drawing conclusions from one matter to the other.
>
> *Midrash Hamevaer*—Elucidative interpretation, that is, explanation and elucidation of the Torah text.

Rule 1

> *Kal Vachomer:* An inference from a minor to a major. (*a minori ad majus*) or from a major to minor (*a majori ad minus*).

The basis of the rule is found in the Torah (*Bereshit* 44:8, *Devarim* 31:27) and the Sages found ten such *kallin vechomarim* in *Tanach* (*Bereshit Rabbah* 92:7).

Generally, the rule looks simple: If A has x, how much more B must have X?[29]

Example

From major to minor:

The laws concerning the prohibition of *melacha* ("work") on *Shabbat* are more strict than those concerning work on the Festivals, since on *Shabbat* one is not allowed to cook anything, while on the festivals this is, to a certain extent, permitted.

---

29. This rule does not find a parallel in the famous Aristotelian syllogism: All men are mortal; Socrates is a man; therefore, Socrates is mortal. First of all, the element of "how much more" is not present; secondly, in the *Kal Vachomer*, the major does not belong to the class of the minor, but that which is true about the minor surely must be true of this major.

Therefore, if something is permitted on *Shabbat*, how much more is it permitted on a Yom Tov (festival) (*Betzah* 20b).

From minor to major:
The opposite is also true. If something is definitely forbidden on the festivals, and nowhere is it mentioned that it is forbidden on *Shabbat*, we say: Since it is forbidden on the festivals, how much more it must be forbidden on the *Shabbat*. (See also *Bava Metzia 95a*.)[30]

Restrictions

1. Although "every person may apply the *Kal Vachomer* according to his reasoning" (i.e., without having received such a tradition from the Sages), obviously such a person must be acquainted with all the *halachot* concerning the minor and the major, since it is possible that what appears to be a major is, in fact, a minor (or the reverse), after which the *Kal Vachomer* can no longer be applied.

2. A second important halachic condition is the principle: *Dajo Lavo Min Hadin—Lihyot Ka-niddon* ("It suffices that the derived inference is equal in stringency to the premise from which it is derived"), but not more so, nor even when it might be argued that logically the inference should be even more stringent than the premises from which it is derived (*Bava Kamma* 2:5). (If A has x, B cannot have x and y.)

---

30. Some examples: *Bava Kamma* 24b, *Hullin* 24a.

3. The *Kal Vachomer* can only be applied in Torah (*Deoraita*) but not in rabbinic law.[31]

The rabbis may have built "a fence around the Torah" in one case of minor importance, while they did not see any need for such a fence in a major case (or the reverse).

4. Nor is it applied to in cases of *Halacha LeMoshe MiSinai*,[32] a Torah law not mentioned in the text itself, but purely an "Oral Law."

5. *Ein Onshin Min Hadin*: We do not impose a penalty on those who have transgressed a prohibition that was derived by *Kal Vachomer* (*Sanhedrin* 54a).[33] (We cannot impose a penalty by using the *Kal Vachomer* reasoning.)

6. *Ein Mazhirim Min Hadin*: We do not use a *Kal Vachomer* to deduce a prohibition otherwise not stated (*Pesachim* 24a).

The *Mishnah* or Talmud do not always introduce the *Kal Vachomer* by using this term. They sometimes use the following phrases as well:

Hen (at the beginning of a sentence)—Indeed
Ve-ech—How (much more)
Ve-af ki—And if already
U-ma—And what if
Hashta-u-ma—Now and what if
Eno din?—Is it not even true?

---

31. *Yadaim* 3:2.
32. P. 101.
33. To this view Rabbi Akiva takes exception (Jerusalem Talmud, *Hagiga* 11:1; see also Rashi, *Hagiga* 11a).

Lo kol sheken?—How much more so
Al achat kamma ve-kamma—all the more so
Mibaye?—Is it necessary?
Tsericha Le-memar?—Need it be said?

Rule 2

Gezerah Shavah: An inference from the analogy
of words (literally, "a comparison with the equal").

When two words are identical, even when they are stated
in completely different contexts, the laws of both passages
are subject to the same regulations and applications.

This rule is an atypical example of a case in which *derash*
reveals a completely new halachic fact by way of a simple
rule.

A maximum of knowledge is derived from a minimum
of words. In such a case the layman will not be capable of
understanding its logic, since he misses the complicated
foundations. The words must not only be similar, but also
superfluous (*mufneh*) so that it appears that they were
placed there for the purpose of indicating a *Gezerah
Shavah* (*Shabbat* 64a).[34]

Rabbi Akiva's school, however, seems to disagree with the
requirement of *mufneh* (Jerusalem Talmud, *Yoma* 8:3, 45a).

There exist two types of *Gezerah Shavah*:

1. A *Gezerah Shavah* that clarifies the text of the Torah;
2. A *Gezerah Shavah* that reconstructs a completely
   new *halachah*, not mentioned in the text.

---

34. See also *Niddah* 22b.

Example 1

In a case of betrothal, it is stated (*Devarim* 22:13): "When a man takes [*yikkach*] a wife," while in the story of Avraham buying the Cave of Machpelah, the patriarch says to Efron, the Hittite: "I have given the money for the field, take [kach] from me" (*Bereshit* 23:13).

Hence, *kicha* refers to acquisition by way of money. Consequently, a man has the possibility of marrying his wife by giving her an object of value.[35]

Example 2

Concerning the Passover offering, it is stated: "On the fourteenth day of this month between the two darkenings shall you make it, *Bemo'ada* [at its appointed time] in accordance with all its laws . . ." (*Bamidbar* 9:3).

In *Bamidbar* (28:12) we read concerning the *tamid*, the daily burnt offering, "You shall guard to bring it unto me *bemo'ada* [at its appointed time] . . , which includes even the *Shabbat*.

By means of a *Gezerah Shavah*, the Sages concluded that since the word *bemo'ado* in the second verse requires man

---

35. This does not mean that a husband "buys" his wife, after which he considers her his "object"; it means that by giving the object of value to *her* (and not to the "seller," her father), her legal status has changed. Until now, she has been permitted to marry everybody; from now on, she can only be married to her husband. (See M. Meiselman, *Jewish Woman in Jewish Law* [New York: Ktav, 1992], p. 96. See also Rabbi S. R. Hirsch's commentary on *Bereshit* 23:19, showing how the Sages interpreted this *Gezerah Shavah*, comparing both cases.)

to bring the *tamid* on *Shabbat* as well, so, too, may the Passover be brought up on *Shabbat*, although this activity would normally be forbidden on *Shabbat* (*Pesachim* 66a).

An important limitation on this rule is that "no one may deduce a *Gezerah Shavah* on his own authority" (Jerusalem Talmud, *Pesachim* 6:11). The reason for this is stated by Nachmanides: "Since the *middah* of *Gezerah Shavah* is an instrument that could be employed all day by someone to refute all the laws of the Torah, since words are repeated many times in the Torah. It is impossible for a large book never to use the same words again" (on *Sefer Hamitsvot* of Maimonides, *Shoresh* 11).

Only the Sages knew, by way of tradition, where an analogous word or sentence could be interpreted as such.

Secondly, both passages must occur in the Torah.

Finally, it must be noted that there cannot exist a "half" *Gezerah Shavah*, meaning that it is impossible to deduce a law from one passage to the other passage and not vice versa (see *Zevachim* 48a).

Another rule, similar to *Gezerah Shavah*, but not explicitly mentioned within the thirteen *middot* of Rabbi Yismael, is called *Hekkesh* ("juxtaposition"), sometimes called *Hekkesh Hakatuv* or *Hishvah Hakatuv* ("comparison of Scripture").

Hekkesh refers to the presence of two laws in the same verse from which it may be inferred that whatever is true of one is also true of the other.

The difference between *Gezerah Shavah* and *Hekkesh* is that the former is constructed from an analogy of words, while the latter is a comparison of cases. Secondly, in a *Gezerah Shavah* the Sages draw the comparison by way of analogy while *Hekkesh* represents an analogy that is drawn by the Torah itself. In fact, it is the basis for reasoning by way of analogy to draw halachic conclusions.[36]

A classic example of *Hekkesh* is found in *Devarim* 22:26, in which the Torah discusses the case of a *na'arah meorasah*, a betrothed maiden, who, by force majeure, was "taken" by a man. Though the man is liable for the death penalty, the girl, despite being betrothed, is exempt from any punishment: "But unto the damsel thou shalt do nothing; there is in the damsel no sin worthy of death, for as a man rises against his neighbor and slays him, even so is this matter."

It is clear that the Torah itself draws that analogy between the case of murder and this case of rape, after which the Sages derived different *halachot* one from the other (*Sanhedrin* 74a).[37]

It is therefore understandable that the Sages preferred a *Hekkesh* over a *Gezerah Shavah* (*Zevachim* 48a).[38] [39]

Another rule similar to *Gezerah Shavah* is *Semuchim* ("juxtaposition") of subjects. It refers to a case in which one verse follows another, after which we conclude that that which is true about one is also true about the other. However, unlike the case of *Gezerah Shavah* and *Hekkesh*, there is neither an analogy of words nor a comparison made by the text itself.

An indication of this rule is found in the *Tehillim* (3:8): "*Semuchim* are truth and justice; faultless are all its precepts."[40]

---

36. See also *Niddah* 19b.

37. Other examples: *Kiddushin* 35a, *Pesachim* 43b.

38. See, however, *Tosafot*, ad loc.

39. Not all authorities are of the opinion that *Hekkesh* is incorporated into *Gezerah Shavah*, but rather into rule 12 (see p. xx).

40. *Yevamot* 4a.

Example

"Thou shalt not suffer a sorceress to live; whoever lies with a beast shall be put to death" (*Shemoth* 22:17–18).

The Talmud derives by way of this juxtaposition that just as somebody who lies with a beast is put to death by stoning, so is the sorceress (*Berachoth* 21b). R. Yehudah rejects this inference and is of the opinion that such a juxtaposition may only be used in *Devarim* (ibid).[41]

Rule 3

> *Binyan Av:* An inference from a biblical text.

This principle is divided into two parts:

1. *Binyan Av Mikatuv Echad*: An inference from a single verse;
2. *Binyan Av Mishne Ketuvim*: An inference from *two* verses.

This *middah* is a construction (*binyan*), in which the text or two texts act(s) as a father (or fathers) (*av*) to the conclusion drawn from it (them).

---

41. This may be the reason why this rule is not incorporated into the rules of Rabbi Yishmael, since these rules should apply to the whole of the Torah. (See Avraham Kurman: *Mavo LaTorah she Beal Peh*, p. 303).

Example 1 (one verse)

"One witness [*ed echad*] shall not rise up against a man for any iniquity or for any sin, in any sin that he sins; by the mouth of two witnesses, shall a matter be established [in court]" (*Devarim* 19:15).

From the word "witness" (*ed*), we may already conclude that the Torah refers to one witness. Consequently, what is the reason for the word "one," *echad*? This seems to be superfluous. The Talmud, however, concludes that we must infer from this that there was an explicit reason to state "one witness," which indicates that the word *ed* ("witness"), mentioned anywhere in the Torah without the word *echad* ("one"), means "more than one."

The construction (*binyan*), in which the text (one witness) acts as father (*av*), teaches us the conclusion that "witness" (without *echad*) means at least two[42] (*Sotah* 2a).

Example 2 (two verses)

A farm laborer, when working in the field of his employer, is allowed to eat from the grapes of this field, and from the standing grain:

> When you come into your neighbor's vineyard, then you may eat grapes until you have enough at your own pleasure, but you shall not put any in your vessel.
> When you come into your neighbor's standing grain, then you may pluck ears with your hand, but you shall not move a sickle unto your neighbor's standing corn. (*Devarim* 23:25–26)

---

42. Other examples: *Yevamoth* 4b; *Shabbat* 22a.

Question: Is he allowed to eat from other things growing in the field of his neighbor?

It is not possible to derive this from the case of the vineyard, since the owner is obliged to leave the gleanings to the poor (*Vayikra* 19:10), and this could be the reason that he is obliged to allow his employee to eat from his field. Nor is it possible to derive any answer from the second verse, discussing the case of the standing grain, since the employer is obliged to give *challah* (a certain portion of the dough) to the priest (*Bamidbar* 15:17–21), which could be the reason for this permission. Secondly, the law of gleanings does not apply to the case of the standing grain, nor does the law of *challah* apply to the case of the vineyard.

So, the only common factor (*av*) is that both are plants (*gedulei karka*), from which we may derive (*binyan*) that the law applies to all plants (*Bava Metzia* 87b).[43]

It would neither have been possible, however, for the text to state "all plants," since "grapes" and "standing grain," as well as the other specifics, stand for other halachic deductions.[44] It appears that the application of this rule could even be extended to derivation of a principle from three verses (*Sifre, Bamidbar* 160) and even from four verses (*Bava Kamma* 1:1).

Sometimes the rule is called *Mah matsinu*[45] ("And what have we found . . .") and in other cases *Chada Mechada*[46] ("One from one"), in the case of a single verse, but not all scholars agree that these are forms of *Binyan Av*.

---

43. Other examples: *Bava Kamma* 6a.
44. See *Torah Temimah* of Rabbi Baruch Halevi Epstein, ad loc.
45. See *Shabbat* 26b (Rashi, *Uferat lecha*).
46. See Avraham Kurman, op. cit., p. 303, and *Encyclopedia Talmudit*, vol. 4, p. 3.

Restriction

The deduction from two verses is only applicable when both texts are required in order to reconstruct a new halachic fact. However, when the second text only repeats what was taught in the first, no *Binyan Av* can be constructed and no general rule may be deduced.

Elucidative interpretation: *Kelal-U-ferat*

This section contains examples of the general and the particular, rules 4–7.

The central problem dealt with in the following three rules may be stated as follows:

When a law lays down a certain directive, which such law renders operative both in particular and in general (which includes the particular), must the directive be held to apply to the particular expressly mentioned and the general be interpreted as including only such a particular and no more, or must it be held that the directive applies to everything embraced by the general and that the particular is quoted only in illustration of the general and not in exhaustion of it?

The fourth rule deals with the case in which the general and the particular serve neither to amplify nor to limit, but the one is merely an elucidation of the other.[47]

Rule 4

> *Kelal* and *Perat:* A general proposition followed by a particular (literally, "the general and the particular").

---

47. Menachem Elon, ed., *The Principles of Jewish Law*, p. 64.

If a law is stated in general terms and followed by particular instances, the law only applies to the specific instances mentioned.

Examples

"If any man of you would bring an offering near unto God from cattle; from the herd and from the flock shall you bring your offering" (*Vayikra* 1:2).[48]

Cattle [*behemah*] is a general term; "herd" and "flock" are particulars. Since the general term (*kelal*) "cattle" includes the "nondomesticated animals" as well, the Torah excludes by way of the particular those types of animals and only allows sacrifices to be brought from the (domesticated) "herd" and the "flock."

We may ask: If so, why did the text start with the supposedly superfluous words "from cattle"? Wouldn't it have been easier to write: "If any man of you would bring an offering, from the herd; from the herd and from the flock shall you bring your offering"?

The answer is that phrase *min habehemah* ("from the cattle") excludes the use of all animals that have been used for bestial, sexual immorality as offerings in the Temple (*Temurah* 28a), a fact that would otherwise not have been known.[49]

Secondly, if the verse would not have started with a general rule, it would not have been possible to apply the rule of *Kelal-U-Ferat*, but rather one of the other *middoth*

---

48. Other examples: *Vayikra* 17:13.
49. See S. R. Hirsch, *Commentary on Vayikra* 1:2.

of Rabbi Yishmael (like *Binyan Av*), after which it would have been possible to *include* some additions to the "particulars"[50] (which are excluded by the rule of *Kelal-U-Ferat*).

Rule 5

> *Perat-U-Kelal:* A particular followed by a general proposition (literally, "the particular and the general").

If the particular instances (*peratim*) are stated first and are afterwards extended by a general term (*kelal*), then others, besides the particular mentioned, are included as well.

Example

> You shall not see your brother's ox or his sheep driven away, and hide yourself from them, you shall surely bring them back unto your brother . . . And so shall you do with his ass, and so shall you do with his garment, and shall you do with every lost thing of your brother's. . . . (*Devarim* 22:1–3)

"Ox," "sheep," "ass," and "garment" are particulars. "And so shall you do with every lost thing of your brother's" is the general term.

Since the particulars are stated first, which would limit the duty to restore a lost article to these alone, therefore,

---

50. See Avraham Kurman (p. 304), quoting Rabbi Samson Ben Isaac Chinon, *Bate Midot* 5.

the text continues with a general rule to include all lost items (*Nazir* 35b).

Again, we may ask why the Torah needed to state the particular first, instead of starting immediately with the general rule. The answer, as stated before, is that otherwise another of these rules of *derash* could have been used, after which different *halachot* would have been deduced, not warranted by the text.[51]

Rule 6

> *Kelal-u-ferat-u-kelal, i atta dan ella ke-en Haperat:*
> A general law limited by specific instances and then again referred to in a general term; in this instance, one may derive only facts similar to the specifics (literally, "general and particular and general, you may derive only similar to the particular").

Example

If a man delivers unto his neighbor money or stuff to keep, and it is stolen out of the man's house, if the thief be found, he shall pay double. If the thief be not found, then the master of the house shall come near to God [i.e., to the judges] to take an oath, to see whether he has not put his hand unto his neighbor's goods.

For every matter of trespass, whether it be for ox, for ass, for sheep, for raiment, or for any matter of lost thing, whereof one says: This is it [the thing lost], the word of both parties shall come before God. (*Shemot* 22:6–8)

---

51. See *Tosafot*, ad loc.

"Every matter" is a general term. "Ox—ass—sheep—raiment" are particulars. "Any matter of lost thing" is again a general term.

The general term "every matter" is followed by some specifics (ox, ass, sheep, raiment) and these again are followed by a general term, "any matter of lost thing."

We now need to look at the common factor of the specifics. This consists of two facts: they are all movable objects, and they have monetary value. This excludes immovable property and documents such as checks, et cetera, which are only drafts for value but have no intrinsic value themselves.

In the last case, no oath can be imposed[52] since this is excluded by the rule of *Kelal-U-ferat U-kelal.*[53]

The differences between the two earlier rules (*Kelal-U-Ferat* and *Perat-U-Kelal*) and this rule are:

Kelal-U-Ferat excludes everything else besides what is explicitly mentioned in the specific;

Perat-U-Kelal includes everything, even those matters that are not all mentioned in the specific;

and *Kelal-Ferat U-Kelal* chooses the middle path, including those matters that are similar to the specifics.

The reverse (*Perat-U-Kelal-U-Ferat*) deduces *halachot* on the same basis as *Kelal-U-Ferat U-Kelal* (*Nazir* 34b) and subsequently belongs to the rule under discussion.

---

52. For the meaning of this, see Rabbi S. R. Hirsch's commentary on *Shemot*, ad loc., p. 356.

53. *Shevuoth* 42b; other examples include *Eruvin* 27b.

Rule 7

Kelal Shehu Tzarich Li-ferat U-ferat Tzarich Lichelal: The general rule requires a specific, or the reverse, to complement each other, being mutually interdependent (literally, "the general requires the particular, and the particular requires the general").

In this case, the general and the particular serve neither to amplify nor to limit, but the one is merely an elucidation of the other.

Example

"Sanctify unto Me all firstborn, whatsoever opens the womb among the children of Israel, both of man and beast . . ." (*Shemot* 13:2).

"Every firstling that is born amongst your herd and your flock, the males shall you sanctify unto God . . ." (*Devarim* 15:19).

"Sanctify unto Me all firstborn" is the general rule. "Every firstling . . . the males" is the specific.

1. From the words "all firstborn," we may conclude this also means the females. However, the word "males" excludes the females.

2. From the word "males" we could, however, derive every "firstborn male," even after a female has already been born. This again is excluded by "whatsoever opens the womb" (for the first time).

3. From the words "whatsoever opens the womb," we would not have excluded one born after a previous caesarean birth. Hence, the general term: "all firstborn" (*Bechorot* 19a).

In this case, the meaning of the general rule would remain obscure without the specifics (see Rashi on *Bechorot* 19a).

Rules 8–11

> *Davar She-hayah Bi-chelal Veyatza min Hakelal:*
> The particular stated separately after forming a part of the general rule.

The problem dealt with is to provide an answer to the following question: "When there are two separate directives referring to the same subject (and not a simple directive with a generality and a specific instance, as in the previous group)—the one a general and the other a special directive—what is the relationship between the two classes of directives and for what reason has the special directive been stated separately from the general one?"[54]

Rule 8

> *Davar She -hayah Be-kelal ve yatza Min Hakelal Le-lamed, Lo Le-Lamed Al Atzmo Yatza Ella Le-lammed Al Hakelal Kullo Yatza:* If a particular has already been included in a general rule and is afterwards repeated by way of an exception, then the exception is not applicable only to its

---

54. Menachem Elon, ed., *The Principles of Jewish Law*, p. 69.

own case but also to the instances embraced by the general rule (literally, "If a matter mentioned in a general rule is singled out to be applied, then it is not only to be applied to itself, but it is singled out for everything included in the general rule").

Example

"But the seventh day is a *Shabbat* unto God, your God, on it you shall not do any *melacha* [work]" (*Shemot* 20:10).

"You shall kindle no fire throughout your habitations upon the *Shabbat* day" (*Shemot* 35:3).

In the first verse ("You shall not do any *melacha*"), the second verse, ("You shall not kindle any fire") is included (being a particular of the general prohibition of "doing any *melacha*").

We may ask: Why was that which was included at first, stated separately afterwards? It is not possible to state that this is done with respect to its own context, since it would not teach us anything new. The answer must be that it follows in order to tell us something that we would otherwise not know.

In our case the answer is clear: Kindling fire is one of the thirty-nine basic forms of *melacha* forbidden on the *Shabbat*.[55] It is mentioned separately, by itself, as the classic example for all the other forms of *melacha*.[56] It is taken out

---

55. *Shabbat* 7:2.
56. See *Shabbat* 70a for an explanation of why the example of kindling fire is used instead of another form of *melacha*.

of the collective idea in which it was included to teach us
that each type of *melacha* constitutes a separate desecration
of the *Shabbat* and needs to be atoned for separately (by
bringing a sacrifice, if done unintentionally) (*Shabbat*
70a).[57]

Rule 9

> *Davar She-hayah Bi-chelal Veyatza Liton To'an*
> *Echad She-hu Ke-inyano, yatza Lehakel Ve-lo*
> *Lehachmir:* When something is first included in a
> general rule and then it is mentioned specifically,
> in order to give information concerning it, then
> one should apply relaxations to this rule and not
> the restrictions (literally, "A matter that was first
> stated in the general rule, and [then] is excluded
> to require a matter in accordance with this fact, is
> excluded to alleviate and not to aggravate).

Example

"He that smites a man, so that he dies, shall surely be put
to death" (*Shemot* 21:12).

"As when a man goes into a forest with his neighbor to
hew wood and his arm is swung with the ax to fell the tree,
and the head drops off from the handle and lights upon his
neighbor and he dies, he has to flee to one of these cities
and remain living" (*Devarim* 19:5).

---

57. Another example: *Sanhedrin* 67b.

The general rule, "He that smites a man so that he dies shall surely be put to death," does not make any distinction between intentional or unintentional murder. All forms of homicide are included in "He that smites." In the specific, an exception is made in the case of unintentional murder so that this committer of homicide could flee to one of the cities of refuge and would not be liable for capital punishment.[58]

In other circumstances, depending on the nature of the text, we find the need to aggravate and not alleviate (*Mechilta, Shemot* 21:38).

This rule differs from the previously cited one, in that it does not limit the entire principle, but rather limits the specific example and excludes it from what is true of the general rule.

Rule 10

> *Kol Davar She-hayah Bichelal Veyatza lit'on To'an Acher She-lo Ke-inyano, Yatza Lehakel Ulehachmir:* When something is first included in the general rule and is then specified in detail, dissimilar from those cases included in the general rule, then such specifying alleviates in some respects and aggravates in other aspects (literally, "A matter that was stated in the general rule and [then] is excluded to require a matter not in accordance with that fact, [then] it is excluded to alleviate and to aggravate").

---

58. See: *Sifra,* Introduction (including other examples).

Example

In Chapter 13 of *Vayikra*, verses 1–3, the different laws concerning *tsara'at* (a type of leprosy), an illness caused by certain moral misdeeds, are discussed, after which a person is declared "impure" in case the priest finds (under certain circumstances) a "white hair on the flesh or the skin" (general rule).

In verses 29–37, the same law is discussed in the case of such a plague on the head under the hair or beard (specific): "And behold, its color is deeper white than the skin and there is short golden [yellow] hair on it, then the priest shall pronounce him 'impure'" (*Vayikra* 13:30).

Now, it is clear that the case of the hair and the beard are included in the previously mentioned plague on the skin and the flesh (general rule). The "specific" of the hair and the beard, however, shows a dissimilarity with the general rule, that is, the golden (yellow) hair, since, in the case of the skin and the flesh, a "white" hair (and not a yellow one) is a sign of impurity.

Instead of saying that the white hair *and* the golden (yellow) hair are signs of impurity, we say of the above-mentioned rule that: (1) the white hair is *not* a sign of impurity in the case of the hair and the beard (alleviation), while it *is* in the case of the skin and flesh; (2) the golden (yellow) hair *is* a sign of impurity in the case of the hair and the beard (aggravation), though it is not a sign of impurity in the case of flesh and skin (*Sifra* 1:3).[59]

---

59. Other examples include *Shemot* 21:7; *Vayikra* 25:15–26:30.

Rule 11

Davar She-hayah Bi-chelal Veyatza lidon Bedavar Chadash, i-attah Yachol Lahachziro likelalo Ad She-yachazirenu Ha-Katuv Likelalo Beferush: When something is first included in the general rule and is then specified to determine a completely new matter, the details of this general rule may not be applied to this instance unless this is expressly done by the text itself (literally, "A matter that was stated in the general rule and [then] is excluded to require a new matter, you are not allowed to restore [this matter] to its general rule, until the text itself specifically restores it to its general rule").

Example

In the case of the guilt offering of the leper, the Torah states:

> And he [the priest] shall slaughter the he-lamb in the place where they kill the sin-offering and the burnt-offering, in the place of the sanctuary; for as the sin-offering is the priest's, so is the guilt offering. . . .
>
> And the priest shall take of the blood of the guilt offering, and the priest shall put it upon the tip of the right ear of him that is to be cleansed, and upon the thumb of his right hand, and upon the great toe of his right foot. (*Vayikra* 14:13–14)

The general rule of the guilt offering (in cases other than that of the leper) is that the sprinkling of the altar is required (*Vayikra* 7:2), as it is in a sin-offering, from which we may presume that this is true of the case of the leper as well.

The question then arises, Why is there any need to state, "So is the guilt offering [of the leper]," a phrase that seems to be superfluous? The answer is that since, in the specific case of the leper, a "new matter" is introduced (the placing of the blood on the ear, thumb, and toe), it is unclear whether this specific rule of the leper still forms a part of the general rule of guilt offerings (sprinkling the blood on the altar) or not.

By stating "as the sin offering . . . so is the guilt offering" (of the leper), the text informs us that this is indeed the case; the text itself brings the specific case back to its general rule, specifically (*Yevamot* 7a, b).[60]

The difference between this rule and the previous one is that the former rule discusses a case in which the "specific" contradicts the general rule, which in our case the specific does not contradict the general rule.

Rule 12

> *Davar Halomed Me'inyano, Vedavar Halomed Mi-sofo:* (1) An interpretation deduced from its context, (2) an interpretation deduced from subsequent terms of the text (literally, "from its end").

Example

In the Decalogue,[61] it is stated: "You shall not steal" (*Shemot* 20:13). From the text alone, it is unclear whether

---

60. Other examples: *Bamidbar* 6:14–15, 15:1–16.
61. See page 46.

this only concerns the stealing of objects or instances of kidnapping as well, which is a capital offense.

However, since it is stated in this context: "You shall not murder" and "You shall not commit adultery," both of which are capital offenses, we must deduce that our verse includes kidnapping as well (*Sanhedrin* 86a).

Example

"I put the plague of leprosy in a house of the land of your possession" (*Vayikra* 14:34).

We may ask, does this apply to every type of house (after which it becomes impure), or not? The answer is deduced from a later reference concerning this plague: "And the priest shall break down the house, the stones of it, and the timber thereof, and all the mortar of the house . . ." (ibid., 45), teaching us that our verse only refers to a house made of "stones *and* timber *and* mortar" (*Sifra*, ad loc.).

This rule shows great similarity to *Semuchim* ("juxtaposition"), mentioned earlier.[62] The difference, however, is that in the case of *semuchim*, we deduce a completely new law by way of a juxtaposition. In our case, no new law is introduced, but instead the meaning of an obscure statement is clarified.[63]

Rule 13

Shene Ketuvim Ha-machhishim zeh et zeh ad Sheyavo hakatuv Hashelishi Veyachria Benehem:

---

62. See page 144.
63. See Avraham Kurman, op. cit., p. 308.

When two verses contradict each other, they are
reconciled by a third verse (literally, "Two verses
that contradict each other, until there comes a
third verse, which decides between them").

This rule is applied to two verses dealing with the same
subject, either in two different chapters,[64] or in the same
chapter.[65] This also applies to two parts of one verse.[66]

Example

"In the beginning God created the heaven and the earth"
(*Bereshit* 1:1).

"In the day that the Lord made earth and heaven" (*Bereshit*
2:4).

There is an obvious contradiction between the two
verses. The first implies that the creation of heaven preceded the creation of earth; the second verse seems to state
the reverse.

A later verse in *Tanach*, however, reconciles both: "My
hand also has laid the foundation of the earth, and My right
hand has spread out the heavens; I call unto them, they
stand up together" (*Jesjaja* 48:13–14).

Rashi, ad loc., remarks: "Like a craftsman who is working
with both hands at two handicrafts at the same time."[67]

---

64. *Bava Metzia* 110b.
65. *Mechilta Mishpatim* 20.
66. *Mechilta Mishpatim* 7.
67. This is not a halachic issue, proving that these rules are not only
used in legal matters, but also in *Aggadah*. See Kurman, op. cit., p. 309.

THE RULES OF RABBI AKIVA

As mentioned before, Rabbi Akiva's approach to Torah exegesis is based on the concept that in the language of the Torah nothing is mere form, but everything is essence.

There are no superfluous words, or syllables, or even a letter. Everything incorporates a deeper meaning.[68]

Rabbi Akiva formulated, among other things, some important rules:

1. *Ribui Umiut*—Extension and limitation. This is a variation of the rule of *kelal* and *perat* of Rabbi Yishmael[69] (*Bava Kamma, Shevu'oth* 26a).

2. *Ribui*—Inclusion or amplification. The words *af*, ("even"), *gam* ("also"), and *et* (a word that introduces a direct object) amplify the halachic meaning of the text.[70]

3. *Mi-ut*—Exclusion or limitation. The words *ach* ("however"), *rak* ("but," or "only"), and *min* ("from") limit the halachic meaning of the text.

4. *Yesh em Lemikra*—There is a preference to the way in which the text is pronounced, that is, the way in which the text is sounded determines the *halachah* (literally, "*Mikra* has a mother").

According to Rabbi Akiva, the traditional vocalization of a word in the Torah, even when it could be read in

---

68. See page 20, concerning the crowns on the Hebrew letters.
69. See *Shevu'oth* 4b (Rashi).
70. The word *kol* ("all") is also included in *Ribui* (*Berachot* 1:5).

different ways, is well-founded, and, consequently, we may deduce *halachah* from it. This rule had already been formulated by Rabbi Judah ben Roetz. Rabbi Yishmael, however, in opposition to Rabbi Akiva, is of the opinion that *Yesh em Lemasoret*. There is a preference for the traditional text, that is, the text as it was written is authoritive. Sometimes this approach is called *Keri U Ketiv*, ("read and written").[71]

Example

"Speak unto the children of Israel, saying: When a woman had given birth to . . . a male child, then shall she be in an impure condition for two weeks [*shevu'ayim*] as in her time of separation . . ." (*Vayikra* 12:2–5).

Since the text is written without vowels, the word *SH-Y-M* could be read as *Shivim* ("seventy"), implying that the Torah requires seventy days of impurity. Tradition, however, tells us that it should be read as *Shevuayim* ("two weeks"), which, however, should have been spelled differently: *SH-VU-IM*,[72] in its full consonantal form. In other words, the *Keri* reads *Shevuayim* ("two weeks"); the *Ketiv* is written *Shiv'im* ("seventy").

In this case Rabbi Akiva, like Rabbi Judah ben Roetz, decided the *halachah* according to the Keri, while it seems that Rabbi Yishmael reached this same conclusion by logical deduction (*Sanhedrin* 4a).

---

71. The *Keri* and *Ketiv* are almost a matter of *Masorah* (see page 22) and incorporate much more than halachic issues.

72. The *U* is a *waw*, a consonant. The *ii* are two *yods*, also consonants.

These and other rules (such as the cases of repetition or redundancy) play a major role in Rabbi Akiva's school of halachic interpretation.

It must be emphasized that Rabbi Akiva and his school had an enormous influence on *Drash*. Nearly all famous scholars since his day are greatly indebted to this halachic interpretation: "The author of an anonymous *mishnah* is Rabbi Meir; an anonymous *Tosefta*, Rabbi Nehemiah; an anonymous [statement] of the *Sifra*, Rabbi Judah; of the *Sifre*, Rabbi Shimon; and all taught according to the views of Rabbi Akiva" (*Sanhedrin* 86a).

AGGADAH

AGGADAH AND HALACHAH

If *halachah* is explained as the system of codes and regulations that govern life, there must be a current system that enables men to formulate a weltanschauung, a teaching that gives man the ability to function on a philosophical, rather than on a concrete, plane. Just as philosophy tries to find metaphysical meaning, so does Judaism give meaning to the rulings of *halachah*. Moreover, even though the halachic system is flexible by its very nature, there must be some manner of dealing with the totality of life's phenomena and of determining a personal course of action that transcends the inherent limitations of every legal system.

Halachah can inform man how to act in any given situation, but it cannot provide insight into the quality of a given act or a sense of the spiritual change that is a result of the performance of, or adherence to, a specific dictate. Because Judaism is a way of living rather than a societal grouping, man must have the means of penetrating the secrets that are the possible reasons for the *mitsvot*. Although some of the reasons are beyond our ability to understand, given our dependence upon the material world, nevertheless, they must exist or else the entire system is meaningless. As we have noted previously, the Torah was given to man and for man; thus, it must contain, along with divine guidance regarding the way in which life should be lived, an indication of what man can aspire to. *Aggadah*—from the Aramaic root *ngd*, "to flow"[1]—is the part of the Torah that deals with the whole of life, rather than the laws in accordance with which it should be lived. *Aggadah* gives man understanding, through which he can choose to follow the dictates of *halachah* based on an acceptance of them, rather than on seeing them as a sort of totalitarian system he is forced to follow. Because there is *Aggadah*, man can accept the *mitzvot* even if he does not understand their purpose. *Aggadah* prevents mechanical observance by freeing man's inner spirit. It is the aspiration of man, whereas *halachah* is the consummation. At times, *Aggadah* is a refinement of *halachah*: thus, whereas the latter, being a code applicable to all men at all times, must base itself on the capabilities of mankind in general, the former is free to suggest a greater degree of Godliness that might be applicable only to a chosen few. While there is no other option but to follow *halachah*, *Aggadah*'s paths are suggestions and offer voluntary choices to each individual.

Aggadah is the aspect of the Torah that draws man toward its teachings. It is the philosophy of the Torah way of life, yet it is not dogmatic or even systematic. It is completely open to all those willing to accept minimal axioms[2] and does not demand that man accept it in

---

1. See Daniel 7:10.

2. In his introduction to the last chapter of *Sanhedrin*, Maimonides lists thirteen articles of faith that every Jew must accept. Rabbi Yosef Albo, in his *Sefer Ha-ikkarim*, maintains that there are but three such principles. Thus, there is even an argument as to what constitutes the

toto.[3] It is a far cry from the theology or catechisms of other religions, for it does not purport to possess or present the "truth," although, as in the case of *halachah*, there is often a consensus of the majority of the Sages. Rather, *Aggadah* was cultivated so as to allow the unseen to enter the visible world and was formulated to give man the ability to go beyond the realms of the definable, perceivable, and demonstrable. Just as language attempts to allow us to comprehend the intangible through use of metaphor, *Aggadah* allows us to begin to comprehend the infinite through the use of symbolism. In this sense, *Aggadah* is a form of religious metaphor, a camera that enables us to form mental images of the indescribable. It answers man's need to understand the reasons for the actions demanded of him and assures him that there is purpose to what he does. When religion becomes frozen in dogmas, its ability to provide meaning to life becomes lost.

Aggadah, by imbuing the practices of Judaism with spirit, insures that the way of the Torah remains ever fresh. Through *Aggadah*, one can perceive, and at times understand, that heaven and earth are one, as well as feel the Divine force that flows through all that lives. History becomes alive, for it is not merely the story of what has occurred but is revealed to be the threads that are woven into the fabric of human development.

Found throughout talmudic literature, *Aggadah* can be

---

minimal axioms that all must accept. It is interesting to note that even Maimonides, who wrote extensively on the subject, was not overly impressed by philosophical study. In his commentary on the *Mishnah* (*Berachot* 9:5), he writes: "It is more precious to me to teach the fundamentals of our religion than any of the other matters that I study."

3. See Maharal, *Beer Hagolah* 17.

defined as all the material that does not determine the practical observances demanded by *halachah*. It includes and emphasizes matters of faith, wisdom, and ethics, and finds its forms in travel tales, parables, business counsel, medical advice, scientific observations, and stories relating to the lives of our forefathers and Sages. *Aggadah* is the source of many of the religious and philosophical foundations of Judaism, such as the immortality of the soul, the coming of the Messiah, reward and punishment in the hereafter, and the nature of prophecy, as well as other principles of our belief that are not directly mentioned in the Written Torah. It, too, is part of the orally transmitted Torah given at Sinai and is transmitted from father to son, at least in its basic ideas. Parts of the *Aggadah* are obscure and difficult to understand; some are hyperbole that go beyond the realm of literal belief. Yet all of the *Aggadah* is authentic, in the sense that it was given and transmitted in order to provide each man with the ability to find his niche within the eternal community of Israel.

We must forcefully point out that the attempts to describe *Aggadah* as legend or folklore are misguided and reveal a basic misunderstanding of its wisdom and sanctity. Aggadic literature was not transmitted and ultimately recorded to make the Jew proud of his ancestry or to provide material for anthropologists concerned with the past. On the contrary, *Aggadah* is meant to serve as an inspiration to man to achieve the level of morality and ethical behavior that once characterized the Jewish people. Those parts that describe wickedness are important, for they reveal the contradictory levels of man's mind, even as the generation that witnessed the Revelation could worship a golden calf. While twentieth-century man has been taught to see history as an evolutionary process, with technological progress a symbol of human advancement, *Aggadah* claims that man's fundamental nature remains unchanged. Man's environment might differ, his understanding of the physical world may be deeper, but his inherent qualities are the same as those of man throughout the generations. The separation from the period of direct Divine intervention in history makes man less capable of fathoming his responsibilities and roles; through study of the *Aggadah*, one can overcome that liability and live as one should. The stories, parables, and homiletic material of the *Aggadah* are not intended to amuse man. Rather, they are the means through which man can develop an ethical personality, when observing the dictates of *halachah*, and which will serve to create a Torah society.

Basically, *Aggadah* finds support within the text of the Torah and serves as a point of departure in filling in the background of the stories, personalities, and motivations of biblical figures. Additionally, it serves as a sort of philosophical commentary to many of the 613 precepts, sometimes providing the reason "for their being ordained. In other instances, the" *Aggadah* deals with the lives of the prophets and the Sages. In general, it is safe to say that *Aggadah* was recorded to allow man to determine what constitutes morality, by comparing his situation with similar occurrences in the past.

Because aggadic literature is replete with highly unusual stories, parables, exaggerations, and sometimes contradictory statements, it is worth our while to mention Maimonides's comments on the intent of the *Aggadah*:

> First of all, it is a way [for teachers] to sharpen the minds of their students. Secondly, it beguiles the fools so that their

minds cannot discern the actual substance, for if the truth was shown to them they would ridicule it, given their destitute nature. Thirdly, the Sages composed these parables and narratives in a manner that even those of limited intellect can still grasp some of their meaning. There are many ways of understanding the *Aggadah* and it is only through intellect and sincerity that one sees that every *Aggadah* can be interpreted on different levels. (Introduction to the *Mishnah*, 8)

He then proceeds to set limits on the study of *Aggadah*:

These subjects do not contain that which is fitting to be publicly taught and demonstrated even in academies [whose students are replete with] wisdom. Indeed, [the subjects] discussed are hinted at in the Torah in well-concealed illusions. When God will remove the veil of ignorance of those whom He chooses—after that person has exerted himself and ingrained himself with wisdom—then that person shall partially comprehend their meaning commensurate with his intellectual capabilities. And when God does remove the veil from that man's eyes and shows him whatever He shows, he must conceal the information from others.[4] (ibid.)

In his introduction to the last chapter of the tractate *Sanhedrin*, Maimonides makes the following comments about interpreting *Aggadah*:

As concerns the words of the Sages, people can be divided into three categories: the first . . . believe them literally and do not see them as containing a hidden message; they

---

4. He goes on to explain that the reason most people cannot grasp the real meaning is because of their poor intellectual abilities, laziness, and desire for instant gratification.

see them as fact. They do so because they do not comprehend wisdom and are far from understanding. They are not
on the level that would give them the ability to discern the
true intent by themselves and lack the teachers who would
give them this ability. They are convinced that the Sages
intended no more than what they [these people] understand
and that all of the Sages' words must be taken literally: a
contention that the simpleton—let alone a wise man—
rejects, for an examination of some of the *Aggadah* leads
one to conclude that there could not possibly be people
who accept them fully or view them as matters of faith.
One must feel sorry for those weak-minded people, for, in
their foolishness, they feel that they are honoring and
elevating the words of the Sages, whereas in reality they
drag them down to the lowest level. . . . This category of
men destroys the glory of the Torah, darkens its brightness,
and perverts the Torah of God into the reverse of what was
intended. God said in the Torah that the nations will hear
its laws and will say how wise and understanding is this
great people. This type of person causes the nations who
hear their [literal] interpretation to comment how foolish
and despicable is this small people. . . .

Aggadah cannot, therefore, always be taken literally;[5]
rather, it must be interpreted with the understanding that a
higher truth is being alluded to—a truth that is beyond
historical perspective, philological expression, or the dimensions of scientific observations. To express these truths
in a manner that man can understand, a vehicle must be
employed that simultaneously frees the mind from the limits
of material constraints and yet keeps it within the bounds
of the intelligible. Thus, if the message intended has meaning
and application, it does not matter that the medium used

---

5. See also Maharal, *Chidushe Aggadoth*, *Bava Kamma* 110 b.

for its expression is inexplicable. What is important is the philosophical or ethical truth that underlies the story. The message of the *Aggadah* is part of the orally transmitted Torah; the medium is often no more than a means used to express ideas.[6] Thus, the *Aggadah* cannot be seen as an invention of the Sages. As is true of *halachah*, *Aggadah* is part of the interpretation given at Sinai so that the Written Torah might be understood and followed. As proof of this, scholars have noted that many of the stories in the *Aggadah* represent traditions that find expression in sources that predate the Talmud. In his *Wars of the Jews*, Josephus tells us of many miracles that occurred in the Temple and that were later recorded in the Talmud (*Taanit* 23a) and in other traditions.[7]

Many of the lives of the patriarchs are quoted in Philo, the Alexandrian philosopher who lived about thirty years before the destruction of the Second Temple. Without falling into the trap of referring to *Aggadah* as the legends of the Jews, we are safe in seeing it as a lore passed on through the generations.

Many of the sayings of the Sages were not recorded in the Talmud, for only those matters whose importance was generally recognized were incorporated. Moreover, not all aggadic statements carry equal weight, for much depends on the standing and level of piety and wisdom of the Sages quoted. One cannot equate the later *tannaim* with Hillel or Rabbi Akiva, for there was something like an unwritten

---

6. That is, in order to make the point understandable to all, the Sages might express their message in a parable that attributed a certain dialogue to our forefathers.

7. Rabbi Z. H. Chajes, *Students Introduction to the Talmud* (New York: Feldheim), pp. 151–152.

law that "the closer one lived to the Revelation, the greater one's level of inspiration."

Thus, confronted with a statement or story in the *Aggadah*, one must first examine in whose name it is said. Perhaps this is the very reason that the *Aggadah* cannot be used in determining *halachah* (Jerusalem Talmud, *Peah* 11:6). Moreover, because the veracity of certain statements is at times questionable, *Aggadah* should not be taught to children or others who might not be able to differentiate between doubt as to their credibility and outright rejection (ibid., *Pesachim* 5:3).

Despite all that what we have said, however, it is interesting to note that some commentators are of the opinion that certain aggadic statements must be taken literally; that is, one cannot see all *aggadot* as being metaphors or hyperbole. This is especially true of the accounts of miracles that happened to certain Sages. It is beyond the scope of this work to discuss the question of real versus perceived miracles. Suffice it to say that there are major commentators who reject the idea completely.[8]

Although most of the masters of *Aggadah* excelled in *halachah* as well, certain Sages seem to have specialized in the former. Generally referred to as *Rabban Deaggadata*— Rabbis of the *Aggadah* (Jerusalem Talmud, *Maaserot* 1:2)— this category seems to have been applied especially to the Palestinian *amoraim*, such as Rabbi Yonathan, Rabbi Abba bar Kahana, Rabbi Tanchuma, and others. Rabbi Akiva was noted for his mastery of *Aggadah*, yet we find that Rabbi Eliezer be Azaryah admonished him, "What do you

---

8. See Nachmanides, *Milchamot Hashem* 39, p. 308, Mosad Harav edition.

have to do with *Aggadah*? Cease your talk and turn to the laws of *nega'im* and *ohalot*" (*Chagiga* 14a). This could be understood to mean that some Sages disapproved of the study of the *Aggadah* and saw it as second-rate material for study and discussion. This conclusion, however, might not necessarily be accurate, for it is possible that the previously mentioned reluctance to teach *Aggadah* to people who might misinterpret its intended message is at issue. As Rabbi Yochanan observes: "There is a tradition transmitted by my father not to teach *Aggadah* to a Babylonian or a southerner, as they are uncouth and unlearned" (Jerusalem Talmud, *Pesachim* 5:3).

Originally, the prohibition against recording the orally transmitted Torah (*Gittin* 60a) applied to *Aggadah* as well. However, when the times called for a partial annulment of that proscription, the question was raised as to whether the various *aggadot* should also be recorded, for there was a great danger of errors and mistakes. This was not necessarily true of the *Aggadah*, for it had always called for an oral interpretation and explanation of its true intention. Indeed, writing down the *Aggadah could* prove to be dangerous and misleading. Thus, we find that Rabbi Yehoshua ben Levi, a third-century c.e. *amora*, says: "Anyone recording it has no share in the world to come and whoever uses a written copy for teaching it is liable to excommunication" (Jerusalem Talmud, *Shabbat* 16:1). Rabbi Zeira considered written *Aggadah* "the work of sorcerers" (ibid., *Maaseroth* 111:4). Other scholars, such as Rabbi Yochanan and Resh Lakish, felt that the importance of remembering the message outweighed other considerations.

THE THIRTY-TWO RULES OF *AGGADAH*

Just as *halachah* has its method of establishing its textual basis, *Aggadah* also employs a system of rules for linking its message with Scripture. These rules are known as the thirty-two rules of Rabbi Eliezer ben Rabbi Yosi the Galilean, a *tanna* of the second century C.E. It should be mentioned that, although mainly aggadic, some of these rules also touch on halachic matters (see, for example, rule 25) and are not so much there to deduce new information from the text, but to show that the Torah has expressed itself in thirty-two ways. While these rules are not explicitly mentioned in the Talmud per se, Rabbi Eliezer's standing as a master of *Aggadah* is indicated by this talmudical statement: "Wherever you find the words of Rabbi Eliezer ben Rabbi Yosi the Galilean in the *Aggadah*, make your ears like a funnel" (*Chullin* 89a).

Our earliest source for these rules is *Sefer Hakeritot*, a work on methodology written by Rabbi Samson ben Isaac Chinon.[9] It would seem that these rules were originally incorporated in a *beraita* (see page 196), similar to the hermeneutic rules of Rabbi Yishmael that were discussed previously. They are also quoted in two post-talmudic works: *Midrash Mishnat* by Rabbi Eliezer and *Midrash hagadol* to *Bereshit*. These sources offer examples of the use of Rabbi Eliezer's rules of aggadic exegesis.

While it is not within the scope of this work to examine closely the applications of each of the rules or to compare and contrast them with those used in halachic exegesis, it is

---

9. See page 150.

important that we at least explain their meaning and offer a short example of how they are used.

1. *Ribui*—Words such as *af*, ("even"), *gam* ("also"), and *et* (used in a verse to indicate that the intention is to include other subjects not explicitly mentioned). For example, the Torah states (in *Bereshit* 1:1), "In the beginning God created [*et hashamaim*] the heavens." The use of the preposition *et* indicates that the phrase is referring to more than just the heavens: that is, to the sun, the moon and planets as well. (See *Bereshit Rabbah*, ad loc.; also *Shemot* 18:18, 19:9)

2. *Miut*—Words such as *ach*, ("only"), *rak* ("just"), and *min*, ("of"), used in a verse indicate a limitation of the application of the statement. For example, the Torah states (in *Bereshit* 7:23) "*ach*—only Noach was left"; that is, he was left alive after the flood but he did not escape unscathed (see *Bereshit Rabbah*, ad loc.; also *Bereshit* 36:29).

3. *Ribui achar ribbui*—When two expressions that indicate an intention to include subjects not explicitly mentioned are used in a verse, we infer that the intention is to broaden the category under discussion even further. For example, 1 Shemuel 17:36 states, "for your servant has slain [*gam*] also the lion, and [*gam*] also the bear." The repetition of *gam* indicates that other animals were also slain. Contrast this with the similar rule used in halachic exegesis, in which such a repetition is taken to indicate that the intent of the second statement is to limit the scope and application (see *Menachot* 89a).

4. _Mi'ut achar mi'ut_—Conversely, when two participles that indicate an intent to limit the application of a subject are used in a verse, we infer that the category under discussion is to be limited even further. For example, the Torah states (in _Bamidbar_ 12:2): "Has God spoken [_ach verak_] only and solely to Moshe?" The repetition indicates that not only were others spoken to in Moshe's presence, but also that God addressed others even when Moshe was not present. Contrast this with the halachic usage in which a repetition of this sort is taken to indicate that the second term serves to broaden the limits established by the first. (See _Bava Batra_ 14a, Megillah 23b, _Bava Kamma_ 86b).

5. _Kal vachomer meforash_—Deductive logic clearly used in a verse. For example, Esther 9:12 states: "And the King said to Queen Esther: 'In Shushan, the capital, the Jews have killed and destroyed five hundred men as well as the ten sons of Haman. What must they have done [_kal vachomer_] in the provinces of the King!'"—That is, if they had been so successful in Haman's stronghold in Shushan, they must surely (_kal vachomer_) have been successful in areas where his influence was not as great (see also _Yirmiyahu_ 12:5).

6. _Kal vachomer satum_—Deductive logic alluded to in a verse but not written outright; for example, _Tehillim_ 15:4 states: "He swears to his detriment but does not retract." If a righteous person does not retract an oath that is to his detriment, he surely (_kal vachomer_) will not retract an oath that is to his benefit.

7. _Gezerah shavah_—An inference based on the use of the same terms. The verse in _Shoftim_ (13:5) states that Shim-

shon was a *nazir* and therefore no razor was used on his hair. Since the same phrase is used concerning the prophet Shemuel (1 Shemuel 1:11), we can infer that he also was a *nazir*. While in halachic exegesis, *gezerah shavah* can only be used if there is a tradition that such an inference was made, in *Aggadah* anyone is permitted to make the comparison (see *Devarim* 2:25 and *Yehoshua* 3:7).

8. *Binyan Av*—A generality deduced from a particular event or instance. The first time God spoke to him, Moshe answered, Hine*ni* ("I am here") (*Shemot* 3:4). We therefore assume that every time God subsequently addressed Moshe, he answered in the same manner (see also *Yeshaya* 10:12).

9. *Derech Ketzarah*—Abbreviated phraseology. A verse (1 *Divre HaYamim* 17:5) states: "And I went from tent to tent and from Tabernacle [to another]." Though the meaning of the verse is "from tabernacle to tabernacle" as well, the verse employs an abbreviated form and one should not assume that the singular usage is significant. (See 2 Shemuel 13:39, *Kiddushin* 21b, and *Yoma* 87a)

10. *Davar shehu shanui*—Repetition of a statement. Aside from the repetition of words already discussed, we find that verses sometimes repeat an entire statement. This is taken as an indication that an additional point, not apparent if the verse is read literally, is being made. For example, the Torah states (in *Bamidbar* 21:4), "from each tribe one thousand men, one thousand men." The repetition indicates that when he, Moshe, conscripted soldiers to do battle with Midyan, he chose one thousand men to fight on the front and one thousand men to pray for victory. (See also *Bereshit Rabbah* 89)

11. *Siddur shenechlak*—A subject whose context is interrupted. We find that a *sof pasuk* or another accent indicating the end of a statement is sometimes used, even though the following verse would seem to be part of the first. This is understood to be an indication that the latter verse is a qualification of the former. For example, the verse (2 *Divre HaYamim* 30:18, 19) states: "For many of the nation . . . ate the Paschal sacrifice in a manner other than that prescribed, for Chezkiyahu prayed for them, saying: 'God, Who is good, will pardon them for this [sin].' To everyone who directed his heart to seek God . . ." The second verse would seem to be a continuation of the first. The use of the *sof pasuk*, however, indicates that Chezkiyahu's prayers were meant for those to whom criteria of the second verse applied.

12. *Davar sheba lelammed venimtza lamed*—A statement brought to shed light on a certain subject, which, instead, is clarified by that subject. For example, *Yeshaya* 64:1 states: "for as the fire of creation burns through and melts . . ." The verse is referring to the punishment meted out to the Egyptians, yet we do not find mention of there being a fire of creation. Thus, not only do we learn that this fire was used as a weapon, we also learn that it was a part of the creation process.

13. *Klal sheacharav ma'aseh veeno ella prato shel rishon*—A general statement followed by a more detailed account of an action to clarify that statement: that is, if a more detailed narrative follows a general statement, we infer that the story clarifies that statement and does not refer to another event. For example, the Torah states (in *Bereshit* 1:27), "And God created man in His image." In chapter 2

of *Bereshit*, we find the creation of man described in detail. The latter verses are not to be taken as a reference to a new creation. Rather, they are understood to be an amplification of the first verse (see also *Shemot* 12:43, 19:6, and *Bamidbar* 19:2).

14. *Davar gadol shenitleh b'davar katan lehashmia la-ozen baderech shehi shoma'at*—An important concept is linked to a concept of lesser importance so as to allow for a clearer understanding. For example, the Torah states (in *Devarim* 32:2): "My lessons drop as the rains, My sayings flow as the dew." Though the reference is to the Torah, which is of far greater signifance than the rain or the dew, the verse uses a metaphor of lesser importance to teach us that just as all people are dependent upon the rain for sustenance, so, too, are we all dependent upon the Torah.

15. *Shene ketuvim hamakchishim*—Two verses that seem to contradict one another (see also page 161). For example, the verse in Shemuel states: "And Israel numbered eight hundred thousand." On the other hand, the verse 1 *Divre HaYamim* 21:5 states: "And Israel numbered one million, one hundred thousand." This contradiction is resolved by a third verse that indicates that the additional three hundred thousand were not enumerated in the Book of Shemuel, for they had already been included in the king's census.

16. *Davar shemeyuchad bimekomo*—An expression used that does not appear elsewhere. This is taken to indicate that the use of the expression is meant to teach a specific lesson. For example, 1 Shemuel 1:11 states: "And she [Channah] took a vow and said: God, Lord of Hosts . . ."

The use of the phrase "Lord of Hosts," which does not appear elsewhere in this type of context, indicates that Channah offered an additional prayer besides the one recorded. According to the *Aggadah*, she prayed: "You have created two legions—one in the spiritual realm who neither procreate nor die, and one in the material world who do procreate and die. If I am part of the material world, permit me to procreate and die. However, if I am not destined to bear children, let me be a part of the spiritual realm." (See also *Malachi* 2:14)

17. *Davar sheeno mitparesh bimekomo umitparesh bemakom acher*—A subject that is not explained in its context but is explained elsewhere. For example, the Garden of Eden is only partially described in *Bereshit*, but its riches are more fully portrayed in *Yechezkel* 28:13 (see also 1 *Divre HaYamim* 24:19).

18. *Davar shenemar bimiktzato vehu noheg bakol*—A subject that seems only to have limited application, yet is applicable to every instance. For example, *Mishle* 22:22 states: "Rob not the poor, for he is poor." Though one is also not permitted to steal from the rich, the verse refers to what commonly occurs and should not be taken literally.

19. *Davar sheneemar bazeh vehu hadin lachavero*—A subject that is stated in reference to one situation but applies to others as well. For example, *Tehillim* 97:11 states: "Light is sown for the righteous and joy for those of upright hearts." Although light is also sown for the upright and joy for the righteous, the verse uses a poetic form and ascribes qualities to each that are, in truth, applicable to

both. This is possible as long as the two subjects are of equal status (see also *Mechilta, Shemoth* 21:18).

20. *Davar shenemar bezeh veeno inyan lo aval hu inyan lechavero*—A subject is stated in reference to a certain situation and although it is not applicable to that situation, it does apply elsewhere. For example, in the blessings that Moshe offered the tribes before his death, we find that the verse *Devarim* 33:7 states: "And this is for Yehudah . . ." Since the verse continues, "God, hear the voice of Yehudah," the first part of the verse must be referring to Shimon, who is not mentioned elsewhere. (See also *Sifre* to *Bamidbar* 18:15)

21. *Davar shehukash bishete middot veatta noten lo koach hayafeh shebishtehen*—A subject that is compared to two objects is considered to have the positive qualities of both. For example, *Tehillim* 92:13 states, "The righteous shall bloom like the palm, they shall flourish like the cedars of Lebanon." The palm bears fruit but offers little shade, whereas the cedar offers shade but bears no fruit, so the righteous possess both qualities (see also *Vayikra* 25:31).

22. *Davar shechavero moshiach alav*—One subject that is clarified by another. For example, *Tehillim* 38:2 states: "God, do not reprove me in wrath; chastise me in Your anger." The Hebrew word *al*, "do not," is applied to the latter half of the verse, as well as to the former, so that the meaning of the verse is: "Do not reprove nor chastise me"—an interpretation that could not be made if the verse were explained as written. (See also *Mechilta, Shemot* 23:1, and *Sanhedrin* 27a)

23. *Davar shehu mochiach al chavero*—One subject that clarifies another. For example, *Tehillim* 29:8 states: "The voice of God shakes the wilderness, the voice of God shakes the wilderness of Kadesh." Though the former phrase already indicates that the voice of God shakes all the wilderness, the phrase is repeated to indicate that the voice of God that shakes the wilderness of Kadesh is even more awesome. (See also *Sifre* to *Devarim* 11:12)

24. *Davar shehaya bichelal veyatza min hakelal lelamed al atzmo yatza*—A subject that, although included in a general statement, is mentioned separately and that indicates that a lesson is to be derived that is specific to that subject. For example, *Yehoshua* 2:1 states: "And Yehoshua sent [spies] to see the land and Jericho." Although Jericho is included in the phrase "the land," it is specifically mentioned to indicate that it was equal in importance to the rest of the land (see also 2 Shemuel 2:30).

25. *Davar shehaya bichelal veyatza min hakelal lelamed al chavero*—A subject that was included in a general statement and that was explicitly mentioned indicates that a lesson is to be derived about another subject. For example, the Torah states (in *Bamidbar* 35:31): "And you shall not take a ransom for a murderer . . ." Although the Torah had already stated that one may not substitute a fine (i.e, a ransom) for the capital punishment due the murderer, the law is specifically stated in this context to teach us that fines are to be levied in case of injury and there is no law to punish the responsible person in the manner that he injured others. There do not seem to be any examples of an aggadic application of this rule.

26. *Mashal*—Parable. For example, *Shoftim* 9:8 states: "And the trees set out to anoint a king to rule them. . . ." The reference is obviously to the people of Israel.[10]

27. *Minneged*—Corresponding to; a number corresponding to another number. For example, the Torah states (in *Bamidbar* 13:25): "And they returned from spying the land for forty years." In the next chapter (14:34) we see that "as the number of days that you spied the land . . . a day for a year, a day for a year, you shall bear your sins for forty years." The punishment of wandering in the desert for forty years was meted out to correspond to the forty days the spies spent in the land of Israel.

28. *Mima'al* (also known as *lashon nofel al lashon*)—A form of alliteration, using the same or similar-sounding words. For example, the Torah states (in *Bamidbar* 21:9): "And Moshe made a [*nachash nechoshet*] a serpent of copper." (See also *Yirmiyahu* 23:2)

---

10. The parable is the most common form of aggadic exegesis and was often used to elucidate difficult concepts, as well as to meet the challenges of skeptics and heretics. The Talmud (*Sanhedrin* 38b–39a) states that Rabbi Meir knew three hundred parables involving foxes as examples, although only three of them are recorded. Our literature is replete with statements made by rocks, trees, hills, and animals. Some scholars maintain that since some of these parables find expression in other cultures, we must conclude that the Sages of the Talmud then Judaized them. However, this is not necessarily true. The Sages may very well have passed judgment on these forms of wisdom, knowing that these types of parables were an efficient means of transmitting the philosophical and moral lessons they wanted to impart. They used the parables to express ideas far loftier than their original intent, but, being pragmatists, they realized that their lessons had to be conveyed in a manner that everyone could understand.

29. *Gimatria*—Numerical values of letters. For example, *Echa* 1:1 states: "How the city sits in solitude." The word *Echa* has the value of *Alef* (1), *Yod* (10), *Kaf* (20), and *Heh* (5), corresponding to 1—the unity of God; *Yod* (10)—the Decalogue; 20—the law of circumcision given to Avraham, twenty generations after creation; and 5—the five books of Moshe. These four values were denigrated by the people of that generation and were the cause for the destruction of the Temple. (See also *Pesikta derav Kahana* to *Bereshit* 14:14 and *Shabbat* 70a)

30. *Notrikon*—Separating one word into two or more words; that is, explaining a term as being a combination of two or more words. For example, the Torah (in *Bereshit* 15:2) refers to Avraham's servant as "*damasek* Eliezer." The term *damasek* is explained as a combination of the words *doleh*, "he drew," and *umashkeh*, "gave to drinks"; that is, Eliezer drew and gave to drink from the spiritual spring of his master Abram. (See also *Shabbat* 105a and *Menachot* 66b)

31. *Mukdam shehu meuchar beinyan*—A subject that occurred earlier but is mentioned after a subject that occurred later. For example, Shemuel 3:3 states: "And the light of God had not yet gone out and Shemuel rested in the Tabernacle of God." The verse cannot be interpreted literally, for it was prohibited to lie down in the Tabernacle. Rather, the phrase "and Shemuel rested" must be removed from its context.

32. *Mukdam umeuchar shebeparashiyot*—Later and earlier occurrences within one section; that is, the stories related in the Torah are not necessarily presented in

chronological order. For example, the Torah states (in *Bamidbar* 1:1): "And God spoke to Moshe in the desert of Sinai in the Tabernacle on the first day of the second month of the second year after they left Egypt." In a later chapter (ibid., 7:1) we find, "And on the day that Moshe completed the construction of the Tabernacle." The latter verse refers to an earlier occurrence, yet is mentioned later.[11]

These thirty-two rules are the fundamentals that the Sages used to penetrate beyond the simple meaning of the texts they studied so that they might discern the underlying messages that, so to speak, were waiting to be deduced. It must be stressed that the rules are of great importance, for the Sages were wary of developing ideas without finding a textual basis. The rules were, and are, the tools these master craftsmen used to build an incredible structure of ethical and philosophical truth, and without them, nothing would have been possible.

As was said earlier regarding the study of *Aggadah*, the reader should always be aware of the fact that the Sages did not create stories to amuse their audiences or to demonstrate their literary creativity. Rather, their purpose was always to develop a vehicle that could impart the lessons that had to be taught. The Sages were prepared to depart from the literal meaning of Scripture in order to make their messages clear. They often used hyperbole, simile, and metaphor toward that end. At the same time, there had to be some connection with the verse they were explaining.

---

11. As we stressed, the Torah is not a history book. Thus, there is no need for chronological accuracy. Rather, the juxtaposition of occurrences mentioned earlier is an indication that there is some lesson to be derived from the text.

Possessing this knowledge, we can accept stories that are unusual or that even contradict our experience or the laws of nature. As Rashba writes, in his commentary to *Berachot*, the Sages would tell stories to ensure that their audiences remained attentive. However, even these stories had to have some linkage to the text, for the Sages were careful not to treat *Tanach* as literature that could freely be expanded on. Even the alterations in the way the text is read reveal that the Sages were careful of making unfounded statements. They would seem to have preferred to intimate that the moral or ethical lesson they expounded was also suggested, rather than being something entirely new. They were, however, willing to go to great lengths to impart their lessons, at times even making statements describing God in corporeal terms despite the fundamental axiom of God's incorporeality. Perhaps the only way we can truly understand just how far they were willing to go is to examine the differences between *Aggadah* and *halachah*.

Halachah, as a system governing action and the interrelationship between people and things, cannot allow for exaggeration or the bending of the rules of nature. Physical laws must be consistent, quantifiable, and comprehensible if they are to have meaning. Dealing as it does with man's inspirations, rather than his achievements, *Aggadah* indulges in flights of fancy, for the message is more important than the medium in which it is expressed.

However, these characteristics of *Aggadah* also limit its application. Thus, no halachic inferences may be drawn from its statements or stories (*Peah* 2:6). As a spiritual and literary source open to different interpretations, we can hardly rely on it as a basis for practical and unchanging guidelines. In no way does this detract from its greatness.

Rather, we must view its materials in proper perspective, accepting its messages as a means of establishing a philosophy of life that is consistent with the laws of *halachah*. The *Aggadah* has enriched Judaism by ensuring that scholars did not lose touch with humanity, closeting themselves in a world of blacks and whites. In a sense, *Aggadah*, when combined with *halachah*, has shown that it is possible to develop a system that enjoys both quality and quantity. By the same token, attempts to create a purely ethical Judaism based only on the teachings of *Aggadah* are doomed to failure, for the moral teachings of the Sages are based on the presupposition that the practitioner accepts the dictates of the *halachah*. Divest *Aggadah* of its link to *halachah* and you are left with a value system you can choose to follow or ignore. Consider them as growing from the same roots and you have a way of life. *Halachah* can afford to be rigid and consistent, for its authorities base themselves on a philosophy of life provided by *Aggadah*. Similarly, *Aggadah* can afford to be free and open because it is based on an unswerving allegiance to the reality of *halachah*.

Throughout Jewish history, the attempts to divorce *halachah* from *Aggadah* have led to misunderstandings and to misguided efforts to create "authentic" practices. In his *Tractatus Theologico Politicus* (V), Spinoza reveals his unawareness of their interdependence and writes: "The Pharisees, in their ignorance, thought that the observance of the state law and the law of Moses was the sum total of morality; whereas such laws merely had reference to the public welfare and aimed not so much at instructing the Jews, as at keeping them under constraint."

When we realize that all of *halachah* was formulated in keeping with the philosophy of life of *Aggadah*, we can understand just how moral a system *halachah* is. Inasmuch as both *Aggadah* and *halachah* are parts of the orally transmitted Torah, revealed at Sinai and faithfully transmitted from generation to generation, we know that it was not the Pharisees who were ignorant!

Conclusion

The Written Torah and the Oral Torah are the pillars of Judaism. Our acceptance of them as the word of God need not—and cannot—depend on scientific proof. This would be as foolish as refusing to look at a painting until we have deciphered the artist's signature, not vice versa. The Torah and its traditions are their own witnesses. Their divine origin is self-evident.

The written word was revealed only once, but the effort to understand it goes on forever. Every moment, another aspect waits to be unveiled. To allow for this continuous revelation, God graced the Jewish people with a minimum of words and a maximum of interpretation. Our study of both must remain an unprecedented event, an ongoing attempt to enrich our understanding and appreciation of the wellsprings of divine wisdom.

ADDENDUM

HALACHIC *MIDRASHIM*

The various methods used to deduce *halachot* find expression in a number of works. The oldest of these are the *midrashe halachah*—halachic expositions—which date back to the early tannaic period. They closely follow the text of four of the books of the Torah; there is no halachic exposition of *Bereshit*.[1] The *halachah* under discussion is integrated into the text so that a source for each ruling is clearly available. In a sense, *Midrash halachah* is a type of biblical interpretation that, by linking text and deduction, serves to facilitate the memorization of the material under study. Secondly, the linkage also establishes the interdependence of the written and orally transmitted Torah; that is, it shows that the *halachah* is contained within the text, rather than being independent of it.

These *midrashim* consist of *beraitot*[2] of various *tannaim*. Like the *Mishnah*, they are couched in simple Hebrew.

---

1. This is due to the fact that hardly any commandments are found in *Bereshit*.
2. See page 196.

Until the middle of the nineteenth century, only four such works were known: the *Mechilta*[3] of Rabbi Yishmael to *Shemot*, the *Sifra*—also known as *Torat Kohanim* to *Vayikra*, and the *Sifre* to *Bamidbar* and *Devarim*. Later, it became clear that other works must have once been compiled, which are divisible into two categories: those written in accordance with Rabbi Yishmael's laws of interpretation and those written in accordance with Rabbi Akiva's.[4] Thus, a *Mechilta* on *Shemot* of Rabbi Shimon bar Yochai—a pupil of Rabbi Akiva—was discovered: a *Sifra* to *Vayikra* of the school of Rabbi Yishmael, as well as a *Sifre Zuta* of the school of Rabbi Akiva to *Bamidbar*, were discovered. In addition, a *Mechilta* of the school of Rabbi Yishmael, known as *Midrash Tannaim*, was discovered, as well as a *Sifre* of the school of Rabbi Akiva. Since none of these works are mentioned in the Talmud, it would appear that some of them were only compiled after its redaction.[5]

MISHNAH

The later form of halachic exegesis of the Torah is referred to as *mishnah*—from the Hebrew root *shanah*, "to repeat," and afterward under the influence of the Aramaic word *tanna*, meaning "to teach." Originally, the term was used to describe the orally transmitted Torah in

---

3. The term *Mechilta* means "measure" in Aramaic.

4. See pages 131 on.

5. Many commentaries have been written on the various *midrashim*; for further readings on the subject, see Dr. David Hoffmann, *Zur Einleitung in die Halachische Midrashim*, and H. Albeck, *Mavo laTalmudim*.

its entirety, as it had developed until the end of the second century C.E. Thus, *mishnah* was the term used describe the total of tannaic teaching, as well as the statements of the individual *tannaim*. When we refer to the *Mishnah* today, however, we refer to the collection of halachic exegesis redacted by Rabbi Yehudah Hanassi—often referred to as Rebbe—the tannaic teacher par excellence. It was during his tenure as head of the Sanhedrin—in the latter part of the second and the beginning of the third century C.E.— that the decision was reached to allow the recording of the orally transmitted Torah in concise form.[6] Unlike the *Midrash halachah*, the *Mishnah* does not follow the verses and the books of the Torah, but is grouped in a systematic way according to different halachic subjects. It hardly ever quotes a biblical verse, and it is written in easy Hebrew. It is concise and therefore meant to be learned by heart, and must, in one way, be seen as Israel's constitution of Oral Law. It is legal, but it includes one tractate that is purely aggadic,[7] called *Pirke Avoth*, the "Ethics of the Fathers." It is clear that Rebbe's redaction was not the first collection of *mishnayot* before his term in office; however, these collections were only circulated privately.[8]

There is considerable discussion among later scholars as to the criteria Rabbi Yehudah Hanassi used in deciding which material should be included in the *Mishnah* and which to omit,[9] and why he divided the *Mishnah* in the manner he did. Whatever his grounds were, his redaction

---

6. See pages 93 on.

7. See pages 167 on.

8. See Rabbi Itzchak Isaac Halevy, *Dorot Harishonim.*

9. See Dr. David Hoffmann, *Die Erste Mishna und die Controversen der Tannaim*, and H. Albeck, *Mevo Lamishnah.*

was accepted by all and has been passed down through the generations without change.

Many commentaries have been written to the *Mishnah*; the most famous are those of Maimonides and Rabbi Ovadya of Bertinoro (fifteenth century).

BERAITA AND TOSEFTA

The *Beraita*—from the Aramaic term for "outside"[10]— refers to tannaic teachings not incorporated into the *Mishnah* of Rabbi Yehudah Hanassi. At times, these teachings are referred to as *Mishnah Chitzonah*—"outside" *Mishnah*. In the Babylonian Talmud, the term is used to designate the tannaic teachings that are found in other sources of halachic exegesis, such as the *Mechilta*, *Sifre*, and *Tosefta*, and often point to a tradition at variance with the view in the *Mishnah* quoted by Rabbi Yehudah Hanassi. In the Jerusalem Talmud, the term is used only once (*Niddah* 3:3). It would seem that the redaction of the *beraitot* took place considerably later than that of the *Mishnah*, for later *tannaim*, as well as some of the early *amoraim*, are sometimes quoted.

In general, the *Beraita* can be subdivided into pre- and post-mishnaic collections and should be seen as being a

---

10. Beraita, from the word *bera* ("outside"), may also refer to those private schools outside the official Palestinian and Babylonian academies, where these teachings were studied, while the *Mishnah* of Rabbi Yehudah Hanassi was studied in the main academies. See *Shabbat* 100a, *Betzah* 13b, *Yevamoth* 77b, *Sanhedrin* 62b; Isaac Ha-levi, *Dorot Harishonim* 111:126ff. Also see H. Albeck, *Mehkarim Ba-Baraita Uva-Tosefta*, 1944.

source of supplementary materials for talmudic discussions. At times, the *Beraita* is offered in corroboration of a statement found in the *Mishnah*. At other times, it is adduced in order to question the authenticity of a statement attributed to a specific *tanna*. In almost all cases, the *Beraita* does not enjoy the authority of the *Mishnah*. The Talmud (*Chullin* 141b) states that no reliance should be placed on *beraitot* not included in the collections of Rabbi Chiya and Rabbi Hoshaya, although even these are only considered authoritative if they do not contradict the *Mishnah*.

Within the Talmud, we distinguish between materials quoted from the *Mishnah* and the *Beraita* by the difference in terminology used to introduce them. Thus, a quotation from the *Mishnah* begins with the term *Tenan*—"We have been taught." If the source is a *beraita*, the terms *Tanu Rabbanan*, "The Sages taught"—or *Tanna*, "It has been taught"—are used.[11] Both the *Mishnah* and *Beraita* originated in the study centers of Israel, although they were known to the schools in Babylon.[12] Unlike the *Mishnah*, which, with the exception of "Ethics of the Fathers," concerns itself solely with *halachah*, the *Beraita* often is aggadic in content.[13] Moreover, unlike the *Mishnah*, which

---

11. Normally introducing different forms of *beraitot*.

12. This is shown by questions such as: "What is the position in Babylon?" (See *Sukkah* 36a, *Bava Batra* 12a.) Still, it seems that some *beraitot* were formulated in Babylonia itself.

13. The Babylonian Talmud, in *Berachot*, quotes fifty aggadic *beraitot*. Famous compilations of *beraitot* are: *Beraita* of thirty-two rules, being the hermeneutic rules for the *Aggadah* (see pages 167 on); *Beraita de Niddah*, concerning ritual purity; *Beraitot de Avot*, sometimes called *Perek Rabbi Meir* or *Perek Kinyan HaTorah*, later incorporated into the "Ethics of the Fathers"; *Beraita de Rabbi Ada*, on the calendar; *Beraita de Melachoth Hamishkan*, concerning the

rarely quotes Scripture and is, in truth, a legal statement concerning a question raised, the *Beraita* uses a more exegetical format and often employs the hermeneutic rules to establish its rulings. The *Tosefta*—literally, "extension" or "addition"—refers to a collection of *beraitot* that are arranged to follow the order of the *Mishnah*. Originally, the halachic statements of the *tannaim* were often amplified by explanatory notes; this is especially true of statements of Rabbi Akiva,[14] Rabbi Eliezer bar Tzadok,[15] and Rabbi Yehudah. The *Tosefta*[16] is extant to all but three of the tractates of the *Talmud Bavli*; the notes on *Kinnim*, *Midot*, and *Tamid* seem to have been lost. The relationship of the *Tosefta* and the *Mishnah* is not completely clear. While it would seem to be a supplement, it also seems to be an independent work. In general, it would seem that the *Tosefta* constitutes a continuation of the *Mishnah*, which quotes from the *Beraita* in order to shed light on the subject under discussion. Although the *Tosefta* is written in mishnaic Hebrew, there are numerous differences in style and terminology. Like the *Beraita*, the *Tosefta* includes aggadic materials.

Even the authorship of the *Tosefta* is unclear. While it is generally assumed that the *tanna* Rabbi Chiya bar Abba is the author, the Talmud (*Sanhedrin* 86a) states that anonymous *toseftot* are to be attributed to Rabbi Nechemyah. Finally, it is questionable whether the *Tosefta* can be seen as a collection of *beraitot* quoted in the Talmud or whether it

---

erection of the Tabernacle. Most famous is the *Beraita of Rabbi Yishmael* (see page 137).

14. See *Eduyot* 2:1, 7:1; *Kilayim* 1:3; *Orlah* 3:7.

15. *Tosefta, Menachot* 10:23.

16. *Shabbat* 75b, *Avodah Zarah* 43a.

is a separate work, which would account for the differences in terminology and style. The *Tosefta*, first published along with the halachic commentary of Rabbi Yitzchak Alfasi in Venice in 1521, is considered to be the most genuine and can be found printed in the back editions of the *Talmud Bavli.*

Many commentaries have been written on the *Tosefta.* The most important commentaries are those of Rabbi Yitzchak Pardo, *Chasde David* (eighteenth century), and *Chazon Yechezkel,* by Rabbi Yeche'kel Abramsky of London and Jerusalem (1886–1976). A new critical edition was published by S. Lieberman, but was not completed.

BIBLE CRITICISM AND ITS COUNTER-ARGUMENTS

A Short History[1]

One of traditional Judaism's most important claims is its total commitment to the divinity of the text of the Torah, the Pentateuch. It is believed that the other books of *Tanach* may contain a human element since "no two prophets prophesied in the same style."[2] But the Torah came to Moshe from God in a manner that is metaphori-

---

1. This essay was written many years ago. Since then, I have updated it several times. To my pleasant surprise, I have found some similarities between this essay and some of the observations made by Chief Rabbi Dr. Jonathan Sacks from Great Britain. I have incorporated some of his insights from his book *Crisis and Covenant* (New York: Manchester University Press, 1992).

2. T. B. *Sanhedrin* 89a.

cally called "speaking," after which Moshe wrote it down "like a scribe writing from dictation."[3]

In the nineteenth century, this belief came under severe attack by a theory called Higher Criticism or *Quellenscheidung*. This theory denied the divinity of the Torah as a verbal account of God's words to Moshe. Instead, the text was seen to be made up of a conglomeration of various sources compiled over many hundreds of years. As such, it could not have been written by Moshe.[4]

The proponent of this theory was Julius Wellhausen (1844–1918), a German Semitic scholar and professor of theology and oriental studies. Wellhausen, however, was not the first to doubt the "authenticity" of the Torah. In the seventeenth century, the famous Dutch philosopher Benedictus de Spinoza (1632–1677), who was a descendant of the Marranos, stated in his *Tractatus Theologico-Politicus* (and in some letters) that he doubted the Mosaic and the divine authorship of the Torah.[5]

---

3. Maimonides, *Commentary to Mishnah: Introduction to Sanhedrin*, Chap. 10, principle 8.

4. See Rabbi Chaim Hirschensohn's interesting discussion, *Malki Ba-Kodesh*, pt. 2. (St. Louis, MO: Moinester Printing Co., 1921), pp. 215–250, concerning the question of whether it is only the divinity of the Torah that is vital to Judaism or Moshe's "authorship" as well.

5. Benedictus de Spinoza, *A Theologic-Political Treatise* (New York: Dover, 1951), p. 165. Spinoza's conclusion was "that the word of God is faulty, mutilated, tampered with, and inconsistent, that we possess it only in fragments and that the original of the covenant which God made with the Jews has been lost." This observation is, for two reasons, most remarkable: First of all, Spinoza leaves the door open for a possible revelational experience. God *may* have spoken to the Jews, but the original text of that conversation was lost. This seems to conflict with Spinoza's understanding of God who lacks all "person-

Spinoza's major point was that the Bible, like many other literary works, should be seen as the product of human spiritual development, mostly of a primitive nature. While accepting the possibility that some parts of the Torah could have originated with Moshe, he contended that it was only many centuries after Moshe died that the Torah, as we know it today, appeared. Ezra the Scribe (fourth century B.C.E.) should be considered the major author and editor of the Torah as well as of the Books of Joshua, Judges, Samuel, and Kings. Because Ezra died prematurely, these works were never revised and are therefore full of contradictions and repetitions.

Because Spinoza never reached any systematic or clear conclusion, Jean Astruc (1684–1766), a French physician, is considered the real founder of classical Bible Criticism. Being a conservative, Astruc concluded in his work (pub-

---

ality" and henceforth is incapable of *ever* conversing with man. Second, it lays the foundation for what later became the attitude of Reform Judaism's understanding of the Pentateuchal text, which sees the text as some kind of human record of the Jews' encounter with God, and as such, "inspired." This idea contradicts Spinoza's general attitude, which sets the text as "primitive literature."

There are even earlier observations of this kind. One famous "Bible critic" was Chivi Al Balkhi (ninth century) of Persia. See "Geniza Speciments—The Oldest Collection of Bible Difficulties by a Jew," Solomon Schechter, *Jewish Quarterly Review* (old series) 13 (190): 345–374.

In Numbers, (Chap. 16) we read of Korach, the first critic of Moses' authority, who claimed that "the Torah was not from heaven" (Jerusalem Talmud, *Sanhedrin* 10, *halachah* 1). Another earlier critic was Menashe the son of Hizkiah (698–543 B.C.E.) "who examined biblical narratives to prove them worthless." Thus, he jeered: had Moses not anything else to write besides, "and Lothan's sister was Timnah"? (Genesis 36:12) (T. B. *Sanhedrin* 99).

lished anonymously in Brussels and Paris, 1753), *Conjectures sur les memoires originaux, dont il parait que Moses s'est servi pour composer le livre de la Genese*, that Moshe, the redactor of Genesis and the first two chapters of Exodus, made use of two parallel sources and ten fragments written before his time. These primary sources refer to God as *Y-H-V-H* and *Elohim*, respectively.

Although Astruc's conclusion aroused intense opposition, scholars like J. G. Einhorn (1752–1827) attached much importance to his work. It was Julius Wellhausen, however, who gave full impetus to this theory, and his name is identified with the Graf-Wellhausen Hypothesis or Documentary Theory.[6]

Wellhausen wanted to prove that the Torah and the Book of Joshua were, in large measure, "doctored" by priestly canonizers under Ezra in the time of the Second Temple. Their purpose was to perpetuate a single falsehood: Moshe's authorship of the Torah and the central worship, first in the Tabernacle and later in the Temple. According to Wellhausen, there never was a Tabernacle and no revelation at Sinai ever took place. Moshe, if he ever

---

6. Karl Heinrich Graf (1815–1869), a German Protestant Bible scholar on whose work Wellhausen founded his theory. Wellhausen's forerunners were Karl David Ilgen (1763–1834), a German Protestant philologist (*Urkunden des Ersten Buchs Moses*, 1798); Wilhelm Martin Leberecht de Wette (1780–1849), (*Beitraege zur Einleitung in das Alte Testament,* 1806–1807); and Wilhelm Vatke (1806–1882) (*Die Geschichte des Heiligen Schriften des Alten Testaments*), who was highly influenced by Hegel. Vatke laid the foundation for Wellhausen's critique, and the latter admitted that he was indebted to Vatke "for the most and the best" of his own work. Ironically, Vatke, in his later days, retracted his conclusions, undermining many theories that Wellhausen later published!

existed, considered the Deity a local thunder god or mountain god. The Torah had, therefore, to be seen as a complete forgery and not as a verbal account of God's words to Moshe and the People Israel.

In 1875, Wellhausen published his *Prolegomena to the History of Ancient Israel*, an unusual work with almost five thousand textual references covering the whole of the Old Testament. In this work, Wellhausen purports to present the *true* biblical story. Relying heavily on his forerunners, he maintained that four major documents could be identified in the Torah. Each had an individual character, both in content and in general outlook. Though they had been skillfully interwoven, their special characteristics made it possible to trace each source throughout the books of the Torah. The earliest was the *-J-Document* (J being the first letter of the Divine Name, which was used throughout this source and so became essential). It was followed soon after by the *Elohist Document -E-*, in which God is designated as Elohim. These documents were thought to have been composed in the early monarchical period, probably in the ninth or eighth century B.C.E.

The Book of Deuteronomy -D-, which gave a narrative framework to the "Book of the Law," promulgated by King Yoshia in the seventh century B.C.E., was primarily a code of law based on prophetic principles.

The Priestly Code (P), a universal history and extensive legal code, was chiefly concerned with matters of cult and was dominated by the priestly interest in prescribing the correct ritual for each ceremonial occasion. K. H. Graf had already assigned it to the post-exilic age and connected it with the Law of Ezra in the fifth century B.C.E.

Wellhausen's method is clear and straightforward. Every passage that fits his theory is authentic; all others are forgeries. Whenever possible, he points out poor grammar, corrupt vocabulary, and alleged internal inconsistencies. In cases where he felt some "need" to change the plain meaning of a Hebrew word to fit into this theory, he offered what he called "conjectural emendation." The fact that thousands of verses contradicted his theory never disturbed Wellhausen. He contended that there was a master forger or interpolator at work who anticipated Wellhausen's theory and consequently inserted passages and changed verses so as to refute it. Wellhausen assumed that the forger had worked, as it were, with scissors and paste, taking all kinds of liberties: carving up the original texts; moving half a sentence here, a few sentences down, and three and a half sentences there, and a few sentences up, while altogether suppressing and omitting large portions of each source that could not be fitted into this patchwork. He claimed to be more clever than the interpolator could have ever imagined and therefore to have divulged the real truth. This obviously was a wonderful theory, for arguments against Wellhausen's theory thereby became his strongest defenders!

With the publication of this masterpiece, Wellhausen introduced a new era in the world of Bible studies, and most of his contemporaries, as well as their students, accepted his conclusions as gospel. His influence on younger scholars was profound and far-reaching. For a full generation, he dominated Old Testament scholarship, not only in his own country but also in England[7] and America.[8]

The most important histories of Israel and of Hebrew

---

7. See H. Wheeler Robinson, "The Contribution of Great Britain to Old Testament Study," *Expository Times* 41 (1929–1930): 46–50.

8. See J. M. Powis Smith, "The Contribution of the United States to

literature, as well as a host of commentaries and introductions, were based more or less directly on the Wellhausen system. The commentaries edited by Wilhelm Nowack and Karl Marti,[9] as well as those of the *International Critical Commentary on the Holy Scriptures*, were indebted to Wellhausen's theories.[10]

His students continued to use his method and discovered within their teacher's *J*, *E*, *P*, and *D* documents at least thirty additional documents. Each document (especially *J* and *E*) contained a number of older elements; each had undergone a certain amount of "editorial" revision in an effort to coordinate and harmonize the various elements within the style of the original. The additional materials were so extensive that they could not have been the products of only a handful of authors, but rather belonged to a complete religious school.[11]

Old Testament Scholarship," *Expository Times* 41 (1929–1930): 169–171.

9. See *Handkommentar zum Alten Testament*, 15 vols., ed. Wilhelm Nowack (Gottingen, 1892–1903); *Kurzer Handkommentar zum Alten Testament*, 20 vols., ed. Karl Marti (Freiburg, 1897–1904).

10. The following works summarize the literary criticism of the Wellhausen schools: John Edgar McFaydon, "The Present Position of Old Testament Criticism," in Arthur S. Peake, *The People and the Book;* "Modern Criticism," in H. Wheeler Robinson, ed., *Record and Revelation* (Oxford, 1938), pp. 74–109. For these and other important works in the field, see Herbert F. Hahn, *The Old Testament in Modern Research* (Philadelphia: Fortress Press, 1966).

11. One of the most important works following this line is Heinrich Holzinger's *Einleitung in den Hexateuch* (Freiburg, 1893). (According to some scholars, the J and E documents could also be traced through the Book of Joshua, so they spoke of the Hexateuch—six books). See Rudolf Smend's "JE in den geschichtlichen Buchern des Alten Testament," *Zeitschrift fuer die Alttestamentliche Wissenschaft*

The materials were cut even finer. Slowly, more and more forgeries were "discovered," until finally half a dozen documents were found for each single verse, and others even went as far as tracing them through some of the other books of *Tanach* as well. The whole theory degenerated into a reductio ad absurdum. Already in his own day, objective and honest scholars raised objections against Wellhausen's incredible guesswork and fantasies. The chancellor of England, the earl of Halsbury, referred to it in 1915 as "great rubbish."[12] The famous historian Lecky sharply criticized it on the basis that it totally lacked evidence.[13]

In 1908 Wellhausen came under heavy attack by B. D. Eerdmans,[14] while in 1925, Professor Rudolf Kittel, originally an admirer of Wellhausen's theories, stated that "the assumption of forgery may be one of those hypotheses which, once set up, is so often repeated that finally everyone believes it. Who nowadays would take upon himself the odium of being 'behind the times'?"[15]

Among the generations of critics who came to maturity after World War I, new insights provided by later ap-

---

49 (1921). Also see Rudolf Smend, *Die Erzaehlung des Hexateuch auf ihre Quellen des Genesis von neuem untersucht* (Giessen, 1916).

12. See J. H. Hertz, *The Pentateuch and the Haftarahs*, 2nd ed., (London: Soncino Press, 1962), p. 199.

13. Ibid.

14. *Alttestamentliche Studien* (Giessen, 1908, 1910, 1912).

15. See Hertz, *The Pentateuch and the Haftarahs*, p. 939. Kittel remarked on another occasion:

> Speaking for all branches of science we may say that a hypothesis which has stood for half a century has done its duty. Measured by this standard, Wellhausen's theory is as good as the best. However, there is increasing evidence that it has had its day and that those scholars, who from the first expressed serious doubts about it, were right. (ibid., p. 941)

proaches to *Tanach* made the Higher Criticism of the preceding generation seem less than adequate. Slowly it appeared to the scholars that new criteria had to be established and that historical criticism had its limitations. Hugo Gressmann declared that "in our field we need not more but less literary-critical research. The Higher Criticism has generally exhausted the problems which it could and had to solve."[16]

Scholars began ascribing the books of the Torah and the rest of *Nach* to earlier periods and stated that the legal principles of the Torah were already well established in the time of the prophet Samuel.[17] This tendency to regard much of the narrative and law in the Torah as more ancient brought into question what had once been accepted as the assured result of criticism.

The dating of Deuteronomy has always been the central point from which the critics had worked forward and backward to determine the age of the other law codes and documents. The description of Deuteronomy as the immediate inspiration for the reform and centralization of the "cultus" had been the starting point for Wellhausen's reconstruction of the religious history of Israel. With the dating of Deuteronomy, the whole critical edifice stood or fell.

---

16. *"Die Aufgabe der Alttestamentlichen Forschung,"* *Zeitschrift fuer die Alttestamentliche Wissenschaft* 42 (1924): 8. See Hahn, *Old Testament in Modern Research*, p. 28.

17. See, for example, Adam C. Welch, *The Code of Deuteronomy: A New Theory of Its Origin* (London, 1924); see also Theodor Oestreicher, *Das Deuteronomische Grundgesetz* (Guthersloh, 1923) and Edward Robertson, *The Old Testament Problem* (Manchester, 1950).

Adam C. Welsh's earlier dating was, therefore, a major blow to the whole critical school and consequently not easily accepted by his contemporaries.[18] His view was, however, strengthened a decade later by certain conclusions of Otto Eissfeldt regarding the nature and history of the Pentateuchal law.[19]

While the origin of much of the law was being moved back in time, the alternative that the final dates of the law codes should be moved down, was also considered. While Gustav Holscher dated Deuteronomy later than had the Wellhausen school, most scholars were of the opinion that earlier dates were more plausible.[20] It became increasingly clear that Wellhausen's theory of the history of Judaism was inadequate.

This does not suggest that the scholars agreed, for different dates were suggested and new theories contradicting each other were published. What became clear was that Bible Criticism was developing into a chaos of conflicting conjectures producing contradictory results and generating the impression that this type of research was ineffective.[21]

Moreover, in Jewish circles, sharp protest was raised. Although these theories did not impress the greatest Jewish scholars, they highly influenced many assimilated Jewish communities (especially in Germany). The Reform movement, perhaps searching for a means to support its objections against observance, embraced this theory and contributed

---

18. A. Welch, *The Code of Deuteronomy*.

19. *Einleitung in das Alte Testament* (Tübingen, 1943).

20. On Holscher, see his *Komposition und Ursprung des Deuteronomiums Zeitschrift fuer die Alttestamentliche Wissenschaft* 40 (1922).

21. See C. R. North, "Pentateuchal Criticism," in H. H. Rowley, ed., *The Old Testament and Modern Study* (Oxford, 1951).

some of its strongest proponents. Rabbi Samson Raphael Hirsch (1808–1888), in his Torah Commentary,[22] Dr. David Hoffmann (1843–1921),[23] an Orthodox Jewish scholar of great erudition, and Professor Jacob Barth (1851–1914),[24] another outstanding philologist of his time, destroyed much of Wellhausen's theory. Also, Rabbi Yitzchak Isaac Halevi (1847–1914), in his historical works, showed the position of Wellhausen and his admirers to be untenable.[25] In non-Orthodox Jewish circles, Wellhausen also came under sharp attack. One of the most profound analyses in this field was written by Benno Jacob (1862–1945) in his book on Genesis, *Das Erste Buch der Torah*, which concludes (p. 1048) with the words, "The theory that the Book of Genesis is composed of various sources that can be singled out and separated has been rejected."

---

22. S. R. Hirsch, *The Pentateuch, Translated and Explained*, tr. I. Levy (New York: Judaica Press, 1971).

23. *Die wichtigsten Instanzen gegen die Graf-Wellhausensche Hypothese* (vol. 1, 1903; vol. 2, 1916); *Das Buch Leviticus, uebersetzt und erklaert* (1905–1906); *Das Buch Deuteronomium, uebersetzt und erklaert* (1913–1922).

Most important are Hoffmann's refutations of the theory that the Priestly Code was a separate document composed after the Book of Deuteronomy and even after Ezekiel. Hoffmann showed that Leviticus was an earlier work than Deuteronomy and that Ezekiel was a derivative of it, rather than the other way around. Interesting is Hoffmann's belief referring to a statement in the Talmud (T. B. *Gittin* 60a) that Moshe composed the Torah in a series of scrolls that were written down after every revelation and later redacted into a single document.

24. In many unpublished papers. See A. Barth, *Dorenu Mul She'elat Ha-Netzach* (Jerusalem, 1952). In this book some important examples of Hoffmann's and Barth's arguments are presented.

25. *Dorot Harishonim*, 7 vols. (1897–1939, repr. 1967).

Later non-Orthodox scholars, in particular Umberto Cassuto (1883–1951)[26] and Yechezkel Kaufmann (1889–1963)[27]
further demolished the theory, showing that Wellhausen's
observations contradicted his conclusions. Kaufmann's main
contribution lies in his thesis that monotheism was not, as
Wellhausen and others had stated, a gradual departure from
paganism, but an entirely new development. Israel's monotheism began with Moshe and was a complete revolution in
religious thought.

Why were these earlier-mentioned theories ever accepted? In Wellhausen's day the theory of evolution was
dominant. Darwin had won the day, and any discipline,
including literature, that accepted the theory of evolution
was welcomed with open arms. Furthermore, the philosopher Hegel (1770–1831) had left a deep impression in
German and European culture by contending that all of

---

26. *The Documentary Hypothesis and the Composition of the
Pentateuch*, trans. Israel Abrahams (English ed. [Jerusalem: Magnes
Press, Hebrew University, 1961–1972]) or "The Theory of Docu-
ments." Cassuto concludes (pp. 100–101):

> I have not shown that it was possible to solve the problems in a different
> way from that of the documentary theory. I have shown that one must
> necessarily solve them otherwise and that it is important to solve them
> according to this system. I did not prove that the pillars are weak or that
> none of them is decisive. I have proved that they are not pillars at all,
> that they are non-existent and imaginary. Hence, I have arrived at the
> conclusion that the complete negation of the theory of documents is
> justified.

Other books by Cassuto in this field are *La questione della genesi*
(1934), his commentaries on the books of Genesis and Exodus, and
many other important papers.

27. *Toledot Ha-Emunah Ha-Yisraelit* (1937); abridged version in
English, *The Religion of Israel*, translated and condensed by M.
Greenberg (Jerusalem: Magnes Press, Hebrew University, 1960).

history is a development from lower to progressively higher stages. It was therefore assumed that the Jewish religion developed from idolatry, and having passed through many intermediate stages, the earlier one of which was the Torah, reached the ultimate pure monotheism of latter days.

Special mention should be made of the famous archaeologist William F. Albright.[28] He convincingly demonstrated that archaeological research did not support, and in fact often contradicted, this view of history. In many of his works, Albright destroyed the very foundations upon which Wellhausen's edifice had been erected.

In retrospect, it is rather surprising that Wellhausen's theories were accepted for so long. How is it possible that so many scholars promulgated similar theories and totally ignored or attacked those who differed?[29] Albright and others have pointed out that besides Hegelian theories, other motivations kept the Wellhausen tradition alive. Christian scholars were eager to attribute greater significance to the New Testament than the Old. In order to make this plausible, it had to be proven that large portions of the Torah were falsified and were not to be taken seriously.

When anti-Semitic tendencies became stronger in the immediate pre-Hitler days, many scholars felt the need to use the Wellhausen and other theories to give a final blow

---

28. William F. Albright, *From the Stone Age to Christianity* (Baltimore: Anchor, 1957), pp. 84, 118–119.

29. W. L. Baxter (1841–1937), a Scottish Bible scholar, wrote, "Witnesses are reliable when they testify in favor of the critics, but their veracity is promptly impeached if their testimony is on the other side" (*Sanctuary and Sacrifice* [1892]); quoted in J. H. Hertz, *The Pentateuch and the Haftarahs* (London: Soncino Press, 1962), p. 556.

to the Jewish People, religion, and Bible. When Friedrich Delitzch (1850–1922) delivered a lecture called "Babel und Bibel," in which *Tanach* was considered devoid of any religious or moral value, Kaiser Wilhelm congratulated him for helping "to dissipate the nimbus of the Chosen People."[30]

The Germans, convinced of their status as *Herrenvolk* suffered from Teutomania and believed that anything must either be German or valueless, according to William F. Albright. Solomon Schechter, who headed the Jewish Theological Seminary in its earlier and more Orthodox days, exclaimed that Higher Criticism was no more than higher anti-Semitism. Albright asked the question, how was it possible that the "scientific community" accepted many of these theories without critical assessment, knowing that many of the scholars had shown that their personal anti-Semitism completely overshadowed their intellectual honesty.[31]

While Wellhausen and other schools of Higher Criticism slowly lost their credibility, a new school developed, introducing the anthropological approach. It saw religion as a general feature of the cultural history of mankind and made it possible to view Torah (and the rest of the *Tanach*) in the broad light of the universal experience of humanity. The anthropological approach to the study of religion was first applied to the whole of *Tanach* by William Robertson Smith.[32]

---

30. On Delitzch, see *Babel und Bibel* (Leipzig, 1902). See also Hugo Winckler, *Géschichte Israels*, vol. 2 (Berlin, 1900).

31. See *History, Archeology and Christian Humanism* (Baltimore: Anchor, 1942).

32. See W. R. Smith, *Lectures on the Religion of the Semites* (Edinburgh, 1889).

The general trend of Smith's interpretation was determined by the view, common to anthropologists, that religion was an integral part of life, not to be treated as an entity separate from a people's social and political culture. Smith suggested that to understand the basic foundations on which the primitive Semitic religions were based, one had to make a thorough study of the ritual (sacrificial) institutions. Since these tended to remain unchanged from the earliest times to the historical period, they reflected the fundamental beliefs that stood at the beginning of religious development. He subsequently found "a consistent unity of scheme," which ran through the whole historical development, from a crude and imperfect understanding of religious truth to a clear and full perception of its spiritual significance.

Working along the lines of Robertson Smith, Sir James G. Frazer published his famous work *The Golden Bough* (1890), which grew from two volumes in the first edition to twelve, twenty years later. This work studies the traditional rites and superstitious practices of primitive peoples and presents a great number of suppositions regarding the evolution of primitive religions. However, the vast accumulation of illustrative data is frequently more impressive than the conclusions drawn from them.

The faults of Frazer's methodology were those of nineteenth-century anthropologists in general, for they failed to understand that monotheistic religion could not be explained as developing out of primitive cults. While other theories were suggested by Wilhelm Wundt[33] and

33. *Voelkerpsychologie*, 2 vols. (Leipzig, 1909).

Johannes Pedersen,[34] these approaches failed to explain the transition from a primitive mentality to the highly developed conceptions of a later age, especially in the framework of the *Tanach* with its distinctive features and its religion.

In the meantime, another school had emerged: the Religio-Historical School of Interpretation. This field of research is known in German as *Religionsgeschichte*. The term "Comparative Religion," which is sometimes applied to it, connotes the early anthropological approach to religion and fails to indicate the importance of its historical aspect. Generally speaking, it is the application of the historical method to the study of religion, under the influence of positivist principles of investigation combined with the use of the comparative method. Auguste Comte made the point that one had to take the concrete and actual into consideration in philosophy; thus, this positive approach became influential in religious studies as well.[35]

No longer were broad generalizations about religion to be permitted. Rather, careful study of the historical manifestation of religion was researched. With the recovery of religious literature of the Far East, the publication of large numbers of inscriptions from the Graeco-Roman world, and the critical reexamination of the surviving documents of classical literature, the new approach acquired rich material with which to work.

The major point that this school propounded was that these discoveries showed that the ancient Orient represented a high cultural maturity—something denied by

---

34. *Israel: Its Life and Culture* (London, 1926; repr., 1940).

35. See E. Hardy, *Zur Geschichte der vergleichenden Religion forschung*, Archiv fur Religionswissenschaft 4 (1901).

Wellhausen and others—and that Torah (and *Nach*) had been the outcome of this maturity. Some scholars rejected the evolutionary view of Israel's religious history and described the religion of *Tanach* as having already reached the full development of its most important features in the age of Moshe. Paul Volz argued that the high ethical principles of the Decalogue, which were usually attributed to prophetic inspiration, were known to the Israelites in Moshe's time.[36] On the basis of the evidence, Volz declared that the Mosaic authorship of the Decalogue could easily be established and that it was as advanced as the later teachings of the Prophets. The most significant attempt to restore the traditional view of the Mosaic religion was made by Bruno Baentsch, who claimed that traces of monotheism can be found in other religions of the ancient Orient.[37] Moreover, the discovery of the Hammurabi Code in 1902—a code of ethics of a remarkably high standard—completely changed the picture of the ancient Far East. Some suggested that this code was the forerunner of the Torah law, a view that was later rejected.[38] The difficulty of this approach is that Hammurabi's monotheistic ideas do not seem to agree with the monotheistic idea of the one Invisible God described in the Old Testament. Also, the laws of the Torah often contradicted the Hammurabi Code.

---

36. Moses, *Ein Beitrag zur Untersuchung ueber die Urspruenge der Israelitischen Religion* (Tübingen, 1907).

37. *Altorientalischer und Israelitischer Monotheismus* (Tübingen, 1906), p. I. For an interesting comparison, see Maimonides, *Mishneh Torah: Hilchot Avodah Zarah*, introduction.

38. For an overview of this debate, see Henry Biberfeld, *Universal Jewish History* (Jerusalem: Feldheim, 1948), appendix, pp. 129–156.

As was the case with other schools, speculation became more and more rife. It became clear that the Torah and the other books of *Tanach* could best be understood on their own merits, without extrabiblical evidence. Israel's religious history had characteristic features of its own that could not be understood without primary attention being given to evidence derived from the Bible itself.

In his classic work *Critique of Religion and Philosophy* (Princeton, NJ: Princeton University Press, 1978) p. 377, Walter Kaufmann discusses Wellhausen's as well as other forms of Higher Criticism and shows one of the major failures of these schools in the following observation:

> Imagine a Higher Critic analyzing Goethe's Faust, which was written by a single human being in the course of sixty years. The scenes in which the heroine of Part One is called Gretchen would be relegated to one author; the conflicting conceptions of the role of Mephistopheles would be taken to call for further divisions, and the Prologue in Heaven would be ascribed to a later editor, while the prelude on the stage would be referred to yet a different author. Our critic would have no doubt whatsoever that Part Two belongs to a different age and must be assigned to a great many writers with widely different ideas. The end of Act IV, for example, points to an anti-Catholic author who lampoons the church, while the end of Act V was written by a man, we should be told, who, though probably no orthodox Catholic, was deeply sympathetic to Catholicism. Where do we find more inconsistencies in style and thought and plan: in Goethe's Faust or in the Five Books of Moses?[39]

---

39. Herman Wouk remarks in his book *This is My God* (Glasgow: Williams Collins Sons and Co., 1973) p. 291:

"Literary analysis has been used for generations by obsessive men to prove that everybody but Shakespeare wrote Shakespeare. I believe

In short, inconsistencies of style and text cannot be taken as proof that a work was written by more than one author.

This is not the only observation Kaufmann makes concerning the nature of *Tanach*. After asking how *Tanach* should be read, he answers (p. 383):

> Any suggestion of the close affinity of religion and poetry is generally met with the retort that a religious scripture is not mere poetry, which is true enough. But at the very least one might accord a religious scripture the same courtesy which one extends to poetry and recall Goethe's dictum: "What issues from a poetic mind wants to be received by a poetic mind. Any cold analyzing destroys the poetry and does not generate any reality. All that remains are potsheds which are good for nothing and only incommode us."

His observation is true in its critical attitude not only toward Higher Criticism but toward most of the other schools of Old Testament research as well. The different schools approached the Old Testament as a collection of historical facts from which to draw only such conclusions as the facts warranted.

It was the theological approach to Old Testament studies that, after long being neglected, made this point. The real value of Torah and the other books of *Tanach* is essentially religious in content and outlook and, as such, the critical schools missed the point the Torah was making. Consequently, they used the wrong tools of investigation. Only an approach to the world of Torah and *Nach* that did justice to what it said about God, man, and the meaning of

---

literary analysis could be used to prove that I wrote both *David Copperfield* and *Farewell to Arms*. I wish it were sound!"

life could offer a means of arriving at the permanent significance of the Torah.

This point, for ages emphasized by traditional Jewish scholars, had been made by Otto Eissfeldt[40] and later by Walter Eihrodt,[41] albeit these studies were also heavily influenced by New Testament sentiments. Still these studies are of major importance, for it took courage to present this view at a time when the Torah and the rest of *Tanach* was rejected as a "Jewish book" of no significance to Germans and Christians. It is only in the last twenty to thirty years, especially in America and England, that full emphasis was given to this approach. One of the most important books accepting the true significance of Torah and *Nach* was written by H. H. Rowley and is entitled, *The Relevance of the Bible.*[42] Norman H. Snaith's important work *The Distinctive Ideas of the Old Testament* (London, 1944) also drew attention to the uniqueness of the Hebrew tradition.

In 1946, the secular German literary critic and theorist Erich Auerbach published an essay called "Odysseus Scar." In this important study he explored the nature of the biblical narrative. In comparing it with the Homeric way of narrative, Auerbach shows how much the biblical narrative

---

40. *Israelitisch-Juedische Religionsgeschichte und alttestament-liche Theologie, Zeitschrift fuer die Alttestamentliche Wissenschaft 44* (1962): 1–12.

41. *Theologie des Alten Testaments,* 3 vols. (Leipzig, 1933–1939). See "Guide to Understanding the Bible," *Journal of Biblical Literature* 65 (1946): 205–207.

42. *The Relevance of the Bible* (London, 1942). See also his *Rediscovery of the Old Testament* (London, 1946); Frank Glen Lankard, *The Bible Speaks to Our Generation* (New York, 1941); and Wyatt A. Smart, *Still the Bible Speaks* (New York, 1948).

is different from the Greek epic. Unlike Homer, the former is "fraught with background," unspoken words, and silence. It can only be understood on its own terms. It is in need of constant interpretation, claims absolute truth, and draws its reader into the world of religious experience. But above all, it is not art but *command* that strikes the student as the most important characteristic of the biblical story.

Auerbach maintained that the text of the Torah clearly shows that it wants to be "heard" as an encounter in which God speaks to man. It was not the later Rabbis or theologians who invented such a claim, but the very intent of the text itself.[43] Auerbach's essay gave impetus to much novel research in the field of Bible studies. Most important are the works of Robert Alter,[44] Roland Barthes,[45] and Harold Fisch.[46] All of them show a remarkable sensitivity for the authentic meaning of the text, reflecting a more "Jewish" approach when discussing some of the most difficult biblical narratives. Meir Weiss,[47] Meir Sternberg,[48] and Shimon bar Efrat,[49] using literary analysis, have dealt with the intricate subtleties of the biblical texts, uncovering

43. Erich Auerbach, *Mimesis* (Princeton, NJ: Princeton University Press, 1971).

44. *The Art of Biblical Literature* (London: George Allen and Unwin, 1981).

45. *Image, Music, Text* (London: Fontana, 1977).

46. *A Remembered Future* (Bloomington, IN: Indiana University Press, 1984).

47. *The Craft of Biblical Narrative* (Hebrew) (Jerusalem: Molad, 1962).

48. *The Poetics of Biblical Narrative* (Bloomington, IN: Indiana University Press, 1985).

49. *Narrative Art in the Bible* (Sheffield, U.K.: Almond Press, 1989).

more traditional interpretations. While these developments fall short in the eyes of traditional Judaism, they indicate a more objective, honest approach toward the Torah. The authors, dissociating themselves from the old schools of Bible Criticism, tried hard to hear the genuine "voice" of the Torah, and therefore moved closer to the traditional Jewish approach then any of their predecessors.

What has become increasingly clear is that the problems raised by Spinoza, Wellhausen, and others were well known to the traditional Jewish commentaries throughout the ages. What is different is the *method* by which these problems were solved. The Bible critics took it for granted that the biblical texts were texts like any other and therefore to be explored by the normal criteria of literary research. Axiomatically, without sincerely considering other possibilities, they rejected the idea of a "personal" God, the possibility of verbal revelation and the authority of tradition in interpreting these texts.[50]

---

50. Most enlightening is Spinoza's observation that some texts of the Torah, such as the ones in Genesis 12:6; 22:14, and Deuteronomy 1:2, must have been written many years after Moshe's death, since they reveal information that refers to latter days. Spinoza relies here on the famous Jewish commentator Ibn Ezra (1088–1167), who wrote that these verses were "mysteries" about "which the wise should be silent" (on Deuteronomy 1:2). The traditional understanding of Ibn Ezra, as also confirmed by the modern Jewish scholar Samuel David Luzzatto (ShaDaL) (1800–1865), is that these passages must be understood as prophetic and anticipating the future. Here, the differences between the traditional approach and the ones of criticism become apparent. The critics were obviously not prepared to accept the "prophetic" dimension as suggested by tradition and consequently concluded that these passages could not have been written by Moshe. In other words, it was not the problems themselves that caused these differences of

Mordechai Breuer, an Orthodox Jewish scholar, goes even as far as to state that he is prepared to accept much of the critic's findings. Using an unusual hybrid of neo-Kantian thought and Jewish mysticism, he concludes (not without major problems) that the traditional and the critical views are both "true." He distinguishes between the Torah as a "document" (phenomenon) and as words "written in black and white fire" (noumenon).[51] Thereupon, he asks why the word of God came down to man in such a way that it seems to support some of the critic's findings. He answers that this was necessary to show all the different religious perspectives of the Torah. For example, when discussing the different Pentateuchal names for God (one of the most important foundations of the Wellhausen theory for the existence of "documents"), he explains that this is connected with the different attributes of God as understood by the Jewish tradition. Sometimes God appears to us as a merciful God (the Tetragrammaton), at another time as Judge (*Elohim*). These, however, are the ways in which God *appears* to us (phenomenon). But behind all this is the mystical meaning of the Torah, which *unites* all these names (noumenon).[52]

The famous Rabbi Avraham Yitzchak Kook (1865–

---

opinion but the very *approach* to the text that created these controversies.

51. See pp. 27–34.

52. "Emunah U-Madda Be-Parashanut Ha-Mikra," *Deot, Cheker Ha-Mikra Be-Machshavah Ha-Yehudit Ha-Datit He-Chaddashah*, 11 (1959): 18–25, 12 (1960): 13–27. See also Zvi Kurzweil, *The Modern Impulse of Traditional Judaism* (New York, 1985), pp. 79–91.

See also the critical comments by Jacob Katz, Uriel Simon, Joseph Heinemann, Meir Weiss, Dr. Halperin, and Jacov Zeidman in *Deot* 13 (1961): 14–23.

1935) added that there could essentially be no conflict between the scientific approach and the religious one. This was due to the fact that the Torah was primarily concerned with the knowledge of God and the sanctification of life, not with astronomy or geology. Scientific statements in the Torah and later prophets have to be understood as parables and analogies and not as primitive scientific statements.[53]

The greatest problem with Bible Criticism must, however, be seen in its failure to understand the crucial role the Oral Torah plays in the proper understanding of the Pentateuchal text. As stated before, the text can be understood only when read in its own spirit. Looking a little deeper, this means that it can be understood only when one "hears" its words in "the doing," in other words, when one "lives" it and is part of its weltanschauung. One can *read* the text of the "Pentateuch" and remain unaffected; in contrast, one can *listen* to the "Torah" as a religious act and be involved.[54]

More and more Bible scholars in the latter years admit that this is possible only when one studies the Pentateuchal text from *within* a certain tradition on which the text heavily relies. This is indeed one of the most important claims made by the Jewish tradition. Many Jewish commentators have convincingly argued that it is wholly *impossible* to understand the text without such a tradition. The point that they were making is that not only is it

---

53. See Ish Shalom, *Avraham Isaac Kook: Between Rationalism and Mysticism* (Hebrew) Tel Aviv: Am Oved, 1990), pp. 98–115. Also see Zvi Yaron, *The Philosophy of Rabbi Kook* (Jerusalem: Eliner Library, 1991), pp. 188–189.

54. See also Franz Rosenzweig, *On Jewish Learning*, ed. Nahum Glatzer (New York: Schocken, 1955).

possible to read the text through the eyes of an Oral Tradition but that the intended meaning is the very one suggested by the Oral Tradition. While some modern commentaries may not go as far as arguing for a talmudic Oral Tradition, they do agree that the Pentateuchal text alludes to a comprehensive Oral Tradition that preceded it.[55]

In his famous commentary on the Torah, Rabbi Samson Raphael Hirsch argues that the Written Torah is the masterful "synopsis" of the Oral Tradition as laid down in the Talmud: first God instructed Moshe concerning the Oral Torah, and only afterward did He give him a dictation of the written text. In much the same way that lecture notes can help us to reproduce the original lecture only *after* we

---

55. See H. S. Nijberg, *Studien zum Hoseabuch: Zugleich ein Beitrag zur Kehrung des Problems der Alttestestamentlichen Textkri-tik*. (Uppsala: Uppsala Universitets, Arskrift, 1935). For an overview, see E. Nielsen, *Oral Tradition: A Modern Problem in the Old Testament Introduction, Studies in Biblical Theology* 11 (Chicago, 1954); C. Stuhlmueller, "The Influence of Oral Tradition upon Exegeses and the Senses of Scripture," *Catholic Biblical Quarterly* 20 (1958): 299–326; B. Gerhardsson, *Memory and Manuscript; Oral Tradition and Written Transmission in Rabbinic Judaism and Early Christianity*, Acta seminarii neo-testamentici upsaliensis 22 (Uppsala, 1961); by the same author, *Muendliche und Schriftliche Tradition der Prophetenbuecher*, Theologische Literaturzeitung 17 (1961), pp. 216–220; and Michael Fishbane, *Biblical Interpretation in Ancient Israel* (Oxford: Clarendon Press, 1985). Herbert Schneidau's *Sacred Discontent* (Berkeley, CA: University of California Press, 1977) argues that textual tensions and apparent inconsistencies function as ways through which the reader becomes involved in the text. See also the important observations by J. F. Molitor, *Philosophie der Geschichte oder ueber die Tradition*, vol. 1 (Frankfurt, 1857), in which the author stresses that fact that in ancient times, the relationship of the written word and the spoken word was very different and much more involved than in modern times.

have heard it in full, so the Written Torah can only be understood after one has studied the Oral Torah in all its aspects: "It is not the Oral Law (Torah) which has to seek the guarantee of its authenticity in the Written Law (Torah); on the contrary, it is the Written Law (Law) which has to look for its warrant in the Oral Tradition."[56]

Yeshayahu Leibowitz, one of the most controversial Orthodox scholars of today, argues on similar lines: The sanctity and the uniqueness of the Written Torah cannot be inferred from any quality of the text itself.[57] Getting very close to the kabbalistic tradition, he states that *as* literature, the Written Torah is inferior to Shakespeare; *as* philosophy, it cannot compete with Plato or Kant, and *as* "moral education," Sophocles' *Antigone* is superior![58] Where the critics went wrong was to try to read and understand the "notes" without having heard the lecture. This would obviously perforce lead to the most absurd propositions. To read the Torah as an autonomous text is therefore an unforgivable mistake: "This kind of bibliolatry is Lutheran," said Leibowitz.

---

56. See the introduction on Hirsch's commentary on the Torah by Dayan Dr. I. Grunfeld in Samson Raphael Hirsch, *The Pentateuch, Translation and Commentary*, Genesis (New York: Judaica Press, 1971), pp. viii–xxx.

57. *Judaism, Human Values, and the Jewish State* (Cambridge, MA: Harvard University Press, 1992), pp. 11–12.

58. Rabbi Simeon said:

Alas for the man who regards the Torah as a book of mere tales and everyday matters! If that were so, even we could compose a Torah dealing with everyday affairs and of *even greater excellence*. Nay, even the princes of the world possess books of *greater worth* which we could use as a model for composing some such Torah. The Torah, however, contains it all, its words are supernal truth. (*Zohar* III:152a) (italics added)

Important in a different way are the observations of
Rabbi J. B. Soloveitchik, who deals with several "contradictions" in the Pentateuchal text. These, he shows, are not
the result of having been written by a different hand but
are rather evidence for different and paradoxical dimensions in the human condition with which the religious
personality has to struggle.[59]

What can be said with certainty is that honest Bible
scholars no longer maintain that the Torah is the result
of different fragments edited and reedited. The Torah is
now taken to be Mosaic in origin and content, and it
has been acknowledged that much of this tradition was
already well established in pre-Mosaic times. Although this
position has moved considerably in the direction of the
Jewish traditional view, it has definitely not thrown in
the towel to the tradition concerning the verbal infallibility
of the Torah.

A sister school of "Higher Criticism," known as "Lower
Criticism," has come to the fore within the last centuries.
This school has taken upon itself to question the reliability
of the text based on outside sources such as the Septuagint.
The proponents of this school have developed recensions
based on variant readings that they regard as more reliable
than the traditional text. As later scholars have pointed out,
these recensions have been accomplished by offering baseless emendations and conjectures that are without rational
foundation.

Nijberg has shown that these methods of critical analysis
were in vogue in the latter part of the nineteenth century

---

59. "The Lonely Man of Faith," *Tradition* 7:2 (Summer 1965).

and were often employed in classical philology.[60] He mentions a scholar who used this approach to analyze *Paradise Lost* and came to the conclusion that this work was full of later interpolations. He also speaks of a scholar who made seven hundred revisions in Horace and finally published a volume that contained, in effect, a revised version of the poems which, while hardly being improved upon, turned out to be rather amusing.

Regarding "Lower Criticism," Nijberg observes:

> The most insane arbitrariness in this field is slowly begin-
> ning to recede. . . . The first step to such reflection, how-
> ever, must be the recognition of the errors in method that
> have so far been made in the treatment of the text. . . .
> In the end we should remember a good old philological
> rule: When one does not understand something, one should
> first mistrust oneself and not the text.[61]

As has been clearly demonstrated, the Jewish Sages and later scribes were extraordinarily careful to guarantee that no changes were made in the text of the Torah and *Nach*.[62] Their precision was such that today, despite the fact that the Jews were dispersed to almost every corner of the globe and their communities often had little contact with each other, there are no essential differences in the text of the Torah scrolls. The Torah text that Jews brought from Cochin, India, is identical to the text used by the community in Cracow, Poland.

---

60. H. S. Nijberg, quoted in Walter Kaufmann, *Critique of Religion and Philosophy* (Princeton, NJ: Princeton University Press, 1958), p. 384.

61. Ibid., p. 385.

62. See pages 18 on.

Still, there are differences in *some* ancient versions. This is not surprising: from the earliest times many individuals wrote scrolls for *private* study. These private scrolls often contained emendations that reflected the Oral Torah connected with a specific phrase or verse. This was done so as to remind oneself of the correct interpretation of the text. These scrolls were not intended for public use and were, in fact, ritually unfit for use because of these changes. Jewish tradition informs us that one of the great earlier Sages, Rabbi Meir, used to mark his allegorical explanations in his own private scroll as a means of remembering them.[63] There is no evidence of these private scrolls ever becoming mixed up with the traditional written Torah, for Jewish law is extremely precise and exacting in its demands of the scrolls used for the Torah reading in the synagogues. Scribes who prepared Torah scrolls were and are required to use a copy of the traditional Torah text as a source and are prohibited from writing a scroll from memory.

It is possible that non-Jewish editions of the Bible, such as the Septuagint or Vulgate, may have used private scrolls as a source, and this would account for the deviations found there.

But perhaps the most devastating blow to these critical theories was delivered by Rabbi Chaim Heller (1878–1960). Not only had he mustered the Oral Torah to the extent that he was one of the greatest talmudic scholars of his time, but he also knew every extant ancient Bible translation in its original target language, whether Aramaic, Greek, Latin, or Syriac. In his *Untersuchungen ueber die*

---

63. See Nachmanides on Ecclesiastes (*Kitvei Ha-Ramban*).

Peschitta (1911), he took issue with those who concluded that apparent divergences from the Torah in their possession were due to *variae lectiones* in the ancient texts. Not so, he asserted. Every translation is a commentary, and the variations result from the translator preferring one explanation in the Oral Torah to another. Thus, the differences were exegetical rather than textual. He further showed that all the apparent differences stemmed from the thirty-two exegetical rules of biblical interpretation enumerated by Rabbi Elazar ben Rabbi Shimon.[64] In the above-mentioned study, he gives examples showing how the translator employed each rule in his version.

Dr. David Hoffmann points out that even to accept the contention that the text in certain places of the Torah has been altered would still leave no choice but to accept the traditional version as the one closest to the original, for "every conjecture, no matter how many exegetical and historical and critical arguments it may be supported, does not offer us even the probability that the Prophet or the writer of Scripture wrote in this form and not in the text before us."[65]

---

64. For a short overview of these thirty-two exegetical rules, see Hermann L. Strack, *Introduction to the Talmud and Midrash* (New York: Atheneum, 1978), pp. 95–98.

65. Quoted by M. Kapustin in "Biblical Criticism, a Traditionalist View," in *Challenge, Torah Views on Science and Its Problems*, ed. C. Domb and A. Carmel (Jerusalem: Feldheim, 1976), pp. 426–427. See also Chaim Hirschensohn, *Malki baKodesh*, vol. 2 (St. Louis, MO: Moinster Printing Co., 1921), pp. 215–250, who points to a talmudic passage (tractate *Sofrim* 6:3) that states that there were three Torah scrolls in the Temple court that contained slight textual misreadings and that the correct reading was determined on the principle of following the majority.

On many occasions, seemingly "unintelligible" words of *Tanach* have suddenly become understandable in light of research and comparison with other oriental languages. It is due to this late research that the traditional text has grown in stature and respectability in the eyes of critical scientists and is increasingly preferred in many cases over other versions that were once considered accurate.

In summation, while Bible Criticism has found its way back to a more traditional approach, as far as the Pentateuchal text, its date, and its origin are concerned, one should never forget that the question of the *verbal infallibility* of the Torah as the expression of an explicit divine revelation lies outside the scope of any literal or scientific investigation.

The modern crisis of religion, of which Bible Criticism is a symptom, is due to the misapplication of scientific research to aspects of reality, like faith and revelation, to which they do not belong. Laws deduced from the world of nature cannot explain supernatural phenomena, in the same way that no scientist would ever accept the position that the rules governing why organic materials react to certain stimuli could apply to inorganic substances. Both are intrinsically different in nature and can only be understood as two completely different systems.

The Torah is a covenantal document and is to be studied as such. It does not inform us of "facts," "history," or "anthropology." It reveals a continuous encounter between God and man, which was set in motion with the revelation at Sinai. It cannot be read but only studied, proclaimed, heard, and experienced. The encounter with its text is a religious act and therefore prefaced with a blessing. For this reason it is untouched and unimpaired by the results of Bible Criticism.

What is important to realize is that the struggle over the origin of the text of the Torah was, and is, not just an academic one. It is foremost a battle between "divine authority" and "human autonomy." Modernity, starting with Spinoza, was looking for ways through which it could liberate itself from the biblical worldview and its far-reaching divine demands. Since it was this biblical text that made man submissive to divine authority, it was necessary to start an assault on the biblical text itself and strip it of its divine nature. The interplay between sociology and theology is a complex one, but what is clear is that *what* man will find and conclude is greatly dependent on the question of *why* he is looking. The Torah can be made to yield whatever meaning its interpreters like to assign to it.

This fact is also of great importance in understanding what has happened within the Jewish community over the last two hundred years. In an attempt to become part of the secular world, many Jews looked to Bible Criticism as a most forceful (and welcome) source of legitimization for the break with tradition. In reference to what Heinrich Heine once called "the portable fatherland of the Jew," the Torah was historicized, secularized, and fragmentized. It is hardly possible to ignore the fact that since the day when this fragmentation theory made inroads into the Jewish community, the Jewish People has lost much of its *élan vital*. It resulted in "nontraditional" forms of Judaism and eventually caused Jews to turn their backs on tradition altogether. The secularization of the Torah had led to secularization of the people.

SHORT INDEX OF THE WRITTEN TORAH

Bereshit—*Genesis*

Part 1

1:1–11:32.	*Universal History*
1:1–6:4	Creation; from Adam to Noach.

1:1–2:3	The story of creation; the *Shabbat*.
1:28	Commandment to multiply.
2:4–3:24	Adam and Chava in the garden of Eden.
2:16	Commandments for the entire human race indicated (*Mitsvot shel bene Noach*).
4:1–16	Kain and Hevel.
4:17–26	The genealogy of Kain; the rise of civilization.
5:1–32	The line of Adam to Noach.
6:1–4	The "sons of God" and the daughters of men.

6:5–11:32	*From Noach to Avraham*

6:5–8:22	The flood.
9:1–17	The blessing and the covenant with man.
9:18–29	Noach's drunkenness.
10:1–32	The lineage of all the nations.
11:1–9	The tower of Babel.
11:10–32	The line of Shem to Avraham.

Part 2

12:1–50:26   *Patriarchal History*

12:1–25:18	Avraham.
12:1–9	The call of Avraham; the migration to Canaan.
12:10–20	Avraham and Sarah in Egypt.
13:1–18	Avraham and Lot.
14:1–24	The battle of the Kings; Avraham blessed by Malchizedek.
15:1–21	The covenant with Avraham.
16:1–16	Avraham, Sarah, and Hagar; Divine promises regarding Ishmael.
17:1–27	*The covenant and commandment concerning circumcision.*
18:1–33	Avraham and the three angels; the intercession for Sodom.
19:1–29	The destruction of Sodom and Gomorrah.
19:30–38	Lot and his daughters; the birth of Moab and Ammon.
20:1–18	Avraham and Sarah at Gerar.
21:1–8	The birth of Yitschak.
21:9–21	The expulsion of Hagar and Ishmael.
21:22–34	Avraham and Avimelech at Beer Sheva.
22:1–19	The binding of Yitschak (*Akedah*).
22:20–24	The line of Nachor.
23:1–20	Death of Sarah, the purchase of Machpela, and the burial of Sarah.
24:1–67	The marriage of Yitschak to Rivka.
25:1–6	The line of Keturah.

| 25:7–18 | The death and burial of Avraham; the line of Ishmael. |

25:19–36:43   *Yitschak and Jacov*

25:19–34	The birth of Yacov and Esav; sale of birthright.
26:1–33	Yitschak, Rivka, and Avimelech at Gerar.
26:34–35	Esav's Hittite wives.
27:1–28:5	Yacov's "deception" of Yitschak.
28:6–9	Esav's wife of Ishmael.
28:10–22	Yacov at Beth El.
29:1–30:43	Yacov with Laban; his marriage to Leah and Rachel.
31:1–54	Yacov's flight from Laban.
32:1–33	Yacov at Machanaim and Penuel.
(32:25–33)	Yacov wrestles with the angel.
(32:33)	Prohibition of the sciatic nerve.
33:1–20	Yacov meets Esav; his purchase of land at Shechem.
34:1–20	The rape of Dinah.
35:1–15	Yacov revisits Beth El.
35:16–29	Family affairs in Canaan.
36:1–43	The lines of Esav and Seir, the Chorite; early kings of Edom.

37:1–50:26   *Joseph and His Brothers*

37:1–36	Joseph and his brothers.
38:1–30	Judah and Tamar.
39:1–23	Joseph in Potiphar's house.

40:1–23	Joseph in prison.
41:1–57	Pharaoh's dream; Joseph's rise to power; the years of abundance; and the start of the famine.
42:1–44:34	Joseph encounters his brothers.
45:1–28	Joseph discloses his identity.
46:1–47:10	The migration of the Israelites to Egypt.
47:11–27	Joseph's agrarian policy.
48:1–50:21	Yacov's farewell blessings; his death and burial.
50:22–26	The death of Joseph.

Shemot—*Exodus*

Part 1

1:1–18:27	*The Liberation*
1:1–2:25	The enslavement of Israel and the advent of Moshe.
3:1–7:13	The call and commissioning of Moshe.
7:14–11:10	The plagues.
12:1–12:2	The precept of establishing the months.
12:3–12:51	Firstborn plague and Pesach rites and laws.
13:1–13:16	Precepts of redeeming of firstborn man and animal.
13:17–15:21	Exodus and the miracle of the Red Sea.
15:22–17:16	Trouble and deliverance on the way to Sinai.

(16:29–16:36)	Some Shabbat laws (Manna).
18:1–18:27	Jetro's visit and the organization of the people.

Part 2

19:1–24:18   *The Covenant*

19:1–20:21	The revelation at Sinai and the Decalogue.
20:22–23:33	(A). Criminal and Civil Law (the Hebrew servant, the sorcerer, proselyte, orphan, and widow; court rules, penalties, damages, plaintiff, defendant, financial matters, sovereign leaders). (B). Agriculture laws, dietary laws, festivals.
24:1–24:18	The covenant encounter (Moshe's forty days on Mount Sinai).

Part 3

25:1–40:38   *The Tabernacle and the Golden Calf*

25:1–27:19	Orders to build the Tabernacle (activities and actors in the Sanctuary—priestly garments, sacrifices, annointment of kings, high priest, appointment of Bezalel.)

32:1–34:35	The golden calf incident.
35:1–40:38	Building of the Tabernacle.

Vayikra—*Leviticus*

Part 1

1:1–7:38   *The Sacrifical System*

1:1–1:2	General introduction.
1:3–1:17	The burnt offerings (*olah*).
2:1–2:16	The tribute (meal) offering (*minchah*).
3:1–3:17	The peace offering (*shelamim*).
4:1–4:35	The sin offering (*chattat*).
5:1–5:13	Borderline cases requiring the purification offering.
5:14–5:26	The guilt offering (*asham*).
6:1–7:38	Supplementary instructions on sacrifices.

Part 2

8:1–10:20   *The Inaugural Service at the Sanctuary*

8:1–8:36	The installation of the priests.
9:1–9:24	The priests assume office.
10:1–10:11	The sin of Nadab and Abihu.
10:12–10:20	The consumption of the initiatory offerings.

Part 3

11:1–16:34   *The Laws of Impurities*

11:1–11:47	Dietary laws.
12:1–12:8	The "impurity" of childbirth.
13:1–14:57	The "impurity" of skin diseases.
15:1–15:33	The "impurity" of genital discharges.
16:1–16:34	The "impurities" concerning the Sanctuary and the nation.

Part 4

17:1–26:46   *Laws of Holiness*

17:1-17:6	Slaughtering of animals.
18:1–18:30	On being holy (sexual relations).
19:1–20:27	Miscellenea (prohibition of idolatry, interhuman relationships.)
21:1–22:33	The disqualifications of priests and sacrifices.
23:1–23:44	The festivals.
24:1–24:23	Miscellenea (the lamp's oil, shewbread, blasphemy, financial compensation).
25:1–26:46	The sabbatical and Jubilee Years; warning of exile and destruction.

Part 5

27:1–27:34	Gifts to the Sanctuary.

Bamidbar—*Numbers*

Part 1

1:1–10:10   *Continued Stay at Sinai*

1:1–4:49	Counting of males; tribes; their relationship with the Tabernacle.
5:1–5:4	The law of the leper.
5:5–5:10	Restitutions for wrongs.
5:11–5:31	Ordeal of jealousy in marriage.
6:1–6:21	Laws of nazarite.
6:22–6:27	Priestly blessings.
7:1–7:89	Gifts offered by tribal leaders for the service of the Tabernacle.
8:1–8:4	The menorah.
8:5–8:26	Dedication of the Levites.
9:1–9:14	The second Pesach.
9:15–9:23	The cloud of fire over the Tabernacle.
10:1–10:10	Clarions of silver.

Part 2

10:11–22:1   *Journey to the Plains of Moab*

10:11–10:34	Departure from Sinai.
10:35–10:36	Invocation prayers for the Ark.
11:1–11:35	Murmurers and rebellion.
12:1–12:16	Miriam and the vindication of Moshe.
13:1–14:45	The spies and their report.
15:1–15:16	Meal offerings and libations.

15:17–15:21	*Challah* (portion of dough set aside for the Priests).
15:22–15:31	Sin offering for unintentional sins.
15:32–15:36	*Shabbat* desecration at the wilderness.
15:37–15:41	*Tsitzit* (fringes on garments).
16:1–18:32	Rebellion of Korach.
19:1–19:22	The red heifer.
20:1	Death of Miriam.
20:2–20:9	Striking of rock; sin of Moshe and Aaron; no permission to pass through Edom; death of Aaron.
21:1–21:9	Battle with Canaan; rebellion; and the brass serpent.
21:10–22:1	Halting places and war.

Part 3

| *22:2–36:13* | *In the Plains of Moab* |

22:2–24:25	Balak-Bileam curse.
25:1–25:19	The sin of Ba'al Peor; Pinchas rewarded.
26:1–26:51	The second census.
26:52–26:56	Division of land.
26:57–26:65	Census of the Levites.
27:1–27:23	Laws of inheritance; Yehoshua; the successor of Moshe.
28:1–28–31	Daily and festival offerings.
29:1–30:1	New Year, Day of Atonement, and Succot offerings.
30:2–30:17	Vows.
31:1–31:54	War against enemies.

32:1–32:42	Tribes remaining east of the Jordan.
33:1–33:49	Intinerary from Egypt to the Jordan.
33:50–33:56	Commands with regard to the settlement in Canaan.
34:1–34:29	Boundaries of Israel.
35:1–35:15	Levitical cities and cities of refuge.
35:16–35:34	Distinction between murder, manslaughter, and accidental homicide.
36:1–36:13	Law of heiresses and daughters of Zelophchad.

Devarim—*Deuteronomy*   Farewell discourses of Moshe and his death.

Part 1

1:1–4:44	*Moshe's First Discourse*
1:1–1:5	Introduction.
1:6–4:44	Review of journey from Sinai to Kadesh, with exhortation to obedience.

Part 2

4:45–26:19	*Moshe's Second Discourse*
4:45–11:32	*Foundations of the covenant.*
4:45–4:49	Title, time, and place of the discourse.
5:1–5:18	Decalogue, repeated.

5:19–5:30	The manner in which the Decalogue was delivered.
6:1–6:9	Introduction to the *Shema* and the *Shema* itself.
6:10–7:26	Matters relating to the commandments mentioned previously.
8:1–10:11	Appeal to history as a motive for fulfilling the fundamental study of loving God and keeping the commandments.
10:12–11:32	Concluding portion, curses, and blessings.
12:1–25:19	*The rehearsal of the code.*
12:1–16:17	Religious institutions.
16:18–18:22	Government of the people.
19:1–21:9	Criminal law.
21:10–25:19	Laws of war, domestic life, miscellanea.
26:1–26:15	Conclusion of code: firstfruits, tithes, and accompanying prayers.
26:16–26:19	Formulation of the covenant between God and Israel.

Part 3

27:1–30:20	*Moshe's Third Discourse* *Enforcement of the Law.*
27:1–29:12	Procedure of crossing the Jordan; blessings, curses, and warnings.
29:13–29:28	Israel, present and future.

30:1–30:20   Omnipotence of repentance—return
                    from exile and encouragement.

Part 4

31:1–34:12   *The Last Days of Moshe*

31:1–31:8   Appointment of Yehoshua.
31:9–31:13   Public reading of the Torah.
31:14–31:23   Introduction to the Song of Moshe.
31:24–31:30   Moshe hands the Torah to the
                    Levites to be deposited in the Ark.
32:1–32:44   Song of Moshe.
32:45–32:47   The Law in Israel's life.
32:48–32:52   Moshe ordered to ascend Mount
                    Nebo.
33:1–33:29   The blessings of Moshe.
34:1–34:12   The death of Moshe.

INDEX OF THE *MISHNAH**

1. *Zeraim*—seeds

	C	B	J
Berachoth (blessings) Recitation of *Shema*; blessings and prayers in general.	9	•	•
Peah (corner) The setting aside of the corners of the field for the use of the poor (*Vayikra* 19:9, 23:22); and the gifts to the poor.	8	—	•
Demai (dubious produce) The requirement for tithing produce; where a doubt exists; whether the proper tithes have already been given.	7	—	•
Kila'im (diverse kinds) The prohibitions of mingling different species of plants, animals, and clothing (*Vayikra* 19:19, *Devarim* 22:9).	9	—	•

245

---

*Number of Chapters: C; Commentary of Babylonian (B); and Jerusalem Talmud (J) are indicated by a (•)

1. Zeraim—seeds (continued)

		C	B	J
Shevi'it (seventh year)	The laws of the sabbatical year and the release of debts (*Shemot* 23:11, *Vayikra* 25:1–7).	10	–	•
Terumot (heave-offerings)	Heave-offerings due to the priest from both the Israelite and the Levite (*Bamidbar* 18:8, *Devarim* 18:4, *Bamidbar* 18:21).	11	–	•
Ma'aseroth (tithes)	The tithe given to the Levites (*Bamidbar* 18:21).	5	–	•
Ma'aser Sheni (second tithe)	The tithes eaten in Jerusalem and how they could be redeemed for money.	5	–	•

---

*Number of Chapters: C; Commentary of Babylonian (B); and Jerusalem Talmud (J) are indicated by a (•)

1. *Zeraim*—seeds (*continued*)

		C	B	J
Challah (dough offering)	Portion of dough given to the priests in Temple times (*Bamidbar* 15:17–21).	4	—	•
Bikkurim (firstfruit)	The offering of the firstfruits in the Temple (*Shemot* 23:19, *Devarim* 26:1–11).	3	—	•
Orlah ("uncircumcized" fruit)	The laws forbidding the use of fruit of trees or vineyards for the first three years after planting (*Vayikra* 19:23).	3	—	•

2. *Moed*—Set feast

		C	B	J
Shabbat (the seventh day)	The general rules concerning *Shabbat* observance.	24	•	•

247

---

*Number of Chapters: C; Commentary of Babylonian (B); and Jerusalem Talmud (J) are indicated by a (•)

2. *Moed*—Set feast *(continued)*

		C	B	J
Eruvin (amalgamations)	Rules concerning carrying on *Shabbat* and the walking distance permitted on *Shabbat*, as well as the rules permitting work on festivals that fall on the evening of *Shabbat*.	10	•	•
Pesachim (Passover)	Regulations appertaining to the Pesach festival.	10	•	•
Shekalim (shekels)	The tax of half a shekel collected for the maintenance of the Temple.	8	—	•
Yoma (the day)	The Temple service of the High Priest on the Day of Atonement; regulations concerning the fast, atonement, and repentance.	8	•	•

248

---

*Number of Chapters: C; Commentary of Babylonian (B); and Jerusalem Talmud (J) are indicated by a (•)

2. *Moed*—Set feast (*continued*)

		C	B	J
Succab (booth)	The Laws concerning the festival of the feast of Succot and the water libation on these days.	5	•	•
Betzah (egg)	Laws concerning the festivals and the differences of opinion between the schools of Hillel and Shammai.	5	•	•
Rosh Hashanah (head of year)	Regulations concerning the sanctification of the New Moon, especially concerning the seventh month (New Year), the blowing of the ram's horn, and the prayers of the day.	4	•	•

249

---

*Number of Chapters: C; Commentary of Babylonian (B); and Jerusalem Talmud (J) are indicated by a (•)

2. *Moed*—Set feast (*continued*)

	C	B	J
Ta'anit (fast day) The designation of fast days in time of drought; the time and form of prayers for rain; other communal affairs.	4	•	•
Meggila (scroll) The scroll of Esther and Purim; the scriptural readings for special *Shabbatot*, festivals, and fast days.	4	•	•
Moed Katan (minor festival) The nature of work permitted during the Intermediate days of Pesach and Succot; mourning on holidays.	3	•	•
Chagiga (festival offerings) Temple sacrificial obligations of the individual during the three Pilgrim Festivals; topics improper for public teaching and discussion.	3	•	•

*Number of Chapters: C; Commentary of Babylonian (B); and Jerusalem Talmud (J) are indicated by a (•)

3. *Nashim*—women

	C	B	J
Yevamoth (levirates) — The status of widows of men who died childless and whose brothers must contract levirate marriage (*Vayikra* 18:16; *Devarim* 25:5, 7:10).	16	•	•
Ketuvoth (marriage contract) — The money to be received by the wife in case of widowhood or divorce; father's right to daughter; mutual rights and duties between husband and wife.	13	•	•
Nedarim (vows) — Regulations concerning vows and invalid vows; interpretation of vows.	11	•	•
Nazir (nazarite) — Nazarite vows (*Bamidbar* 6:1–21).	9	•	•
Gittin (divorce) — Laws of divorce (*Devarim* 24:1–4).	9	•	•

251

*Number of Chapters: C; Commentary of Babylonian (B); and Jerusalem Talmud (J) are indicated by a (•)

3. *Nashim*—women (*continued*)

	C	B	J
Sotah (errant woman) Laws concerning the woman suspected of adultery (*Bamidbar* 5:11–31); liturgical readings; the heifer whose neck is broken in a case of unsolved murder (*Devarim* 21:1–9); last chapter discusses the decline of standards since the destruction of the Temple, and the anarchy that will precede the messianic times.	9	•	•
Kiddushin (betrothals) Betrothals, prohibited marriages.			

---

*Number of Chapters: C; Commentary of Babylonian (B); and Jerusalem Talmud (J) are indicated by a (•)

4. Nezikin—damages

	C	B	J
Bava Kamma (first gate, concerning legal matters) Damages caused by property or agents (ox, pit, cattle, fire) or man (theft, assault, robbery).	10	•	•
Bava Metzia (middle gate) Laws of chattels; lost and found property; caretakers; embezzlement; fraud.	10	•	•
Bava Batra (last gate) Real estate; inheritance; partnership; usucaption; drawing up legal documents; interest; hired laborers; partnership.	10	•	•

253

*Number of Chapters: C; Commentary of Babylonian (B); and Jerusalem Talmud (J) are indicated by a (•)

4. *Nezikin*—damages (*continued*)

	C	B	J
Sanhedrin (high court) — Court of justice; judicial procedures, especially in criminal law; execution; rebellious son (*Devarim* 21:18–21); city tempted to evil (*Devarim* 13:13–15); a list of sins that exclude a man from future life.	11	•	•
Makkot (stripes) — Lashings administered in accordance with court decisions; false witnesses (*Devarim* 19:15–21); cities of refuge (*Devarim* 35:9–28).	3	•	•
Shevu'oth (oaths) — The various types of oath (*Vayikra* 5:4); "uncleanness" (*Vayikra* 5:2–3).	8	•	•
Eduyot (testimonies) — Testimonies given before the High Court at Yavneh, concerning statements of older authorities.	8	–	–

254

*Number of Chapters: C; Commentary of Babylonian (B); and Jerusalem Talmud (J) are indicated by a (•)

4. Nezikin—damages (continued)

		C	B	J
Avodah Zarah (idolatry)	Prohibitions against idol worship; regulations to prevent close association with idolaters.	5	•	•
Avoth (fathers)	Saying on religious, ethical teachings; later, a sixth chapter was added.	5 (6)	—	—
Horayot (decisions)	Decisions in matters of religious law made in error by the High Priest or the Sanhedrin (*Vayikra* 4:1–21).	3	•	•

5. Kodashim—holy things

		C	B	J
Zevachim (animal sacrifices)	The laws concerning the offering of sacrificial animals; successive locations of sacrifice.	14	•	—

255

*Number of Chapters: C; Commentary of Babylonian (B); and Jerusalem Talmud (J) are indicated by a (•)

5. Kodashim—holy things (continued)

	C	B	J
Menachot (meal offerings) Preparation of the meal offering (*Vayikra* 2:1–14, 5:11–13); the shewbread (*Vayikra* 24:5–9), the two loaves brought on *Shavuoth* (*Vayikra* 23:17).	13	•	—
Chullin (profane matters) Ritual slaughtering and other regulations connected with the preparation of animal food.	12	•	—
Bechorot (firstlings) Laws relating to the firstborn, both men and animals.	9	•	—
Arachin (estimations) Valuation for purposes of redemption of men and of things vowed to the Sanctuary (*Vayikra* 27:2–29).	9	•	•

*Number of Chapters: C; Commentary of Babylonian (B); and Jerusalem Talmud (J) are indicated by a (•)

256

5. Kodashim—holy things (continued)

		C	B	J
Temurah (exchange)	Regulations concerning the exchange of an animal consecrated for sacrifice (*Vayikra* 27:10, 33).	7	•	•
Keritot (excisions)	The punishment of *Karet* (excision), frequently mentioned in the Torah; an enumeration of the offenses to which this applies.	6	•	—
Meilah (trespass)	Trespass with respect to holy things, that is, making profane use of things consecrated for holy use (*Vayikra* 5:5–16).	6	•	•

257

*Number of Chapters: C; Commentary of Babylonian (B); and Jerusalem Talmud (J) are indicated by a (•)

5. Kodashim—holy things (continued)

	C	B	J
Tamid (perpetual offering) The prescription for the daily burnt offerings (*Shemot* 29:38, *Bamidbar* 28:1–8); the Temple service organization and the apportionment of the various priestly duties by lot.	7	•	•
Middot (measures) Architecture, organization, and dimensions of the Second Temple.	5	—	—
Kinnim (bird nests) The regulations for the bringing of an offering after childbirth (*Vayikra* 12:8), or by the poor who might commit the offenses enumerated in *Vayikra* 5; cases in which sacrifices are interchanged.	3	—	—

*Number of Chapters: C; Commentary of Babylonian (B); and Jerusalem Talmud (J) are indicated by a (•)

6. Toborot—purification

			C	B	J
Kelim (utensils)	The ritual uncleanness of vessels (*Vayikra* 11:32, *Bamidbar* 19:14, 31:20), especially concerning metal, wood, earthenware, glass, (etc.) vessels.	30	—	—	—
Ohalot (tents)	The ritual impurity conveyed by a corpse (*Bamidbar* 19:13–20) and anything lying under the same roof.	18	—	—	—
Negaim (plague of leprosy)	The laws of the various types of "leprosy" affecting a person, clothes, or dwellings (*Vayikra* 13:14).	14	—	—	—
Parah (heifer)	The regulations concerning the heifer (*Bamidbar* 19).	12	—	—	—

259

---

*Number of Chapters: C; Commentary of Babylonian (B); and Jerusalem Talmud (J) are indicated by a (•)

6. *Toborot*—purification (*continued*)

	C	B	J
Toborot (purification) — The minor degrees of ritual uncleanness of vessels, the effects of which only last till sunset (*Vayikra* 6:20).	10	–	–
Mikvaoth (ritual baths) — The regulations of the ritual bath (*Vayikra* 14:8, 15:5).	10	–	–
Niddah (menstruating woman) — Ritual "uncleanness" conveyed by menstruation (*Vayikra* 15:19–24) and by childbirth (*Vayikra* 12:1–5).	10	–	–
Machshirin (predisposings) — The laws of ritual impurity in connection with food that is liable to impurity when wet (*Vayikra* 11:34, 38).	6	–	–

*Number of Chapters: C; Commentary of Babylonian (B); and Jerusalem Talmud (J) are indicated by a (•)

6. *Tohorot*—purification (*continued*)

		C	B	J
Zavim (sufferers from flux)	The ritual uncleanness caused by flux, whether in man or woman (*Vayikra* 15); ritual uncleanness through contact with a person affected with an issue.	5	—	—
Tevul Yom (one who has bathed that day)	Minor degrees of ritual uncleanliness after ritual bathing, which continues until sunset (*Vayikra* 15:7–18).	4	—	—
Yadayim (hands)	Rabbinic enactments concerning the ritual impurity of hands and their ablution; the canonicity of the Song of Songs and Ecclesiastes; the aramaic language of Ezra and Daniel; the ancient Hebrew script; and disputations between the Pharisees and Sadducees.	4	—	—

261

*Number of Chapters: C; Commentary of Babylonian (B); and Jerusalem Talmud (J) are indicated by a (•)

6. *Tohorot*—purification (*continued*)

	C	B	J
Utzkin (stalks) The conveyance of ritual impurity to a harvested plant when its roots, stalks, or pods come into contact with an unclean person or thing.	3	–	–

*Number of Chapters: C; Commentary of Babylonian (B); and Jerusalem Talmud (J) are indicated by a (•)

INDEX OF MAIMONIDES'S CODE OF JEWISH LAW: *MISHNEH TORAH*

In the eleventh century, the famous Jewish thinker and halachic authority Moshe ben Maimon wrote a most comprehensive codex on all of Jewish law. Since this code has become a standard work in Jewish law and is daily consulted by all students of Jewish law, we present here, for the insider, an index of the complete work. It is subdivided in fourteen parts.

Term	Hilchoth	Laws of
1. *Mada*—knowledge	*Yesode hatorah*	Foundations of Torah
	De'oth	Ethical ideas
	Talmud Torah	Idolatry and Heathenism
	Avodath Kochavim	Repentance
2. *Ahavah*—love	*Kiryath Shema*	Reading of *Shema*
	Tefilla	Prayer
	Tefillin	*Tefillin*
	Mezuzah	*Mezuzah*
	Sefer Torah	Scroll of Torah
	Tsistsit	*Tsitsit*
	Berachoth	Blessings
	Milah	Circumcision
3. *Zemanim*—times	*Shabbat*	*Shabbat*
	Eruvin	*Eruvin* (concerning carrying on *Shabbat*)
	Shevitath Asor	Yom Kippur
	Yom Tov	Festivals
	Chametz umatza	Festival of Pesach

Term	Hilchoth	Laws of
	Shofar	Ram's horn and Rosh Hashanah
	Succah	The festival of Succot
	Lulav	The four species for Succot
	Shekalim	Shekels, Temple contributions
	Kidush ha-chodesh	Sanctification of the moon
	Ta'anioth	Fastdays
	Megilla	Purim
	Chanukah	Chanukah
4. *Nashim*—women	*Ishuth*	Marriage
	Gerushin	Divorce
	Yibum ve-chalitzah	Levirate marriage
	Na'arah betulah	Rape
	Sotah	Suspected woman
5. *Kedusha*—holiness	*Isure bi'ah*	Forbidden sexual relationship
	Ma'achaloth asuroth	Forbidden food
	Shechita	Ritual slaughter

Term	Hilchoth	Laws of
6. *Haflaah*—distinction of vows	*Shevuoth* *Nedarim* *Neziroth* *Arachin*	Oaths Vows Naziriteship Estimating "value" of people, animals, and objects in relationship to the Temple
7. *Zera'im*—seed	*Kila'im* *Matenot Aniyim* *Terumoth* *Ma'aser* *Ma'aser sheni* *Bikurim* *Shemita ve-yovel*	Mixtures Gifts to the poor Priestly offerings Tithes Second tithes Firstlings Sabbatical and Jubilee year
8. *Avodah*—service	*Beth ha-bechira* *Kele ha-mikdash* *Bi'ath ha-mikdash* *Isure mizbeach* *Ma'ase ha-korbanoth*	Temple Temple utensils Entrance to the Temple Prohibitions related to the altar Sacrifices

Term	Hilchoth	Laws of
	Temidin u-musafin	Daily offerings and extra offerings
	Pesule ha-mukdashin	Invalidation of offerings
	Avodath yom ha-kipurim	Day of atonement service
	Me'ila	Trespass of holy matters
9. *Korbanoth*—sacrifices	*Korban Pesach*	Pesach lamb
	Chagiga	Festival offerings
	Bechoroth	Firstlings
	Shegagoth	Sacrifices brought for mistakes
	Mechusre kappara	Sacrifices brought after purification
	Temurah	Exchange of sacrifices
10. *Tahara*—purification	*Tumath met*	Impurity of dead corpse
	Para adumah	Red heifer
	Tumath tsara'ath	Impurity of leprosy
	Metame mishkav u-moshav	Different ritual impurities after menstruation, et cetera
	Shear avoth hatume'oth	Other forms of ritual impurity

Term	Hilchoth	Laws of
	Tume'ath ochlin	Ritual impurities of food
	Kelim	Utensils that can become ritually impure
	Mikvaoth	Ritual baths
11. *Nezikin*—damages	*Nizke mamon*	Damages
	Geneva	Theft
	Gezela va-aveda	Robbery and lost property
	Chovel u-mazik	Assault and battery
	Rotseach	Homicide
12. *Kinyan*—acquisition	*Mechira*	Sales
	Zechiya u-matana	Acquisition and gifts
	Shechenim	Neighbors
	Sheluchin ve-shutafin	Agents and partners
	Avadim	Slaves
13. *Mishpatim*—laws	*Sechiruth*	Hiring
	She'ela u-fikadon	Borrowing and depositing
	Malve ve-love	Creditor and debtor

Term	Hilchoth	Laws of
	To'en we-nitan	Plaintiff and defendant
	Nachaloth	Inheritance
14. *Shoftim*—judges	*Sanhedrin*	High Court
	Eduth	Evidence
	Mamrim	Rebels
	Avel	Mourning
	Melachim	Kings

INDEX

About the Author

Nathan T. Lopes Cardozo was schooled in Amsterdam, Holland. He received his rabbinical ordination from Gateshead Talmudical College, England in 1972. In 1976 he moved to Israel, where he studied at the Rabbinical Institute for Higher Rabbinical Studies of Chief Rabbi Unterman and at Yeshivath Mir in Jerusalem. He taught at Neve Yerushalaim College for Women and Michlala Jerusalem College for Women. Presently, he is Associate Dean at the Isralight Institute in the Old City of Jerusalem. Cardozo travels extensively throughout the United States, Canada, South Africa, and Europe to deliver lectures on Jewish Thought of which there are more than 150 audiotapes. He is a guest lecturer at different universities in Israel and in other countries. He holds a Ph.D. in Philosophy and heads the Cardozo School for Jewish Studies and Human Dignity, which sponsors his books and other publications. He is the author of *Between Silence and Speech, Essays in Jewish Thought* (Jason Aronson Inc.). He resides in Jerusalem with his wife, five children, and eight grandchildren.